Murnau

Lotte H. Eisner

Murnau during the making of *Tabu*

MURNAU

by
Lotte H. Eisner

UNIVERSITY OF CALIFORNIA PRESS
Berkeley and Los Angeles

F. W. Murnau by Lotte H. Eisner
first published by Le Terrain Vague, Paris
© Le Terrain Vague 1964

Awarded the Prix Armand Tallier in 1965

This English translation, revised and enlarged,
first published in 1973 by
Martin Secker & Warburg Limited, London

A Shadows book
Cover design by Michael Farrell

University of California Press
Berkeley & Los Angeles

ISBN: 0-520-02285-8 (Clothbound)
          0-520-02425-7 (Paperbound)

LC: 72-82222

Printed in Great Britain

Preface to English-language edition

Unlike Fritz Lang and G. W. Pabst, the two other great directors of the German cinema, F. W. Murnau has been mostly loved and admired by a specialist minority. His films are not widely known to the larger cinema public. In Germany, indeed, he is today practically unknown,[1] even though he is one of the rare directors of German origin (Lang and Pabst are both Austrian by birth). In France, mainly on the strength of *Nosferatu* and *Tabu*, he has always had his admirers; and when he died in a car accident in California, in 1931, when talking pictures were just getting into their stride and he, at 42, was in his prime, it was particularly in French journals that his work was recalled with enthusiasm. In the United States, on the other hand, his death was virtually ignored and he was quickly forgotten. By 1958, however, the time seemed ripe for revaluation. In that year *The Last Laugh* was voted among the ten best films in the history of the cinema, by an international jury of critics at the Brussels International Exposition. It was in 1957 that I began to write this book, which was first published in Paris in 1964.

The particular problem which Murnau poses for the film historian is that of the loss of nearly half his work. Of the twenty-one films listed in the filmography at the end of this book nine are missing; and some of the other

---

[1] Though there is the F. W. Murnau Stiftung at Wiesbaden.

5

twelve are in a very incomplete state. Of course, the publication of a book like this can bring films to light, and we may be lucky enough to find some of those missing nine. A copy of *Gang in die Nacht* was discovered in East Berlin, and a copy of *Phantom* in Moscow, only recently; both, alas, incomplete, but both priceless in the fresh light they throw on Murnau's artistic progress. Murnau has been singularly unfortunate in the way his films have disappeared. Virtually all Pabst's films survive. Only a few of Lang's very early films have vanished.

In common with Pabst and Lang, however, surviving Murnau prints are very often poor copies, dupes of dupes, quite without the subtleties of shading and light values of their originals. A print from the original negative is a rare thing. When inflammable nitrate film is copied on to safety acetate, there is always a loss in tone-values and contrast. When a 35 mm. copy is duped in 16 mm. there is usually a loss of quality of a similar kind. Not always, however: recently I saw a 16 mm. copy of *Tartuffe*, with Spanish titles, of which even the framing prologue and epilogue had astonishingly subtle qualities of light and shade, far surpassing any of the 35 mm. copies known to me. Seeing this print is to understand Murnau's intentions: the lighting of the framing sequences forms a dramatic contrast with the visual style of the *Tartuffe* play.

The hazards are immense: poor duplicates, the mutilations of distributors or cinema owners (cuts were easier in silent days), destruction. As I attempt to show in discussing *Nosferatu*, even a print from an original negative can be tampered with.

I know Lang and knew Pabst; but I never met Murnau. By the time I came to the cinema, in 1927, Murnau had already left for the United States. From *Faust* onwards I had of course seen his films at the time of their first showings; but that is now a long time ago. I do not believe in books written in haste, and during the seven years I worked on this book I saw – thanks to Henri Langlois and the Cinémathèque Française – Murnau's films again and again, in as many different copies and versions as I could find. Even so, the fragmented nature of the material is such that I am aware that others may yet find more aspects of Murnau's style than I have been able to discover in my 'archaeological' pursuit. As to his working methods, my approach was to interview his surviving collaborators, the designers, cameramen, and others from his film units. I also had the great good fortune to meet Murnau's brother, Robert Plumpe Murnau, who entrusted to me a number of scripts annotated in Murnau's own hand, among them the shooting script of *Nosferatu* itself, reproduced in translation at the end of this book.

In my previous book *L'Ecran Démoniaque* (Paris 1952; new edition, revised, 1965; English translation *The Haunted Screen*, 1969) I made a first attempt at an evaluation of Murnau, devoting separate chapters to *Nosferatu*,

The Last Laugh, Tartuffe, and *Faust*. Consequently, although in this book the reader will find constant reference to these films, I have felt it more important to put the most emphasis on his other works. I hope this will explain the disproportionately little space devoted specifically to these major films.

Murnau died prematurely; he stays eternally young. My aim has been to trace the development of his style through that brief life, and to demonstrate the often intransigent continuity of his artistic will, a will expressed in films made in Germany, in the United States, and on his island in the Pacific.

L.H.E.

Acknowledgements

The author thanks the following people, either for information about Murnau's life and work, or for sending photographs, programmes, posters, and other documents. In West Germany, first and foremost Gerhard Lamprecht. The author also thanks Murnau's colleagues: Messrs Hermann Warm, Rochus Gliese, Heinrich Richter, and Arno Richter; and Murnau's relatives: Mmes Ursula Plumpe, Eva Dieckmann, and Mr Hans Plumpe.

The author pays tribute to Robert Plumpe-Murnau, and to those colleagues and friends of Murnau who are now dead: Ruth Landshoff York, David Flaherty, E. Savitry, Robert Herlth, the designer, Dr Ludwig Berger, and the cameramen Fritz Arno Wagner, Karl Freund and Robert Baberske.

Her thanks are also offered to Mrs Hanna Hofmann and to Messrs Erwin Goelz, Friedrich von Zglinicki, Engelbert von Mallinckrodt, Hubert Schonger, Rolf Burgmer, and to Mrs Eva Diehl-Schmid of Recklinghausen; and to Professor Giuseppe Becce for the musical score from *The Last Laugh*.

The author cordially thanks Mrs Erika Ulbrich of Munich and Mr Werner Zurbuch of Munich, who, like Dr Agnes Bleier-Brody of Vienna, have most kindly carried out valuable researches among various German newspapers and film reviews which the author was unable to consult personally, and which have made an effective contribution to establishing the filmography and the quotations in the chapter on the lost films.

In East Germany the author thanks: Wolfgang Klaue, of the Staatliches Filmarchiv der D.D.R., Berlin; Dr Baumert, Klaus Lippert, Dr Herbert Müller-Jena, and Murnau's former colleagues (now working at Defa), Messrs Eduard Kubat and Erich Nitzschmann, and Mrs Lena Neumann.

She also gives grateful acknowledgments to *Filmforum, Der Neue Film, Deutsche Filmkunst* and *Le Théatre Européen*.

Acknowledgements

In the USA she thanks: Mrs Francis Flaherty, Miss Louise Brooks, Mrs Salka Viertel, Mr Fitzroy-Davis, Mrs Belli Heerman-Baer, and Mr George Pratt, of George Eastman House, Rochester, Mr Ernst Jaeger, and Murnau's cameramen, Mr Paul Ivano and Mr Charles Rosher; also his assistants Frank Hansen, Edgar G. Ulmer, and Eugen Sharin, and the film historians Mr Herman G. Weinberg and Mr Seymour Stern. She is grateful also to Mr Albert Johnson of the San Francisco Film Festival for help with stills of *Tabu*.

For the photographs the author thanks first the Cinémathèque Française, Paris; the late Mrs Norah Traylen, and Mr Liam O'Leary, both formerly of the British Film Institute, London; Mr Freddy Buache of the Swiss Cinémathèque; Herr Heinz Berg, Deutsche Kinemathek (Berlin); the Cinémathèques of East Berlin, Czechoslovakia, Denmark, Sweden, and Holland. Thanks also to Mr Rudolf Leutner of Vienna for photographs, and to Mr Rudolf Meyer of Amsterdam for information; to Mr H. Feld of London; M. Jean-Claude Kress and Mlle Marie Epstein of Paris; to Mr Kenneth Thompson of London and to M. Denis Bablet of Paris. Thanks also for information to Mr Viggo Holm Jensen and for photographs to Mr Carl Nørrested of Denmark and M. Jean Pierre Jeancolas of Louhan, France.

Contents

Contents

10

To HENRI LANGLOIS, founder and director of the Cinémathèque Française, whose devotion to retrieving and showing film classics has enabled me to study Murnau's work.

In his house at Grunewald

1. Murnau Remembered

Robert Plumpe Murnau: My brother Wilhelm

A fugitive and a vagabond . . . our family has exemplified these words from the Bible.

For a thousand years none of my people has remained anywhere more than five or ten years without growing uneasy, without being seized by wanderlust; they have constantly moved backwards and forwards from the country to the town and from the town to the country. They came to Germany from Sweden, settling first somewhere in the west, among strangers with different ways from theirs; then they set off again towards the east. Our oldest ancestors were knights and peasants, officials, ministers of the church, and mayors. They would halt somewhere, work, produce something; then, without waiting to see the full results of their labours, they would set off again.

Friedrich Wilhelm Murnau must have been thinking of this destiny when he wrote to his mother from Tahiti: '. . . I am at home in no house and in no country. . . .'

He was born on 28 December 1888 in Bielefeld, in a house on the Bahnhofstrasse where the Capitol Cinema now stands. He spent his childhood in Bielefeld. The town where he received his earliest impressions was then a place full of life and activity.

From the very beginning my brother overflowed with imagination. The dreams that seemed to weave themselves round his being at night surrounded

13

him by day as well. When we were out for a walk my mother used to have to keep saying to him: 'Look where you're going – you're dreaming again.'

Although my father had taken over his uncle's big textile business and was related to the best families in the town, he made hardly any attempt to establish contact with them. He sold the business and bought a magnificent estate at Wilhelmshöhe, near Kassel, with a lot of land, hunting, a carriage, and a horse. We children were delighted. There was everything we could wish for in that garden – a see-saw, a horizontal bar, a trapeze, all the things provided nowadays in playgrounds. It was a miniature paradise.

The huge park was bound to encourage our imaginations and make our thoughts turn to fairy tales. Every morning our elder half-sister, who was sixteen, used to sit at her easel painting the dew-drenched flowers, or the rose-bordered garden path, or the pond surrounded by birches and weeping willows. She was very gifted, and was studying painting in Kassel.

She outdid us all in imagination, and it was she who got up a theatre in the enormous attics. She wrote spectacles and plays for it, in which her brothers and girl-friends from the art-school all had to take part. Wilhelm was always present at these performances: he used to stand there staring, all eyes. When he was seven he started to act in them too, and when our sister went away to school the next year he became director of the theatre.

As soon as he could read he fell on every book that came his way, whether it was a novel or a classical drama. Our father used to get angry, seeing him with his nose always stuck in a book.

The families in the neighbouring houses used to invite us round: there were garden-parties, fireworks, illuminations: each tried to outdo the other.

But one day all this came to an end. We moved into a rented apartment in Kassel: my father had sold the estate to finance an invention that was supposed to revolutionize industry, but which in fact turned out to be disastrous.

For Christmas Wilhelm was given one of the little puppet theatres that were currently fashionable. He was then at school, in the fourth grade, and used to dramatize Grimm's and Andersen's fairy tales for our family audience.

But he soon found this too childish. The tiny stage was not large enough for *William Tell* or *The Brigands* – he wanted a big theatre with changeable scenery and a revolving stage. We, his brothers, decided to help him build a theatre four times the size of the one he already had. Wilhelm himself played no great part in the work – he was no good at practical things nor at working with his hands. The new theatre turned out to be very good, with lighting, a trap, and flies. We couldn't find the sets we wanted in the shops, so we made them ourselves, and although my father looked rather sternly on all this childishness, he allowed us to use his lathe to turn the ·columns for the proscenium, and other wooden parts.

Hedda Hofmann with Murnau (*right*) and Schweizer, young actors, in 1913

Wilhelm was happy; now he could put on any play he liked. He used to hand us out little paper-bound books and we all had to learn our parts. In the afternoon, as soon as we had finished our homework (Wilhelm didn't need to do any serious preparation), we began rehearsing, and every Sunday we gave a performance. There were tickets, and we had to find people to buy them, for we needed money for new productions.

Whenever Wilhelm saw a play that interested him at the theatre in Kassel he adapted it for his own theatre.

Our father, who had more serious plans for him, was not very pleased with these activities, but he was persuaded not to interfere by our mother and his sister Anna. Aunt Anna had an excellent library, and fed the book-hungry Wilhelm with classical plays and poetry. By the time he was twelve my brother was already familiar with Schopenhauer, Ibsen, Nietzsche, Dostoievski, and Shakespeare.

But he was not at all misanthropic; on the contrary, he liked watching people and the things that went on around him. His observation was remarkable, and always on the alert.

Ever since we had come to live in an apartment in town our parents had taken us every summer to the island of Juist, partly to give us a change of air, but mainly to stop Wilhelm, who was rather delicate, from staying indoors reading all day. Reading had become a sort of mania with him, and father, with the support of our headmaster, did all he could to combat it. During our holidays on the island he took the books out of Wilhelm's hands and told him to look at the beauties of nature instead. And Wilhelm began to join in our games on the beach. He liked swimming, and thereafter was often to be found either in the water or on the dunes. He would spend hours gazing out to sea at a sailing-boat that went back and forth there every day. One morning he got to know the fisherman it belonged to, and astonished us by asking if he could go out with him. He often did so after that, and the fisherman told my parents that their son was a born sailor!

Opposite our apartment were the grounds of the castle and a lake poetically surrounded with trees. It was an ideal place for skating in the winter, and Wilhelm and I were always there, heedless of lunch or homework or the rows we would get into for being late.

Wilhelm was by now fourteen, and we were both at the age when boys start to be interested in girls. Wilhelm was not captivated by the pretty ones; he was attracted rather by those who were sensitive or a bit odd, especially if they were witty too. This was the case with the graceful and intelligent Emmy Virchov, and, later, Rose Spier, a young Jewish girl very keen on music and painting, who was a friend of our mother's for many years.

Up to the *baccalauréat* he was always top of his class, though he was never vain about it. There was nothing of the climber about him, and he always remained friendly and unassuming. He went to Paris several times during the holidays, and must have been very impressed by the city, the people, their way of living, and their feeling for art. Between 1905 and 1910, when he was a student, he spent the vacations visiting other countries. During the last holidays he made long excursions in Switzerland.

It was probably in 1909 that father got a letter one day from my brother's landlady in Charlottenburg, Berlin, insisting that he pay his son's debts at once. Father was furious and decided to go to Berlin immediately. 'You come with me,' he told me, and we set off together the same night. When we arrived we found ourselves not in a student's lodgings but in the best drawing-room of an apartment on the Krummestrasse, decorated in a very personal style that was unmistakably my brother's. Wilhelm knew how to appease father. He hurried him through the salon and out on to the balcony, where he installed him in a comfortable armchair, to give himself the chance to whisk out of sight the modern paintings and prints that might have hampered financial discussion. The negotiations nevertheless became stormy enough. The landlady kept popping up to say there was still something else owing, that the tailor had come complaining the day before, and that there was even a fine outstanding. 'If this ever happens again,' said my father, 'I shan't let you finish your studies, and you can just be a village schoolmaster.' During the months that followed, Wilhelm kept an eye on expenses and saw that they didn't exceed the amount of his monthly cheque.

But soon after this some friends who had been in Berlin told us they had seen Wilhelm acting in a play at the Deutsches Theater. Of course he was using an assumed name, but he was easily recognizable because of his height. My father said nothing, but got up and left the room. Later I heard him say to mother: 'No, not another penny. I paid for him to become a professor, not a starving actor.'

So mother asked my grandfather to send Wilhelm the monthly cheque he needed to continue his studies. They had to be careful, for father would never take presents from his father-in-law.

Murnau's closest friend from this time was Hans Ehrenbaum Degele, the son of the opera singer Degele and a Jewish banker. They were both interested in literature, shared the same views on artistic matters, and had the same conception of the world. It was a fruitful friendship: one of them became an actor, the other a poet. The Ehrenbaums treated Wilhelm like a son, and he accompanied them on Sunday excursions and on their travels. With characteristic generosity, Hans's father gave them both everything they could desire.[1]

Ottilie Plumpe: My son Wilhelm
In Berlin my son studied philology with his friend Hans Ehrenbaum Degele, then they both went on to Heidelberg to study art-history and literature.[2] It was there that the students performed a play in the presence of the grand duke of Baden. Max Reinhardt was there, and when the play was over he offered

---

[1] It must have been at the Ehrenbaums' that Murnau met the Jewish poetess Else Lasker Schüler, celebrated for her shimmering oriental fantasies. When writing to her friends she used to give them all resounding nicknames from history or legend. She herself was 'Jussuf, Prince of Thebes', and in the many letters she wrote to Murnau when, later in the war, he was interned in Switzerland, she addressed him as 'Ulrich von Hutten'. Other friends used to call him 'Bayard, the knight sans peur et sans reproche'. Murnau's friendship with the sculptress Renée Sintenis and the painter Franz Marc also dates from this time.

[2] In the studio people often addressed Murnau as 'Herr Doktor', and an assistant once wrote this title on one of his working scripts. But Dr Ludwig Berger told me that having become an actor Murnau abandoned his studies without taking his doctorate, and research at both Universities seems to confirm this. In an interview published in *Cahiers du Cinéma*, August 1961, Edgar G. Ulmer, who praises Murnau's cosmopolitanism and universality, and says how well he spoke French, maintains there has never been such a cultured film director.

my son a place in his newly founded theatre school, which would cost him absolutely nothing if he agreed to stay at the theatre for six years.[3]

From the letters Wilhelm wrote me from Budapest, Salzburg, and Vienna, I learned that he was on tour, acting in *The Miracle* and *Henry IV*. At the Reinhardt school he had already done some directing. It interested him more than acting. He also realized that his height would be a handicap in getting parts.

Then the war came and he was called up into the First Regiment of the Foot Guards at Potsdam. He took part in some heavy fighting and was made an officer. He became a company commander at Riga, then transferred to the air force, crashing eight times without being wounded. One day he got lost in a thick fog and landed in Switzerland. He was interned at Andermatt.

A competition was then being organized in Switzerland for the best production of *Marignano*, a popular national drama. Every canton could compete, and so could the internees.[4] My son won a first prize, and was acclaimed when the play was performed in Berne.

Major Wolfgang Schramm

It was 1917 and our regiment of flyers was quartered near Verdun, in a beautiful but rather melancholy château abandoned by its owners. Murnau was then a young actor who had been with Max Reinhardt. He was very tall and thin, and stooped a little. His eyes were brown and full of life. He was always to be seen by his aircraft, personally making sure that it was serviced properly. He was a curious mixture of wandering gypsy and cultivated gentleman. He had the largest room in the château, arranged in perfect taste. Everything in it was clean and well-appointed; when you went to see him you forgot about the war, and made a polite and civilized visit. On every mission, every flight, he did all he had to do as carefully and conscientiously as he arranged his room, and in spite of the toughness of our job he managed to bring to things a touch of beauty, even of tenderness. One didn't need to be a psychologist to know that someone like that would make his mark.

In the evening, after dinner, when we sat around in the mess, Murnau had another duty to perform. It was always the same. As the fire threw its

[3] Murnau's companions at the Reinhardt school were Lothar Müthel, Ernst Hofmann, Walter Storm, Else Eckersberg, and Alexander Granach. In his memoirs Granach tells how Murnau, always chivalrous, defended him, a little Jew from Galicia whose German was still imperfect, from the anti-Semitic attacks of Professor Held, who was himself Jewish. Granach also recalls how he and Murnau used to lie on the floor of a stage-box in order to see and hear Reinhardt working with his actors (Reinhardt would not allow anyone to be present at rehearsals). See Alexander Granach, *Da geht ein Mensch*, Frankfurter Verlagsanstalt, Frankfurt n.d., pp. 252, 253, 260.

[4] A cousin of the author, Belli Heermann, also remembers playing opposite Murnau in a production of *Der Graf von Charolais* by Richard Beer-Hofmann (1866–1945), during the period of Murnau's internment in Switzerland.

Lieutenant Murnau, 1916

dancing, changing shadows on the shifting group of young officers, Murnau had to recite 'Der Todspieler' (The Pianist of Death). I don't know whether he used to do it to please himself, but he did it conscientiously, with the emphasis and the strange intonation, half pathetic and half comic, that proclaimed him the pupil of his great master. He would recite the poem in a ringing voice, his gaunt face quivering: 'There, on that bier, behold the last of my sons.' Our captain was completely captivated. He would listen with his little wine-reddened eyes half-shut, then applaud enthusiastically, shouting to everyone else to do the same. Then, after a carefully calculated pause, Murnau had to recite another poem, 'Three old troopers sat round the hearth of heaven'.

Since then, whenever I recall Murnau – and with that vitality of his that led him straight to his goal, he is not easily forgotten – I always see him sitting there in front of the fire with his long legs stretched out comfortably, his slender nervous fingers beating in time to the 'trum trum trum' of the refrain, which he would intone slowly, rolling the r's.

Outside it was dark and cold, with every so often the dull rumble of the guns. But we sat there quietly, and we were all moved as we listened to the tall Murnau reciting.

Next morning, like all the rest of His Majesty's pilots, he would go off to his work again, his lofty silhouette, dressed with studied negligence, creating around him an atmosphere that was somehow disquieting. His uniform was correct, the only eccentricity being a long stick made out of a bullet-riddled propeller, with a handle shaped like a mushroom. Soon all of us were carrying the same sort of stick. Murnau used to create our fashions and customs. He was the accepted authority in his section on all cultural activities, and accepted with a smile of pride any praise of his creative gifts.

He came through the war, one of the few survivors of the Verdun group, was transferred to another section, and I lost sight of him.

Once, during the revolution, I glimpsed his tall form, looking rather bowed down and sad, on the platform of a Berlin railway station, standing amid the depressed and nondescript lower-middle-class passengers. I was leaning out of the window of a train. For a moment we looked at each other, then the train moved off again and he disappeared among the crowd.

Robert Plumpe Murnau

Hans Ehrenbaum Degele served in the 1914 war as a volunteer. He sent Wilhelm many letters and a volume of poems from the front. One of the poems seems to express a sort of presentiment of his early death:

> *The hours go slowly*
> *You are awake, you dig trenches and sometimes softly sing*
> *You dream of country, happiness and going home*
> *Patience becomes duty, waiting becomes action*
> *Oh, grey night, oh, grey and misty night*
> *Soon will come death, sharp as a terrible blow.*
>
> *Dig your grave deeper, soldier!*
> *Perhaps one day peace will be born*
> *To the sound of bells*
> *From one tower to another; and everything will shine again*
>
> *And all over the German earth everyone will be joyful.*
> *Dig your grave, soldier, full of nostalgia, and faithful;*
> *The flakes of a dreary winter fall in silence*
> *On you and your moth-eaten coat.*

Not long afterwards the presentiment became a reality. Murnau was deeply stricken by his friend's death. Hans's father died soon after. When Murnau came back from the war Hans's mother, Mary Ehrenbaum Degele, offered him hospitality, and when she died a few years later she left her house in the Grunewald to the University of Berlin on condition that my brother was allowed to live in it for the rest of his life.

When he became an actor, Wilhelm completely dropped his family and former friends and schoolmates. He did not see them or answer their letters;

Murnau and a brother officer: a Christmas during the war

he severed all connection with the people of the past. The only person he wrote to was his mother, and, on exceptional occasions, his brothers. He wanted to work without hindrance and to be quite free to do as he wished. So our youngest brother, Bernhard, who was a student at the technical college in Berlin, was strictly forbidden to introduce himself into the circles Wilhelm frequented. But Bernhard wanted to see what our brother was doing; he loved art, and was particularly interested in the cinema. He had already managed to get unrestricted entry into the studios near the Zoo. One afternoon he took me there, and as we went from one stage to another he said, 'We must be careful not to meet Wilhelm.'

But certain things that had happened during the war, and other experiences such as the solitude of his internment, and perhaps even his new activity in the freer atmosphere of film-making gradually brought about a change in Wilhelm and reawakened his family feeling. In 1920 he came to spend Christmas with me and my wife in our new home. He went round the apartment making friendly suggestions for improvements, and in the little room I had converted into a bar I showed him our family tree. Not being met with his usual mocking smile, I plucked up courage and showed him the arms

Four faces and the man

dating from 1350, which had been found at our cousin's in Berlin. He was interested enough to ask me where our family came from, and I told him it had emigrated from Sweden towards the beginning of the year one thousand and settled in Pomerania. It had titles of nobility, belonged to the knightly order, and had included craftsmen, priests, and mayors among its members. For a long time our ancestors owned an estate at Varzmin, but towards the end of the Thirty Years War the family decided to leave this dangerous area. They had been told it was safer and more peaceful in the west. So Peter von Plumpe sold his estate and took his family to Westphalia.

When I told Wilhelm that two women of our family had been burned as witches at Recklinghausen, he looked at me doubtfully, but eager to be convinced.

'Yes,' I said. 'It's true. It happened in 1650. I still have to do some more research to find out whether one of their daughters, Trine Plumpe, was burnt too. At any rate, her mother and grandmother were, and she herself was accused of witchcraft and imprisoned in the Tower at Horneburg.'

Wilhelm seemed very struck by this, and remained deep in thought.

Ottilie Plumpe

When he got back to Berlin he devoted himself entirely to the cinema in order to express his conception of the art of the image.

In 1919, together with several colleagues from the Reinhardt school, he founded a film company called the Murnau Veidt Filmgesellschaft, and made his first films, with Conrad Veidt, Ernst Hofmann, Alfred Abel, Eugen Klöpfer, Paul Hartmann, Werner Krauss, Olga Tchechowa, Lya de Putti, and Adele Sandrock.[5] The films were well received for their artistic quality and the humanity of their subjects.

American producers began to be interested in him, and in 1926 William Fox, through his representative Sheehan, invited him to Hollywood.

The success of *Sunrise* and *Four Devils* enabled my son to fulfil his childhood dream of going on an expedition to the South Seas. He had bought a sailing-ship and passed his master's certificate in navigation, and after a long voyage, with several stops, he reached the island of Tahiti, where he made his last film, *Tabu*.

It was his intention to go back to the islands. He had started a plantation at Punaavia, and built himself a convenient, colonial house, a model of which was shown in the colonial exhibition in Paris. The main building, a huge tropical mansion, was unfortunately destroyed by fire. The construction of the roof was managed with perfect geometrical harmony, and the furnishing and decoration were carried out in exquisite taste.

[5] Francesco von Mendelssohn must also have been among those concerned.

My son wanted to go on making films about the South Seas. *The Island of Demons* was his idea, and he entrusted the preparatory stages to his friend Walther Spiess, a very gifted painter who had been living in Bali since 1919. After Wilhelm's death the film was made by Baron von Plessen. Walther Spiess, well-known to most visitors to Bali, died in April 1942 when the ship taking him to an internment camp was torpedoed.

Almost immediately after Wilhelm's death I lost my youngest son, Bernhard. To console me, my son Robert brought me Reri, the Tahitian girl in *Tabu*. I was impressed with the nobility of her mind and the intelligence of her conversation and she showed me great affection. Wilhelm's pets – his dog Tommy, his cats Lindi and Tscheko, the parrot, and the tortoises – and my two grand-daughters became Reri's playmates.

Wilhelm had had Reri living in his house in Tahiti to work with her on her part. She stayed there until he left. When he said goodbye he told her: 'Always stay my nice little girl.'

I should have liked to be able to keep Reri in our family, but the tours she went on took her far away. We used to write to each other until this terrible war, which broke that bond too.

Robert Plumpe Murnau
When I arrived in Tahiti some while after the tragic death of my brother, the huge port of Papeete was crowded with people who had come there that day to meet our ship. Their brown bodies were all draped in pareos mainly ornamented with red, with garlands of flowers round their necks and luminous, wonderfully scented gardenias in their dark hair.

They watched everyone come down the narrow gang-plank, and gave each one a suitable nickname, which was taken up by the whole crowd. I was the only person who did not receive this cheerful spontaneous welcome; they didn't even look at me. The only one there to meet me was the caretaker of the house. He explained the people's attitude: my brother was supposed to have built on the sacred soil of the temples of Punaavia, thus defying the ancient law of tabu. He had been warned that he would meet with misfortune, and the vengeance of the gods must have pursued him and struck him down. Now the natives were afraid my arrival might bring them harm, and were avoiding me.

It was true that the land my brother had chosen to build on had long been considered tabu. The natives were afraid to go there, and none of them had set foot on it in human memory. Murnau had been stirred by the picture of decay that it presented: it was completely abandoned, the temple had fallen into ruin, not one stone stood upon another. The whole site was strewn with debris; somewhere under all the ruins were the throne and the flag-stones of the place of sacrifice. All the splendour had become a wilderness.

Paradise

My brother decided to transform it into a paradise. Before long he had made a garden and built on it in the ancient Polynesian style, showing the present generation what the art of its ancestors had been. He knew the history and culture of this people. He respected their traditions and their laws. But he did not fear their gods. Visitors from all over the world admired the splendour of the place, but they were all oppressed by the strange atmosphere of foreboding that hung over it.

Once I had met the natives I realized that to obtain their confidence I had to convince them that my brother had never meant to break their ancient laws. But it was only later, when I knew them better, when I had been present at their feasts and dancing and taken part in their conversations, that I succeeded in overcoming their fear and shyness, and in reawakening their former veneration for my brother.

I received the proof that I had done so a few days before I left the island. I was leaning against the balustrade in front of the main building of the house, gazing out dreamily towards the sea, which lay gold and purple beneath the setting sun, and to the tall mountains of the island of Moorea, when suddenly I heard the sound of many voices singing in the garden below. I turned round to see the Chief of Punaavia coming along the corridor towards me, surrounded by his entourage and followed by the notables and ancients of his council, all dressed in the historical costumes of their tribe. When he was within a few yards of me the chief stopped, the others assembled round him, and they all bowed. From the solemnity of their manner I realized that this was a special visit, so I took a step towards them and returned their bow.

By this time the song had ended, and the forty singers, men and women, silently came and joined the others. I saluted them, praised their singing, and invited them all to be seated on benches and cushions. At first they hesitated, but their chief signed to them to accept my invitation. Then they sang their most beautiful song: 'The hibiscus will flower, the coral will grow, but man will die.' I listened, moved. An oppressive silence followed. Then, seized by a kind of inspiration, I stood up and went and took my place in the midst of their circle. The tense atmosphere was suddenly transformed: they breathed freely as if relieved of some burden, heads were lifted, eyes shone, they made friendly gestures towards me, their chief embraced me.

Then he started to talk about my brother. He said how much they had all loved and revered him, and told me of the kindnesses he had done many of them. He spoke of his own friendship for 'Frederic', and thanked me for the photograph I had given him a few days before. But he wanted me to take it back. A photograph is a dead thing, and it made him sad. They all wished to keep him alive in their thoughts and in their hearts, just as he had been when he lived among them. They said they would never forget him, and they didn't need any object to make them remember.

I had drinks brought, and was happy to be in the company of such magnificent people. When they left they sang a song dedicated to my brother: 'Jaorana oe Murnau tane. . . .'

2. Murnau and his Scriptwriters

Through the kindness of Robert Plumpe Murnau, I have had the rare opportunity of being able to study some of the scripts left by his brother. Many others, unfortunately, were lost during the fall of Berlin. Those which survive are all to some degree annotated in Murnau's own hand. He concerned himself with the smallest detail, so that after every sequence we find precise instructions concerning costumes and props. He often notes also the time of day or night when the scene is supposed to take place. Sometimes, in the margin, there is a note as to the studio or location; now and then he gives the exact date on which a certain scene was shot, and with what sets. This is the case with *Schloss Vogelöd*, for example, which suggests that this must be the final shooting-script.[1] Sometimes he even indicates the proposed or eventual duration of the shots, as in the case of *Nosferatu*.[2]

As we shall see later, Murnau's more extensive notes are extremely informative about the style of his whole work. These scripts also enable us to

[1] According to the details given on the script, *Schloss Vogelöd* was shot between Thursday 10 February and Wednesday 2 March 1921 inclusive. Discounting Sundays and the two days, Monday 21 February and Tuesday 1 March, which were entirely taken up with building sets, the whole film was shot in sixteen days, of which two, Tuesday 22 February and Saturday 26 February, were devoted to outside shots. This was record time, but it must be remembered that everything had been minutely discussed and worked out before shooting began.

[2] There are also titles and sketches of furniture on the backs of the pages of this script.

27

observe, for the first time, the methods of the scenarists of the German silent cinema: Carl Mayer, Hans Janowitz, Henrik Galeen, Willy Haas, Thea von Harbou, and Hans Kyser.

Der Bucklige und die Tänzerin (Carl Mayer)

Carl Mayer's first script for Murnau, *Der Bucklige und die Tänzerin* (1920), does not show the writer's characteristic style as it was later to be seen in *Sylvester*, published in 1924.[3]

Certain passages recall *Caligari*:

A suburb. Night. Narrow winding street. Crooked and contorted houses.

Sometimes Murnau adds a few words on the decor. Thus for the 'elegant' boudoir of the dancer, Gina, he notes 'a large mirror', and suggests 'a mirror in several sections' for the hunchback's apartment, described by Mayer as

a suite of rooms furnished luxuriously and bizarrely in Indo-Japanese style. Thick carpets. Statuettes. Hangings and cushions. As in a fairy story. The Arabian Nights.

In each case the added detail permits certain lighting and other effects: Gina admires herself in the glass, and the hunchback suffers when he sees his own reflection. Apart from that, Murnau did not make many additions, and gave his scriptwriter *carte blanche*. The film has not survived.

Der Januskopf (Hans Janowitz)

The script of *Der Januskopf*, another lost film, written for Murnau in 1920 by Hans Janowitz, throws light on the nature of the collaboration between Carl Mayer and Janowitz in *Das Kabinett des Dr Caligari* in 1919.

Apparently we owe the greater part of the strange story of *Caligari* to Janowitz.[4] But it is clear now that Mayer – who from the beginning conceived all his scripts in an extraordinarily filmic manner – was responsible for the form. It was this strangely stylized form which called for the Expressionist structure of the sets and a corresponding style from the actors.[5]

One can see just from reading the script of *Januskopf* that Janowitz was not responsible for those aspects of *Caligari* that were most characteristic of it. While other writers, including Murnau, were more or less influenced by Mayer's abrupt, tortured – in short, Expressionist – style, Janowitz uses a

[3] For further information on the script of this film, see Eisner, *The Haunted Screen*, Thames and Hudson and University of California Press, 1969, p. 184.

[4] See Janowitz on the subject in Siegfried Kracauer: *From Caligari to Hitler*, Princeton University Press, 1947, p. 61 etc.

[5] Warm tells how Walter Reimann, on reading the scenario, suggested that only Expressionist sets would do for it. Unlike the other Expressionists who condemned psychology, Carl Mayer, the Expressionist writer *par excellence*, was led to the 'Kammerspiel' by his interest in everything to do with the emotions.

Der Januskopf: Conrad Veidt

vocabulary that is often flat, always normal, typically 'epic'. It is very rarely that he touches on the characters' psychology, never venturing beyond an occasional 'pondering sadly'. In Carl Mayer, on the other hand, an adjective or present participle, or some purely rhetorical question, or an inversion, will suggest a vague state of mind or half-expressed idea in one of the characters, or hint at the underlying meaning of a situation.

Janowitz gives practically no acting directions for Conrad Veidt, apparently having complete confidence in the actor's own ability to bring out all the subtleties of his part. There are none of the complicated psychological suggestions that Mayer loved. Janowitz slows down the action of his script, moreover, with a superfluity of linking scenes, giving each of his characters elaborate theatrical entrances and exits. Mayer, in spite of a certain Middle European deliberation, was primarily concerned with rhythm and the succession of images, and preferred to treat such matters elliptically. Janowitz's characters also read and write far too many explanatory letters, and his titles are often needlessly discursive. He seems, in short, not to remember the essentially pictorial style which had been found for *Caligari* the previous year. The only parallel with the earlier film is where Enfield, standing in front

Der Januskopf

of the strange house, says to Utterson: 'Hier habe ich einmal eine seltsame Geschichte erlebt' (A strange thing happened to me here once), which recalls what Feher says in *Caligari*: 'Mit der habe ich einmal eine seltsame Geschichte erlebt' (A strange thing happened to me with her once).

Januskopf is a sort of transposition of Stevenson's *Dr Jekyll and Mr Hyde*. In an antique shop Dr Jekyll buys a bust which has two faces, one godlike, one diabolical. The idea of the statue begins to haunt the doctor, who sees it as a symbol of the duality of human nature. He offers it as a present to the girl he is courting, Jane Lanyon, who refuses with horror. She is kidnapped and taken by Hyde to a sinister house in Whitechapel, where she is horrified to encounter the bust once more. It is sent to auction, and Jekyll is forced against his will to buy it back. He returns with it to his laboratory, which he had thought he had left forever. Janowitz writes at this point:

> Laboratory. Dusty, cobwebs, dark. The room gives off an atmosphere of horrors and memories that makes Jeskyll[6] shudder. He hurriedly undoes the parcel, looks at the face, and utters a cry.
> Cross-fade to the grimace of the satyr. Jeskyll hastily puts the statue back in its old place and rushes from the room.

Again he falls under the power of the bust that is to be his ruin. Inevitably he becomes Hyde again, and when, unable to escape, he takes poison, he clings to the bust before collapsing dead on the ground.

Though there are many clumsinesses in Janowitz's script, there are also some very good inventions, such as the high-angle shot from an attic window of Hyde committing a murder, or the close-up of the pool of water into which Jekyll, in an attempt to rid himself of his obsession, has just thrown the key of his laboratory. Unlike *Caligari*, the script contains quite a number of scenes to be shot in natural exteriors. Janowitz has realized how a rapid succession of very short scenes, such as those showing the police chasing Hyde through the street, and the one where he is in hiding, can contribute to the creation of suspense. He is also aware of the *visual* effect of sound. When the terrified servants are waiting for the monster to manifest his presence in the laboratory, he suggests a close-up of a bell ringing – a device that was used later in *Tartuffe*. But here Murnau, who unlike Carl Mayer was always preoccupied with camera angles, added 'angle-shot', then 'reverse angle-shot'. When the doctor is going up the narrow stairs to the laboratory, Janowitz adds the direction:

> Camera follows him up the stairs.

Is this a use of the mobile camera, in 1920, long before Lupu Pick and his so-called 'unchained camera' (*Entfesselte Kamera*)? Or did Janowitz simply

---

[6] Janowitz throughout writes 'Jeskyll' instead of 'Jekyll'.

mean to indicate that a normal fixed camera should cover the whole ascent? Without the actual film we cannot say.

Some of the lighting suggestions must have pleased Murnau.

Underground bar. Nocturnal shapes. Lamp smoking.

Or,

Side-altar of a church. Half-light. Jane kneeling in silent prayer. Sacristan extinguishing the candles.

Or the back-lit shot where Jekyll takes Jane, who is ill, to a large window overlooking the terrace:

They look out at the landscape (camera behind them). The two figures are silhouetted against the wide and beautiful sky-line in which float light clouds.

Murnau added only a few notes to the script, simply indicating studios and locations, and, as in the case of *Nosferatu*, the length of the scenes. For an outside scene he notes, for example:

the street leading from the Charlottenburg station to the Kurfürstendamm.

He alters the courtyard outside the house to 'a covered passage'. He puts a word of approval beside a suggested close-up of Jane and Utterson in front of the Janus bust in Hyde's house in Whitechapel, and cuts out several unnecessary shots. It is significant that the only point at which he finds it absolutely necessary to intervene is the big dream sequence, though for Utterson's nightmare Janowitz had found a much more striking form than for any other part of the film. His script gives:

Dr Jeskyll in black pyjamas, sitting in a deep armchair, thinking. Sad thoughts. Anxiety. Behind him, against a dark background, appears the terrible head of Hyde. It hypnotizes him, and he follows it.

(Murnau simply notes: To begin with, just enormous eyes.)

Janowitz goes on:

Dark background still: slowly, as if materializing out of the mist, the square in front of the strange house appears. Hyde and the little girl run on in opposite directions and collide with one another. The incident in sequence 11 [Hyde trampling on the child and beating its body with his stick] is repeated several times. Both figures are multiplied, and Hyde tramples on the child more and more brutally.

(Here Murnau writes in the margin: Enormous shadows!)

Janowitz continues:

Jeskyll appears near them, desperate but drawn there in spite of himself. Cheques keep flying out of his hand, one after the other, towards the crying child. The cheques dissolve in mid-air and disappear. Hyde grows more and more furious, and the children disappear under his feet as if he were stamping them into the ground. In his fury he suddenly throws himself on Jeskyll, raising his stick in his hairy claws. Jeskyll staggers back. Quick fade.

Murnau transforms all this into:

1. The empty square.
2. Veidt appears by the obelisk.[7]
3. Fade to angle shot of Hyde approaching. He knocks over the little girl, then another, then another, on his way to the obelisk. More and more little girls come towards him, then disappear. Hyde, at the obelisk, throws himself on Veidt, who puts up his hands to defend himself. Fade to close-up.
4. Veidt throws away the cheques. Fade to
5. As the cheques fly away, the Hydes double, triple and multiply and all try avidly to get hold of them. The Hydes grow more and more numerous. Veidt can no longer escape, and runs towards the camera, the Hydes pursuing.
6. The Hydes all combine to form one single horrible figure. He lifts his stick against Veidt. Fade. . . .

By not multiplying the figures of Hyde and of the child at the same time, Murnau avoids confusion, but as the film is lost we do not know exactly how this nightmare sequence was really filmed. However, a single still, recently discovered in the Swedish Cinémathèque, shows this precise scene at the obelisk, and it is surprising to see that different actors made up with beards and cloaks to look like Hyde, are used to produce his doubles; and meanwhile numerous children are outstretched on the ground, little girls who are even differently dressed. So perhaps Murnau changed his mind when it came to the actual shooting.   One cannot help wondering whether fantastically inter-woven and superimposed shots of the one character (in the style of Marey's chronophotographic images) would not have produced a more effective rendering of this vision. Of course Murnau used a similar method later in the dream sequence of *Der Letzte Mann* (*The Last Laugh*), where several extras made up with the same livid impersonal masks try vainly to lift the big trunk which Jannings himself easily and triumphantly shifts.

Schloss Vogelöd (Carl Mayer)

The script of *Schloss Vogelöd* was written by Carl Mayer in 1921. Like *Der Bucklige und die Tänzerin*, it is not of the depth and complexity of *Sylvester*, written two years later. Nevertheless Mayer is already capable of revealing situation and crystallizing atmosphere. Here is the arrival of the Capuchin monk; the curious syntax has been kept as far as possible.

Fade into:	The garden gate, inside.
More general	
shot:	The night storm rages. Pouring rain. And trees bent low. But silent, the gate. A bell above it, silent. A few

[7] By 'Veidt' Murnau means Jekyll as distinct from Hyde.

seconds. But! Now the tongue of the bell
moves. Once. Then goes silent again, quite
silent. But then: at the porter's window. The light
shining out.
The porter creeps out. An old man. He turns the key.
Thus opening the door. A form appears in the doorway.
Like a shadow. Thin. A long robe. Hands crossed.
Spectacles, behind which a piercing glance. The
priest draws himself up.
A carriage can be seen, darkly.

Or the description of the characters' states of mind and reactions on the arrival of Father Faramund: the lady of the house is glad, but the baroness's behaviour is very strange.

Closer shot:	But! The baroness. Is she smiling now? Bitterly? The châtelaine is completely at a loss. Looking at her friend. The baroness trembling terribly. She gasps for breath. Then: suddenly: clutching the châtelaine's hand? Jumping up suddenly. Shuddering from head to foot. The châtelaine very frightened. Ready to cry out. But! The Baroness. Stifling the cry? With a wild look, eyes flashing. She stands there thus. Seconds. Then she tears herself away. Suddenly. Runs towards the door. The châtelaine terrified, rigid. She is motionless. Then. The baroness. Turning towards her again. Clasping her friend round the neck. As if desperate, embracing her. And she whispers:
Title:	'Still . . . be . . . my friend!' She stays for a few more seconds. Then: She goes. Silent. Calm. Heavy. Like lead. Now: The door: Then: the châtelaine. Alone.
Close-up:	She is shuddering too.

By chance, after selecting this passage, I came across an account of this sequence in the *Film Kurier* for 18 February 1921, in which a journalist describes what he saw on a visit to the studio. His impressions enable us to catch a brief glimpse of Murnau at work.

The director F. W. Murnau at work. In the studio an intimate interior set. Two women. Dense shadows form and gather near the face of one of them: presentiments. The message of fate gets through to her. Only by being there could one realize how two characters can shed all personal life and become simply artistic material shaped under the creator's hand; how that hand can bring forth life and expression and draw from the body and skill of the actor the deepest and most delicate nuances, transforming the interpreter's own psychology into a living, changing mould. . . .

Fate lays its hand on two people: one staggers out, broken, and the other remains plunged in reflection, her face mirroring the reactions of her friend.

I cannot imagine any more complete and deep psychological expression than the one I saw come into being and then slowly fade under Murnau's hand. In such a case can one still regret the absence of words? I do not think so.

This was Murnau, interpreting Mayer's script in the studio. It is on-the-spot testimony of his ability to handle actors.

Mayer uses questions to prepare the spectator for a new situation or mystery. The count, whom everyone suspects, hears that the baroness, though frightened by his presence and wanting to leave, agrees to stay and wait for Father Faramund. Mayer notes:

Close-up: The count. Did he hear? Is he thinking? For long?

Mayer is fond of these changes of tense. The idiosyncrasy of his German makes it difficult to render his style in another language, but the staccato phrases, sometimes unfinished, the personifications, the apparently fortuitous interjections, form an internal rhythm of their own. His scripts read almost like a poem by Apollinaire, or sometimes like the stage-directions in a play by Büchner:

> Evening. Dark. Rain. A coach.
> Like a shadow.
> Approaches.

It is difficult to say why it was that Murnau added so little to Mayer's script: perhaps it was chance, or perhaps the final script did not need much further improvement; Mayer, who had collaborated with Murnau in 1920 in *Der Bucklige und die Tänzerin* and *Der Gang in die Nacht*, was already perfectly at home with Murnau's cinematographic style.

Tartuffe (Carl Mayer)
It is curious to see how, when he had to add some sequences to the script for *Tartuffe*, begun by Mayer in 1925, Murnau clearly imitated Mayer's tortured, rhythmical style. For example, when Mayer writes:

> rubbing her hands, she returns . . .

Murnau completes it with:

> to the gate
> which soon shuts.
> And stands silent.
> A few seconds.

Murnau also adds several passages about the handsome André Mattoni, the old man's nephew in Mayer's prologue, though he becomes his grandson in Murnau's annotations:

The grandson's whole person should give an impression of harmony and charm, even down to the way he knocks at the gate.

Here is how Murnau describes him:

	Then: smiling, he turns. Is he going away now?
	No! Or does he rather turn
	Towards the camera? Indeed
	Smiling, charming, indolent
	like a successful entertainer
	he says to the audience
	with an amusing pathos:
Title:	You, the witnesses of this!
	Do not think that I
	am going away just like
	that. I shall come back
	to unmask this wicked creature!
	And so he remains for a few more moments
	Looking with a smile at the audience.
	As if saying charmingly,
	'well, now'. So once more
	he takes off his hat, but not with exaggerated
	irony, but politely, charmingly
	even?
	And leaves
	elegantly.
	So he is
	now already gone.
	The gate, however, is still there for a few moments.
	But now slowly
	It grows dim. Fade.
	Which lasts some time.

Even when he writes in camera directions in Mayer's style, Murnau for the most part does not rise to the ardent poetic accents of Mayer himself. His writing is still rather clumsy, rough, and commonplace. Later, for *Faust*, the scenario of which was not by Mayer, he was to find bold and poetic expressions which Mayer himself would not have disowned.

The *Tartuffe* script is informative. It is the final shooting-script for the 'prologue' and 'epilogue', the part that deals with the old man, the housekeeper who hopes to be left his money, and the legitimate heir. These scenes, annotated by Murnau and crossed through on the script as they were shot, were filmed, as the marked typescript shows, between 20 and 25 February 1925, at the rate of two to four sequences a day, depending on their length. The script contains sketches for camera positions and studio directions.

The main action of the film, also annotated here by Murnau but not struck through, must have been filmed from a different copy of the script. An odd scrap of paper in this one shows that certain sequences of the main part of the film were not shot until 2–9 April. Only sixteen sequences were shot in this period, which shows that Murnau worked much more slowly on *Tartuffe* than he did on, for example, *Schloss Vogelöd*, the whole of which was shot in sixteen days.

It is interesting to examine in Mayer's script the sequences which introduced brilliant lighting effects in the film itself: for instance, the scene in which Tartuffe goes at night to Elmire's room.

49

Closer shot: The first floor	Night. Dark.
	But! Coming down the first stair:
	like a shadow: almost indistinguishable.
	Tartuffe?
	Yes. There he stands.
	Just a black shape.
	Is he looking up, slightly?
Slow	For:
pan upwards:	Above Tartuffe's door.
	Another door.
	An attic room.
	With a glass door.
	Lit from within.
	And there: Dorine's silhouette.
	Combing her hair.
	Seconds pass
	Then: suddenly: has
	The light gone out?
	Yes.
	And lo!
Close-up:	Tartuffe.
	Looking down again now.
	Here.
	Slowly. Ghastly in all this
	Black darkness.

Mayer gives a long description of him creeping down the stairs, his mouth open with desire, step by step, on tiptoe, but heavily. The camera is to precede him at a slightly faster pace, but when he reaches the foot of the stair it swings round slightly to the right:

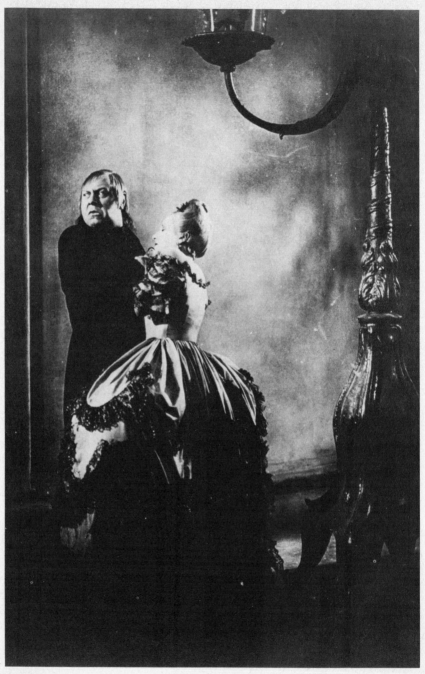

Tartuffe

> As if to reveal Tartuffe's object.
> Which he is now approaching.
> Creeping faster and faster.
> For:
> Here is Elmire's door.
> Standing there silent.
> Only a crack underneath
> Shows there is a light within.

Mayer takes all this much more slowly than Murnau, showing in detail what Tartuffe does outside the door, whereas Murnau cuts this scene very short. He even omits the glass door to Dorine's room. Dorine comes out with a candlestick, lighting up the staircase somewhat, then peers down, the camera doing likewise. Here Murnau follows Mayer:

> And! Now she holds her breath:
> And so leans down over the banister.
> To see down the stairs.
> And lo!
>
> What Dorine sees: Seen from right up
> Above:
> A door opens.
> Slowly.
> So that light falls on the floor.

In the film, as in the script, the only sign that Elmire's door has opened is a ray of light falling across the black and white tiles.

Mayer cannot resist giving another view of Elmire's door:

> But at the same time:
> The same moment:
>
> Close-up: Elmire's door
> Was shutting.
> And! Then:
> It stands there silent.
> Only the crack under the door
> betrays the light within.
> For a few seconds.

Murnau treats this more subtly and elliptically. We have seen the ray of light fall across the tiles. This ray narrows and disappears as Tartuffe, whom we do not see, falls into the trap and enters the room. Then, as in the film, Mayer draws the camera slowly back:

> The hall thus comes into view again.
> And lo! Dorine? Yes.
> Holding up a candlestick
> Which sheds the strangest beams.

> And so she gropes her way down.
> With waddling gait.
> Quite soundlessly.
> Only her enormous shadow
> gliding all over the walls.

Murnau wisely omits a rather complicated signal arranged, according to the script, with Elmire: it would have interfered with the musical play of the other, more important lighting effects. But he uses Mayer's directions for Orgon:

Slow fade-in:	a room dark as night.
Closer shot:	Just a gleam of a candle.
	Flickering on a table.
	By it: pale:
	His cheeks hollow and shadowed
	Orgon.
	Writing? Apparently. For:
	He has a pen in his hand . . .

For some the strange constructions of Mayer's style must have seemed incomprehensible. In a letter to Erich Pommer, written on 21 January 1925 (after *The Last Laugh*), Murnau complains of the insinuations of a director of Ufa whom he met in New York, who said to him:

> You've a lot to learn in America. I've had a great many disappointments here. The films we make in Germany won't sell in the States. I've just seen a film without titles. What's the point of wanting to make art films? Who wants to see films without titles? You have to have them. Who's interested in films about old men? What people want to see are nice young couples and a nice simple love story; and that's what I want to see too.

By an irony of fate *The Last Laugh*, that 'unsaleable' film, was a great success with intellectuals in the United States, and for the first two films he made in America, *Sunrise* and *Four Devils*, Murnau continued to work in collaboration with his favourite writer, though Mayer had remained in Germany.[8]

Nosferatu (Henrik Galeen)

It is bold, perhaps, to assert that Henrik Galeen (who in 1914 had collaborated with Paul Wegener on the script of the first *Golem*, and who was to

[8] Mayer even began work on a third film, *Our Daily Bread*. Murnau cabled him on 19 December 1928 to ask if it was true that Winfield Sheehan had given him an ultimatum either to send him the script straight away or to send back the money he had already received. The film was finally attributed only to Marion Orth and Berthold Viertel, who had collaborated on Mayer's script for *Four Devils*.

direct the second *Der Student von Prag* and the first *Alraune*) was influenced by the style of Carl Mayer, since no script of his is known to us except *Nosferatu*. That scenario, however, is certainly rhythmical and full of poetry. As in Mayer, the sentences are set out like lines of poetry, but though they are often rather abrupt they are less broken, less Expressionist than Mayer's. He does, however, use similar inversions, rhetorical questions, and conjunctions like Mayer's famous 'And so . . .'.

In the scene at the port, where the men open an earth-filled coffin and the rats swarm out, Galeen writes:

> Did not one of them . . . reeling from the blow . . .
> bite his foot?

And, describing the ghost ship:

> The ship.
> Dead and forsaken. A rope is dangling
> from the deck. Is it swaying in the wind?

Murnau added very little to this final script. Here and there he did change certain scenes, as for example the passage where Nosferatu leaves the ship.

Galeen writes:

Medium close up:	An endless number of rats climbing down the swaying
Shot of deck.	rope. The hatch. It opens slowly. N O S F E R A T U climbs out. He carries the last coffin. Remains standing. Motionless. The image of death. Then he approaches slowly.

Murnau substitutes for this:

> 1. Ship anchored in the harbour. Dissolve.
> 2. Ship's hatch with a piece of deck.
> Trick: 1. Canvas glides away from hatch.
>   2. Hatch lid is lifted.
>   3. Rats are rushing on deck.
>   4. Nosferatu coffin in arm climbs out.

In the film Murnau shows Nosferatu without the coffin, rising up slowly and stiffly, which gives a much more supernatural effect. Scene 3, with the rats, is the only one not struck through in the script: it was shot differently and edited in after number 4.

For the 'race against death', the scenes where the vampire travels by sea and Hutter by land, while Ellen is waiting for her husband and Knock watches for the arrival of the 'master', Murnau with a few rapid notes reinforces the cross-cuts sketched in by Galeen. He reverses the order of

Nosferatu: end of Act 11

some scenes, and adds others, particularly silhouette shots of the ship and shots of waves off Heligoland. These brief images increase the suspense, which is sustained even after the monster goes ashore.

Here is a part of that sequence as annotated by Murnau:

> Ellen runs out of her room.
> The wheel of the coach breaks.
> Ellen runs across the garden.
> The ship speeds towards its goal.
> Knock [first scene, where he realises that the master has come.]
> Ship in harbour.
> Hutter running along the street, Knock [the master is here]
> Ship in harbour. Nosferatu [coming out of the hatch]
> Hutter running along the street.
> Nosferatu, with the coffin, goes through the gate
> Gate, Hutter [Arrival at the house]
> Knock's flight.
> Nosferatu, square or street.
> Room – [Hutter and Ellen]

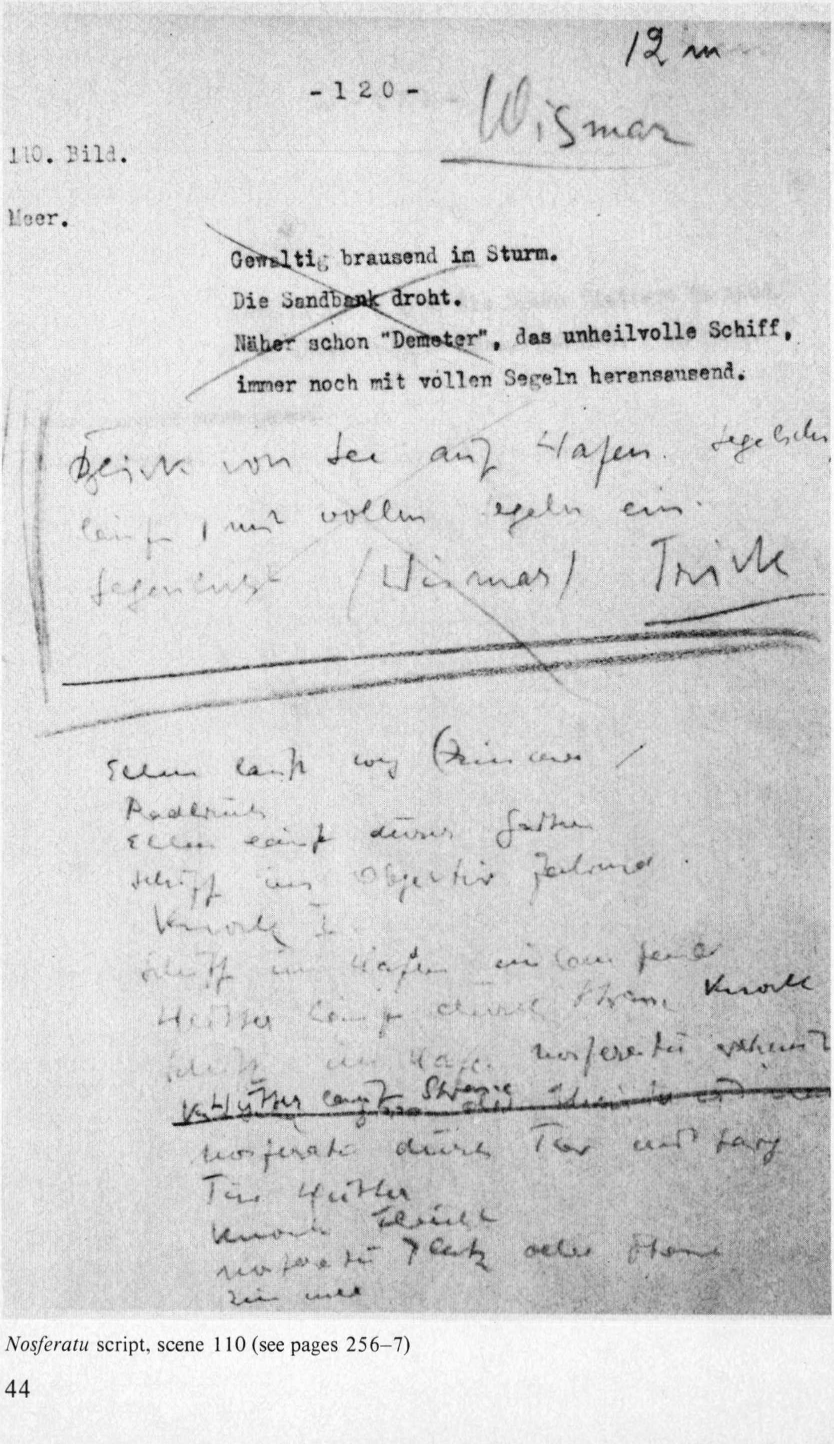
12 m

-120-

Wismar

110. Bild.

Meer.

~~Gewaltig brausend im Sturm.~~

~~Die Sandbank droht.~~

~~Näher schon "Demeter", das unheilvolle Schiff,~~

~~immer noch mit vollen Segeln heransausend.~~

Blick von See auf Hafen. Segelschiff läuft mit vollen Segeln ein. Gegenlicht (Wismar) Trick

Nosferatu script, scene 110 (see pages 256–7)

Nosferatu: a shot not mentioned in the script

Sometimes the film is different from the scenario though Murnau has not indicated any change in the script. For example, when the town-crier announces that in order to prevent the plague from spreading people are no longer to be taken to hospital, Galeen has a woman, already very ill, at a window. In the film however we see several peaceful and healthy citizens lean out of the window to see what is the matter, then withdraw hastily when they realize that it is a warning about the plague.

But there is a more surprising passage, in which nearly twelve pages (thirteen sequences) have been rewritten by Murnau. We do not have the same passage from Galeen's script with which to compare it. It is the section that begins with Nosferatu watching from his window like a spider; then Ellen decides to sacrifice herself, and the monster comes.

Here are the last lines of the passage:

General shot:
Deserted house:
Nosferatu approaches
and disappears out of camera range
The house stands there deserted!
5m.

In front of Hutter's house:	Nobody is about. Nosferatu is approaching. He comes to a halt. (He is preparing to jump, looks up.) He enters the house.
Ellen's room:	Ellen turns round suddenly. She is shaking with fear, anticipating the horror about to happen. And it is coming – slowly, tensed like a predatory animal. She recoils, moves backwards, step by step, and step by step it follows her.

In the film, we see nothing but the shadow of Nosferatu first outlined against the wall of the stairs, then mounting with dreadful slowness, then more quickly, until the gigantic shade pauses outside the door before going in. Then, inside the room, Ellen shrinks back before the monster we, the spectators, still do not see, except as the shadow falling across the body of the young woman.

Murnau's script gives no indication of this nightmare scene on the stairs. Yet he could not have improvised on the floor a scene which in fact necessitated a new set by Albin Grau. Could he have added it after shooting all the exteriors, without recording it in the book that explicitly notes all the locations in the Carpathian and the Baltic towns of Wismar, Rostock, and Lubeck, as well as the sea shots of Heligoland and the North Sea, including the actual footages involved?

It is yet another of the enigmas which remain about *Nosferatu* in spite of the survival of the script.

Phantom (Thea von Harbou)

Thea von Harbou wrote a screenplay for *Phantom* in 1922, in collaboration with Hans Heinrich von Twardowski, who played the friend murdered in *Caligari*. She did not bother with the Expressionist efforts of a writer like Mayer. In the first half of the script (Acts 1 to 3 inclusive) she follows Gerhart Hauptmann's short story 'Phantom' faithfully enough, but in a ponderous style overburdened with detail. The sentences are long and regular, often as elaborate as in a story meant to be read.[9] She even kept the prologue

[9] The making of *Phantom*, first shown in November 1922, was beset with difficulties. Shooting had to be interrupted for some time because Murnau was suffering from kidney trouble. Decla Bioskop wrote to him on 21 August 1922, at the Bühlershoh sanatorium near Baden-Baden, to tell him that the rest of the shooting must be finished from 4 September onwards, and that Hermann Warm was working on the studio sets of Breslau, which had been seriously damaged by the bad weather. Murnau was informed that he must work more sensibly and economically, and avoid unnecessary travelling. Film negative already cost thirty marks per metre. 'It is necessary to make do', said the letter, 'for even with the help of the big banks it is

to Hauptmann's short story as a *Rahmenhandlung*, a sort of framing device often used in German films at that time.

In a mountain village Lorenz Lubota, a former convict, at his wife's request writes the eventful story of his life. He is sitting by a window, darkly silhouetted against the bright sunlight outside – an image which, it was clear, even before the film was rediscovered, Murnau would not have neglected to exploit.

Lorenz, a minor clerk in the town hall at Breslau, has lived an uneventful, drab life until the day when he is run over, though not hurt, by a strangely beautiful girl, Veronika Harlan. At first stunned, he then runs after her in a frenzy, to see her disappear into the house of her father, a rich iron-founder. Then, instead of going to work, he returns home again like a sleepwalker. When he gets there he suddenly realizes the poverty of his surroundings. Murnau, who had so far modified the script very little, drew two lines beside this passage.

General shot:
He looks round the room which seems to him quite changed. All that was wretched and ugly before is now doubly so. The damp wall-paper, the stains on the floor, the cheap furniture, the uncurtained windows and the depressing well of the courtyard beyond. All these things seem to exude a bleak hostility, a hostility directed against him. It is as if the walls were leaning in on him, as if the ceiling were sinking down to stifle him.[10]

It is not surprising that this transformation of a shabby room, which so lent itself to Expressionist interpretation, should have appealed to Murnau. But the room's transformation was carried even further, and at this point, as in the nightmare sequence in *Januskopf*, Murnau took a decisive hand.

Thea von Harbou writes:

The room grows blurred and changes into:
A street.
Exactly like an ordinary street. But giving impression of a street seen in a dream. Nothing solid and definite except the two things that matter: Veronika's carriage bowling along with her borzoi bounding beside the wheels, and Lorenz following. He is running, panting along out of breath, but he stays in the same place. People turn to look at him, and laugh at him with twisted smiles.
He feels his strength failing. The distance between him and the carriage is increasing. Veronika turns towards him, laughs, and calls her dog. She drives on towards a dazzling wedge-shaped light, while everything else, including Lorenz, grows darker

---

impossible to raise money'. These financial difficulties in Germany were eventually to grow into inflation.

[10] Hauptmann also speaks of this subjective and 'incomprehensible transformation', and in the story Lubota even finds his mother changed.

40. Bild.

Strasse einer Stadt.
-x-x-x-x-x-x-x-x-x-x

Es ist das getreue Abbild einer alltäglichen
Strasse. Dennoch wirkt sie wie eine Strasse,
die man im Traum sieht. Nichts ist an ihr we-
sentlich und klar als die beiden Dingen auf
die es ankommt: Das Ponygespann Veronikas,
das umsprungen von dem russischen Windhund in
schärfster Gangart die Strasse entlangrollt
und der das Ponygespann verfolgende Lorenz
Lubota. Er rennt mit keuchenden Lungen und
kommt doch nicht vom Fleck. Die Menschen scha-
en sich nach ihm um und lachen mit verzerrten
Gesichtern. Er fühlt, dass ihm die Kräfte ver-
sagen. Der Abstand zwischen ihm und dem Wagen
vergrössert sich. Veronika schaut über die
Schultern nach ihm zurück, lacht, ruft ihren
Hund. Sie fährt in einem blendenden Licht-
keil, während alles Andere, auch Lorenz, mehr
und mehr im Schatten versinkt. Zuletzt ver-
schwindet sie. Nahe am Apparat steht das
schweissüberronnene, keuchende, verzweifelte
Gesicht Lorenz Lubotas und versinkt in einem
Wirbel von Schatten. Das Bild verwandelt sich
in

Phantom script, scene 40

and darker. Finally she disappears. Close to the camera, the desperate face of Lorenz Lubota, panting, streaming with sweat; then it is swallowed up in a maelstrom of shadows. The picture changes into:
Madame Lubota's dining-room.

Murnau notes:

becoming vague and dark
1. (*a*) Street with strong, projected shadows. The ground entirely dark, the lower parts of the houses opposite dark also. (Seen through a glass screen.)
(*b*) Shot of the carriage driving over the dark ground, with spotlights on Lorenz running alongside.
2. Darken the street in the foreground completely by means of a mask gradually thinning upwards. Mask sky also.
Yellow filter. Nothing luminous but the eaves of the houses.
3. As 2. The other aspect of the houses not to be shown till later!

There is a sketch of this dream street in the margin of the script, presumably drawn by Murnau.

In his book *Grossmacht Film*, published in 1928, Curt Wesse (who dates *Phantom* eight or ten years before the time of writing whereas it was actually made in 1922), says that Veronika in her phantom carriage appears, superimposed, throughout the film, driving in ghostly fashion across the action whenever Lorenz feels his destiny dragging him towards the abyss. Sometimes she would just drive across the corner of the screen and disappear. The rediscovered copy of the film confirms this. There is nothing of this in Thea von Harbou's script, but it sounds very much like Murnau.

A review of 23 November 1922 in the *Roland von Berlin* adds confirmation. It speaks of certain scenes which come off perfectly: where the houses threaten to fall in on the guilty one, and giant shadows pursue him; where the superimposed image of the carriage with the white horse keeps reappearing, as in Victor Sjöström's *Phantom Carriage* (1920). Lorenz pays no heed to the laments of his mother for Melanie, the daughter who has just left her forever. He dashes out into the street. Starke the bookbinder stops him: he has read his poems, and has even given them to a famous professor, for Lorenz may yet be a great poet! Here there comes another vision that must have appealed to Murnau. Lorenz imagines himself famous, going up the steps to the town hall while Veronika presents him with a bouquet of flowers. Again he is drawn towards Veronika's house, but realizing how shabbily he is dressed he goes first to borrow some money from his old aunt Schwabe, a rich money-lender for whom he works as book-keeper in his spare time. He pretends that a well-known professor is going to introduce him to an important publisher and show him his poems, and that he has nothing suitable to wear.

Wigottschinski, old Mrs Schwabe's shady lover, thinks he sees an opportunity to make some money and accompanies Lorenz when he goes to buy his fine clothes. In the evening he takes him to a low tavern, where Lorenz is horrified to find his sister Melanie, garishly dressed. He is wounded in a fight with one of her temporary lovers, and driven off in a cab by Wigottschinski and Melanie. In front of the Harlans' house, Lorenz leaps from the cab – Wigottschinski has mentioned that Veronika is about to become engaged to a rich suitor. In spite of the late hour, Lorenz rings at the door. Thea von Harbou writes:

	Veronika's head in close-up leaning out of the window.
Shot of:	Lorenz looking up with an expression of painful ecstasy.
	As if struck by an irresistible force he kneels, without
	taking his eyes off Veronika.

Melanie at last drags her brother away and Veronika's head disappears from the window. The next day the chief clerk at the town hall will not accept the excuse that Lorenz has been ill: he has heard of the two scandals; Lorenz has lost his job. Lorenz, not knowing that the professor has found his poems very undistinguished, goes off proudly to ask the Harlans for their daughter's hand. He is politely shown the door. Then, afraid to go back to his miserable hovel, of which Thea von Harbou gives us a non-realistic flash-back, Lorenz jumps into a cab and drives to a fashionable restaurant. There he is irresistibly drawn towards two ladies sitting alone at a table: a so-called 'baroness' and her daughter Melitta, who bears an extraordinary resemblance to Veronika.

All the *Stimmung*,[11] or atmosphere, missing in Thea von Harbou, Murnau could find in Hauptmann:

The artificial light that was necessary there even during the daytime, except beside the single window, increased his feeling of well-being. It was intensified further by the twilight veil produced by the clouds of tobacco smoke, which seemed to isolate each of the guests.

Lorenz follows the ladies out into the street. As he is well-dressed, they take him along with them.

In *Grossmacht Film* Wesse mentions another of Lorenz's visions, which seems to have taken place in the restaurant, in which everything around him begins to lose its stability. The table goes round faster and faster and in ever-increasing circles, all is drawn into the vortex, and the audience itself is dragged to the brink of the abyss. A man's mental sense of the ground giving way under his feet is translated into a visual event on the surface of the screen. There is not much of this in the script, nor, alas, in the film as it survives.

[11] For *Stimmung*, see Eisner, *The Haunted Screen* (1969), pages 199–206.

These images are rather reminiscent of the cafe episode in Dupont's film *Variety* (1925). And Murnau must have remembered this sequence in *Phantom*, sub-titled 'Der schwankende Tag' (The Tottering Day), when he came to film the temptation of the city in the swamp in *Sunrise*.

Here is part of the last sequence in this copy of the script of *Phantom*. It takes place in the apartment of the 'baroness', who has discreetly disappeared. Thea von Harbou suggests:

	subdued light, but not too dim.
Different angle:	Melitta and Lorenz in profile. He has come close to her, and stammers, still without touching her:
	'You!' As soon as he touches her,
	she shrinks back, uttering a little gurgling cry,
	eluding his hand nimbly, like a beautiful animal, so
	that she is now with her back to the camera, leaning
	away from Lorenz and drawing him to her with her whole
	body.
Close-up of Lorenz, murmuring:	'No . . . no! Don't you run away from me too!'
	Close shot of Lorenz and Melitta. She stands in front of
	him, still drawing back but trying to attract him to her.
	Seeing the expression on his face, she is touched. She
	leans towards him, hands suddenly outstretched. Lorenz
	comes into view and takes her hands. She snatches them
	away: throughout this scene her whole being seems
	possessed by a continual trembling.
	Close-up of the two heads. Melitta takes Lorenz's face in
	her hands, looks at it closely, and asks:
	'Who are you? . . . Who are you?! . . .'
	Lorenz goes still at the touch of her hands, shuts his
	eyes, then opens them. Distraught, obsessed expression.
	He stares at Melitta and says, looking like someone
	risking all or nothing;
	'I'm . . . I'm a clerk at the town hall who's just been
	sacked!'
	Close shot of Melitta and Lorenz: she still holds his face
	in her hands as she waits for his answer. Now she lets
	it go and bursts out laughing, a jubilant child-like
	laugh that goes on and on. She twirls round on her toes
	and claps her hands, delighted at his fancifulness.
	Close-up of Lorenz, who looks at her not understanding
	what she is laughing at.
	Close shot of Melitta trying to stop laughing. She falls
	into a chair and gasps, still shaken with mirth:

'Don't tell that nonsense to my mother, or she'll throw
you out!'
Shot of Lorenz, who wants to explain that it is the truth.
Close shot of Melitta, now a little calmer, who goes on,
stretching out her hand, still somewhat nervously, to
Lorenz:
'. . . and don't tell *me* any more like it, either! It sounds
like stuffy rooms and dirty linen and cabbage soup. I
don't want to hear you talk about things like that!'
She drops her hand, leans forward charmingly, and says,
looking at Lorenz, childishly and coaxingly at the same
time:
'Tell me who you are!'
Close shot of Lorenz, who stares into space and says slowly:
'I'm . . . a poet . . . an unlucky man . . . pursuing a shadow
. . . a ghost!'

This, with its play of camera angles, is real *Kammerspiel*,[12] which must
have pleased Murnau.

The rest of the script – 'acts' 4 to 6 – more or less follows Hauptmann's
story in its original form, in which the baroness takes increasing advantage of
Lorenz, who with the help of Wigottschinski and Melanie gets large sums of
money out of old Schwabe, ostensibly for his career as a poet.

One day the old woman sees through his deceit, and Wigottschinski and
Melanie hatch a complicated plot to burgle her house; Lorenz, by now
apathetic, agrees. But the old woman wakes, sees Lorenz, cries for help, and
Wigottschinski strangles her. He is condemned to death, and Lorenz, as his
accomplice, is sent to forced labour. After many years he is released; his
mother is dead, but now he is cured of his obsession, and he begins a new life
with Starke and his daughter Marie, who has always loved him.

Without Harbou, Murnau could have made use of certain passages in
Hauptmann's story. There, when the police, in civilian clothing, bring Lorenz
to the dead woman's apartment, he sees the unappetizing remains of dinner on
the table: the head and bones of some smoked fish. This dinner shared by his
aunt and Wigottschinski strikes Lorenz as a sort of ghost meal. Even the most
ordinary things, like simple bread and butter, seem on that table to have
something odd and ghostly about them. And this atmosphere hovers round
Lorenz, who is instinctively aware that it means more to him than horrible
crude reality. Then he sees the grotesque, shapeless, almost indecent mass of
flesh that was his aunt, in the next room, become almost as unreal as the food
on the table.

This could of course have given Murnau a great opportunity for some

[12] For *Kammerspiel*, see Eisner, *The Haunted Screen* (1969), pages 177–99, 207–21.

marvellous scenes halfway between reality and unreality. But Thea von Harbou's script extracts only a detective-story plot from the last part of Hauptmann's story, which she tries on the other hand to endow with a sentimental element.

Faust (Hans Kyser)

There is also a first script for *Faust*, by Hans Kyser, a fairly well-known German poet who himself made several films, including *Luther*. It is only a first attempt, and many passages in it were eliminated or altered later. There is a Walpurgisnacht, for example, which does not appear in the final version, though it must have appealed to Murnau, with his love of fantastic visions; he even made a note in one place: '*Hexenküche* here', i.e. a witch's kitchen, *à la* Goethe.

Another element that disappears is an evocation of a medieval town, with steep streets and flights of steps. The only allusion to it is a note by Murnau to the effect that Mephisto, when crying out 'murder', runs towards an alley that is entered by a flight of steps. In Kyser's version, moreover, Gretchen is not absolved. The angel, with a flaming sword as in the picture of the Last Judgment, grows more and more huge and drives the sinner out of the cathedral as the mass for the dead is being said for her mother and brother. In the midst of this scene of the fainting Gretchen is inserted a shot of Faust pursued by the Furies. Gretchen falls half unconscious and the scenario ends with her despair.

(It is not generally known that Ludwig Berger, not Murnau, was originally to have made *Faust*. I have even seen a script by Berger himself, with which Kyser must have been familiar, for he makes extensive use of its contents. Berger wanted Conrad Veidt for Mephisto, but he was anticipated by Jannings, who wanted the part for himself and the film for Murnau, for whom he had just played Tartuffe.)

Murnau annotated Kyser's text throughout, transforming it, pencilling in whole pages in his rounded handwriting. He even had typed pages incorporated, gathering together his own pencilled notes. This may have been because it was only a first draft, but perhaps it was rather that Murnau himself was developing, and coming more and more to understand how to construct a script, to translate a text into visual terms, and give directions to actors in terms of images.[13]

[13] This first version already gives indications of the dates planned for the actors' bookings. Jannings was to be engaged to shoot from 10 October 1925 till the end of the film; Ekman from 15 September 1925 till 1 February 1926; Lillian Gish, who was to have played Gretchen, from 10 November to 15 February; Frieda Richard, the mother, from 10 November to 31 December; Dieterle, the brother, from 10 November to 15 January; Rosa Valetti, who was at first to have played Marthe instead of Yvette Guilbert, from 10 November to 15

Murnau surpassed the poet Kyser, surpassed – even though he retained a modified form of his style – the verve of Carl Mayer himself. This mode of expression had become natural to him, and his writing was full of life, yet flawless and limpid. He invented, creating daring combinations of words untranslatable into another language. He used vivid expressions, imaginative comparisons, and vigorously replaced Kyser's phrases with phrases of his own. As we examine the process we can really see Murnau at work.

For example, Kyser writes:

Without a moment's hesitation, Faust snatches the pact away from him, goes to a table, and picks up a pen.

Much more plastically and dramatically, Murnau has:

Faust looks at him fixedly. Then he takes the pact from him as though hypnotized, and still as if under the effect of hypnosis, gropes behind him for the pen.

After the scene in which the pact is signed in Faust's blood, Kyser has:

Mephisto has already seized the pact and overturned the hour-glass. Faust, as if freed from an enormous burden, takes a deep breath; then pointing to the window, he says:

Title: Now I can help. . . .

He goes quickly out through the door, signing to Mephisto to follow. Mephisto, with a look of triumph on his face, puts the pact in his pocket and hurries after him.

Here is the same passage in Murnau's version:

Trembling, conscious of this moment's terrible significance, Faust gulps down a glass of water in such haste that he spills it on his beard and clothes. And so he goes out, staggering heavily like Lear.

Title: I shall help you, then, in the name of the devil.

Meanwhile Mephisto, who has been looking lovingly at the signature, dries it with sand. Then he folds up the paper with a look of delight, glee. And although Faust has already staggered out, Mephisto draws himself up, still smiling, and looks after him. He continues to do so. Then he somehow increases in stature; his smile gradually vanishes and he becomes threatening: the triumph of evil makes him grow gigantic.

January. The role of the duchess of Parma was to have been a much longer one, so Hanna Ralph was to be booked from 1 November to 10 November; in the same way Wangenheim was to be engaged from 21 September to 1 October to play the part of the violinist in the procession, a part which hardly exists in the film; Twardowski, the monk, was to work from 21 September to 1 October.

Plans were already made at this stage even for the actual shooting. From Thursday 10 September to the 14th was allocated to preliminary shots of the amphitheatre, Faust's study, and the bedchamber of the dying woman. Tuesday the 15th, the amphitheatre. Wednesday and Thursday, 16 and 17 September, Faust's study. 18 and 19 September, the dying woman's room; from Monday the 21st till the 29th, the Fair. These details show how slowly and precisely Murnau prepared his shooting.

Faust and Mephisto: the pact

And then suddenly he bursts out laughing, laughter as sharp as a flint, but brief. He cuts it short and overturns the hour-glass. [As in Kyser, the hour-glass gets larger and larger until it fills the whole screen.]

The scene outside Gretchen's house is described as follows by Kyser:

Stealthily, like a hunter after his prey, Mephisto comes on the scene. He beckons Faust after him, points out the mother's window, and steals towards the house.

Murnau deletes this scene and replaces it with:

Outside the house: for a few seconds all is peaceful and quiet. But now a head peers round a corner of the house. Mephisto? Apparently. But the head is at once withdrawn.

Only now:

Close shot: Mephisto creeps round the corner, beckoning to Faust, who appears behind him. Faust contemplates the house happily. But Mephisto is busy rubbing his hands. . . .

Or here is Kyser's account of Gretchen's anxiety in her room:

Now she goes over to the little statue of the Madonna, as if she was going to pray. But, as if realizing that her conscience is not as peaceful as it used to be, she turns

Death of Valentin

away, and now, as if making a sudden decision, snatches the chain from its hiding-place and runs out with it.

Murnau gives a fuller explanation of what lies behind all this, with detailed instructions for the benefit of the actress, Camilla Horn, who was new to films.

But her thoughts are wandering. She can't concentrate enough to pray. So she turns away abruptly from the statue. She walks up and down. Her face is sad and drawn. Suddenly she straightens up. Looks at the chest of drawers, fearful, timid. Is she going over to it? Apparently! But suddenly she stops, her expression growing more and more worried. What is she to do? Ah! She suddenly catches sight of her spinning-wheel, and starts to look more cheerful. Yes, that's what she'll do. Work, and forget all these thoughts. She busies herself, almost exaggeratedly, with her wheel, and begins to spin. Seconds go by. She is still at work. Still at work even now. But suddenly she pauses. Sits there thinking – it is touching to see her. She looks almost like a child. Who doesn't know what to do. And then: she runs, almost as if she could not help herself, to the chest of drawers. She opens it and then: takes out the chain and looks at it happily, and yet with a little air of resentment, as if addressing a sort of maidenly reproach to the man she is thinking of.

When Gretchen's brother dies in the duel with Faust, Kyser says briefly:

Valentin, run through by Faust's sword,
falls, dying. . . .

Murnau elaborates:

Valentin, run through by Faust's sword, draws himself up for a moment. Stands there stiffly, with the weapon in his breast. Then; as Faust looks at him, terribly tense, Valentin totters. But now. Like a giant impossible to fell, he seems to grow taller, and still with the sword in his breast, like a wounded bull, he comes nearer and nearer to Faust, who seems quite small and overshadowed by him: does Valentin, immense now and threatening, mean to strangle him? But see: this same giant freezes as if gravely injured, wheels round, and falls heavily, like a tree.

Murnau eventually discarded some of these details in order not to slow up the action. But even so, and even though such long sequences as the one in Auerbach's cellar, which show how boldly Murnau altered Kyser's text, were condensed, this script of *Faust* is very instructive. For it categorically disproves the contentions of those who have maintained that Murnau owed all his visions to his designers and cameramen, or, when he worked with him, to Carl Mayer.

A second version of the script for *Faust* is further proof of how Murnau himself always heightens the visual element, as in the superimposed travelling shot of peaks and valleys which signify the cry of anguish that goes up to Faust from Gretchen in her misery − a cry of despair which is itself made concrete by a shot of her open mouth.

For it is Murnau who pencils these notes:

Big picture of Gretchen crying out. Then wild cry across the chaotic landscapes.
Ranges of mountains split open to the left; behind them boiling waves.
Above all these images hovers a ghostly image of Gretchen's face, tortured by woe.

Murnau's loyal collaborator Robert Herlth, whose great modesty always makes him efface his own contribution to the films, has pointed out to me the example of the dream in *The Last Laugh*. Mayer's script gave only a few vague suggestions, without going into practical visual detail. Murnau pondered over this for a long time. Then he telephoned Herlth to tell him what he had in mind and ask if he thought it could be carried out. Was it possible? Could Herlth set it down in the form of designs? Following Murnau's indications, Herlth made drawings for the dream images. Then Murnau got the whole team together in the Babelsberg Casino. With the sketches spread out on the table he explained what he was aiming at, discussing intently every possibility, every difficulty.

The ever matter-of-fact Jannings objected that this was all *Wunschträume*, over-theoretical examples of wish-fulfilment dreams. Murnau patted him on the shoulder and laughed; and there was always something serious about him when he pretended to joke. 'You're playing the devil,' he said. 'When will you realize you've fallen among a covey of inventors and specialists? You haven't the least idea of what we're up to all round you. So just you leave us to get on with it!'

And Jannings grumbled and kept quiet.

This episode, together with the annotations in the scripts, is an indication of the poetic and plastic force of Murnau's style.

3. With Murnau on the Set

by Robert Herlth

[Robert Herlth who, with Walter Röhrig, was designer of sets for *The Last Laugh, Tartuffe, Faust,* and *The Four Devils,* has given me this account of his working relationship with Murnau.]

One day I got a note inviting me to go and see Murnau, who was then making a film in the studio at Tempelhof, near Berlin.

When I entered the studio I was very much surprised at how quiet it was. For in the days of silent films it was the custom to build sets while the shooting was actually going on, while there was usually a crowd of people talking at the tops of their voices, people who were there simply out of curiosity and had nothing to do with the actual shooting. But here there was no one to be seen but the cameramen and one of the actors, Alfred Abel,[1] and also, standing in the dark out of the way, a tall slim gentleman in his white work-coat, issuing directions in a very low voice. This was Murnau.

When the sequence was finished I introduced myself, and was received like an old acquaintance; it was as if we were simply resuming an interrupted conversation. We had to discuss a sketch for a set,[2] and I needed to know what he had in mind for entrances and exits, and where the doors and various pieces of furniture ought to be. He gave a faintly ironic smile, and said in his calm, precise way: 'A plan? That would be like in the theatre. The cinema is a

---

[1] The film was *Die Finanzen des Grossherzogs* (1923).
[2] This sketch was used for *The Last Laugh* (1924).

matter of projection. You either see something or you don't: all that matters is the impression. If I were a painter myself I wouldn't need anyone else's help.'

When I brought him the sketches, later, he made no comment on the layout as a whole. All he was interested in were the proportions, the lights and shadows, in short the actual realization. It was as if he himself had designed that 'pale grey room', as he called it. I thought how other directors would have reacted. They would have talked about 'distance' and the positions of the props, whereas he was only interested in atmosphere and stylistic effects. I thought then that I should never have any difficulties with him, but in fact we had occasion to argue often and fiercely about stylistic interpretations.[3] But as soon as I had convinced him about anything, the sketch became the equivalent of a contract, and then it was he who was inflexible and insisted that every stroke of the pen should be faithfully rendered in the execution.

Up till then I had always designed the sets first and drawn in the figures afterwards. But under the influence of Murnau I now began to sketch the people first; that is to say, I would begin by drawing what happened in the scene, and then the appropriate space seemed to grow out of it. Murnau used to encourage me in this method. In this way the interiors became more and more simple and more and more empty. It was the actor who had to fill them. We thus came, by our third film, *Faust*, to adapt the space to the actor: for example, Gretchen's mother's room became merely a frame for the robust presence of Dieterle, who was playing Valentin. And Faust's study was not designed as a single room, but, in accordance with the shots that had been decided on, in four separate parts, built one after the other.

The hall in *Tartuffe* consisted merely of a wall: its dimensions were suggested by the shape of Jannings walking up and down with his breviary in his hand – all that was needed was an effect of relief. Depth of field, which all the specialists made such a fuss about at that time, was to us, in this particular case, immaterial.

The prologue and epilogue preceding and following the 'Tartuffe plot' were created entirely by means of perspectives.[4]

When the set had been built in the studio and Murnau strode in, we were all

---

[3] Herlth tells of a dispute over a chimney which he had had made for *The Last Laugh* and which Murnau said was too low and too wide. Herlth was obstinate and told Murnau he would have to find another architect. Murnau replied, 'That's a child's answer', and Herlth said angrily, 'Thank you, Herr Oberlehrer [Schoolmaster]'. They did not see each other for the rest of that day, but when Herlth went to his room in the evening he found a basket with two bottles of champagne and a note: 'Good health! Yours, The Schoolmaster.'

[4] In a letter to the author Herlth writes: 'In *Tartuffe*, everything was done to heighten the black-and-white effects. The rooms were small and round, with smooth, creamy white-painted walls devoid of detail or ornament. All the moulding was done by hand. The costumes too were designed for graphic effect.'

Faust: 'adapting the space to the actor'

tense: we knew we were in for some surprises, for lighting often produced quite a different effect from the one anticipated on paper. Then without the slightest hesitation everything would be changed. Murnau would never imply that it was the designer's fault; he would simply make ironical, almost mischievous comments. The atmosphere, in fact, was always cheerful and gay, as if he and his colleagues were children larking about together. He was very excited, for instance, by my idea of building the market-place in *Faust* obliquely, so that the crowd had difficulty in moving about. He was often to be seen sunk in an armchair, trying to improve on some unsatisfactory move by an actor, or ticking off the studio manager. But on such occasions he was always good-humoured: he was never really angry when he sounded angry. Our team was extremely happy, always ready for jokes and teasing one another. It was partly the exuberance of people who know they are in the process of creating something exceptional; partly the spirit of that time, when people were always trying to spring surprises on one another.

It went without saying that we were all stimulated to be enthusiasts, with an immense capacity for work whenever it was a question of art or technique. So we had no fixed working hours in the usual sense of the term. Even if shooting was scheduled to begin at nine in the morning, the cameras would often not start turning until eleven, or even until two in the afternoon.

But this is not to say that Murnau did not work like a demon. He worked fast, but he was so interested in every detail that he did not bother about questions of time. One never knew in advance whether it would be possible to film a certain set at a certain time. It must of course be remembered that at that time a director was in a completely different situation from now: in the technical sphere there were still an enormous number of unknowns and imponderables. Every day presented us with new problems that had to be solved there on the set itself.

But Murnau's perfectionism made even the simplest thing a problem. I had designed an interior for *The Last Laugh*, in which a gas-light burned over a sofa. We experimented with that lamp for weeks: the difficulty then was to create a lighting effect that was at the same time a real source of illumination. Nowadays such effects are no longer sought after: people haven't the endless patience necessary for exhaustive experiment. So there were endless discussions over every effect of lighting. Murnau listened to us talking and said: 'All the things you're doing now with artificial sets I shall do one day in a natural one.' We laughed then, but when we saw his masterpiece, *Tabu*, we were astonished to see that he had kept his word.

There is one thing Murnau said that I shall never forget. 'Art,' he would often repeat, 'consists in eliminating. But in the cinema it would be more correct to talk of "masking". For just as you and Röhrig suggest light by drawing shadows, so the cameraman ought to create shadow too. That's much more important than creating light!'

And when Carl Hoffmann lit the first set for *Faust*, Murnau said: 'Now how are we going to get the effect in the design? This is too light. Everything must be made much more shadowy.'

And so all four of us set about trying to cut out the light, with screens 23 cm. wide by 50 m. high. We used them to define the space and create shadows on the wall and in the air. For Murnau the lighting became part of the actual directing of the film. He would never have shot a scene without first 'seeing' the lighting and adapting it to his intentions. Hoffmann has made masterly use, ever since, of what emerged from a single one of Murnau's experiments.

I still remember how we had the idea of the mobile, or as it was then called, 'entfesselte Kamera'.

We were making *The Last Laugh*, this time without Röhrig. Erich Pommer had told us to 'try to invent something mad!'

So far we hadn't succeeded, in spite of nights of brain-racking. We were using the cloakroom set, and Murnau was making preparations for the scene in which the millionaire gets the poor cloakroom attendant (not yet cast as

Jannings) to light his fat cigar. The millionaire goes out through the door, which swings to slowly; I had made it 2 metres high so that it would take a long time to close. The attendant was supposed to sniff the cigar smoke after the millionaire had already departed up the stairs.

At this point Murnau said: 'No, that doesn't work.'

'Why not?' Karl Freund and I asked.

'Because you don't see anything – it doesn't have any effect,' answered Murnau emphatically.

'What are we to do then?'

'We need something more intense, if only we could fly with the smoke.'

'What? . . .'

'The stairs . . .' said Murnau.

'With the camera?' asked Freund.

'Of course – what else?'

'We'd need a fireman's ladder,' I said timidly.

Everyone laughed at the idea of a ladder.

I stuck to my guns. Freund looked at me, then tossed his head, which meant that he agreed.[5]

We didn't realize that we were already assuming the existence of a mobile camera; for us it was the stairs that presented the difficulty. We had made the first step without knowing it.

Someone was sent for a ladder, the camera was fixed at the top, and the not insubstantial Freund took up his position. We removed half the set and moved the ladder slowly towards the stairs; the camera followed the smoke, rising with it up the stairs as the ladder was wound upwards.

'We've got it!' cried Murnau.

After this there was no stopping us. 'Now at last we know why you built an open lift', Murnau said to me, smiling. The camera was attached to a bicycle and made to descend, focused on the hotel vestibule; the bicycle went across the hall to the porter, and then, with a cut between shots, continued into the street, which had been built on the lot.

Sometimes the camera was fixed to Freund's stomach, sometimes it flew through the air attached to a scaffolding, or moved forward with Freund on a rubber-wheeled trolley I had built.[6]

One day we had worked till ten in the evening, and Murnau, as he often did, took the whole team back to his apartment to discuss the plans for the next day's shooting. Of course we had dinner first, but as soon as the servant

[5] See Freund, in *A Tribute to Carl Mayer, 1894–1944*, Memorial Programme (Scala Theatre, London 1947) where all the inventive skill is attributed to Carl Mayer.

[6] Lupu Pick and his cameraman, Guido Seeber, had already used a trolley for *Sylvester* (1923).

The Last Laugh: Murnau (right) next to Freund with the *entfesselte Kamera* on his chest

poured the wine for him to taste he cried, 'Oh no, this won't do!', and sent for another bottle. It wasn't until the fourth had been brought that he was satisfied. Yet he himself didn't touch a drop because of kidney trouble resulting from a plane crash in the First World War; it was just that he wanted his guests to be entertained as well as possible.

We had our meeting in the room that the painter Walter Spiess had decorated for him. The walls were black, and painted with enlargements of Persian miniatures. The only furniture was a huge divan with a Persian carpet over it in one corner, and in another a sort of seat to accommodate several people. Apart from that the room was completely empty. Everyone wandered about, talking.

The last set for *The Last Laugh* was Jannings's room. The longer we went on shooting the more completely the walls disappeared, until finally all that was left was the mirror in one corner and the ceiling. In front of the glass was Jannings, and the camera took a reverse angle-shot of him from behind, including just his head and the ceiling, on which shadows swirled and on which his dream vision was to be superimposed. We worked on this one shot the whole of one day, from morning till night. Then, on the set, we took the additional shots for the dream, to be superimposed later above Jannings's head.

Jannings was supposed to feel extraordinarily strong in his dream, and to toss enormous cases about. In fact they were trick cases that were really as light as feathers: they were attached to wires that ran over pulleys, and as soon as Jannings touched them they were to fly up into the air and then fall down again into his hands. But Emil was no acrobat, and the huge cases made him nervous. He kept hanging on to the handles, and the wires kept snapping and having to be re-soldered. Hours went by like this, and a crowd of two hundred extras and a team of fifty technicians had to wait about until midnight. Everyone was moaning and groaning. Emil was ready to burst into tears. Four buses were waiting to take people home. Murnau alone sat there smiling on his little chair. There was no question, with him, of giving up. Finally, at two in the morning, it worked.

In such situations Murnau always remained completely calm. One never knew whether the difficulties got on his nerves or simply amused him. He stayed as unperturbed as if everything were perfectly normal; indeed, for him, difficulties that came up in the course of work were entirely natural. His attitude was the attitude of an artist. The only differences of opinion among us occurred while we were still at the planning stage, before the final shooting.

Each day on the set was a fresh opportunity for us to surpass ourselves in inventiveness and ingenuity. At each shot we were anxious for the rest of the team's reactions; we were enthusiasts, although none of us could help feeling a twinge of jealousy when it was someone else who thought of the solution to some knotty problem. In short, we all of us felt we had invented new visual processes. And we had not 'unchained' the camera for merely technical reasons. On the contrary, we had found a new and more exact way of isolating the image, and of intensifying dramatic incident.

For instance, when we came to the scene before the porter's dream in *The Last Laugh*, where Jannings hears the sound of a trumpet in the courtyard, we puzzled our brains about how to represent a sound travelling through space. The solution of the problem was as follows. The back-yard set had been built on the lot at Babelsberg. We now fitted Jannings's house with a sort of hoist, with the camera in a basket on rails, so that it could slide downwards for about 20 metres, i.e. from Jannings's ear to the mouth of the trumpet: silent films demanded this kind of ingenuity. But it may be that the filmic effect was more striking than the real sound of the trumpet would be nowadays.[7]

When we all took a curtain with Murnau after the first showing of *The Last Laugh*, the film-makers present, even men like Lang and Dupont who were

[7] See also what Freund writes in the Memorial Programme for Carl Mayer, and what Baberske says on p. 81 below.

The Last Laugh: sketch and realization

his rivals, shouted 'bravo' and applauded. There was a telegram from Hollywood addressed to Ufa, asking what camera we had used to shoot the film. It added that in the USA there was no such camera, and no town to compare with the one in our film. The Americans, used to a precise technique, didn't dream that we had discovered new methods with only the most primitive means at our disposal.

We had been helped by our use of perspective models, too. In order to make convincing the sequence where the man who thinks he is the most important person in the hotel whistles to summon motor-cars, the hotel behind him had to appear enormous, at least thirty storeys high. So we used a model. This was a technique that was already known, but it had rarely been used with such success.

We realized that something moving in the foreground would produce an effect of realism, so we had a train rushing by in the front of the picture. It was a railway enthusiast's model train, four times larger than a mere toy and actually driven by steam. But the shot itself was an exterior one, and the cars it included sent up so much dust that the model of the hotel seemed to float in the air, cut off from its base. What was to be done? Every minute's delay cost at first hundreds, then later thousands of marks. But one of us found the solution at once: 'Water!' Once again it was firemen's ladders that came to the rescue. With their aid we sent down a fine drizzle which made the actual scene and the three-dimensional model seem equally real.

The view, or rather 'background', seen from the revolving door was managed by means of a perspective shot of a sloping street 15 metres high in the foreground diminishing to 5 in the 'distance'. The street ran between model skyscrapers as much as 17 metres high – this again caused Hollywood a good deal of astonishment. To make the 'perspective' work we had big buses and Mercedes cars in the foreground; in the middle-ground middle-sized cars; and in the background small ones, with behind them again children's toy cars. Farthest away of all, in front of the shops, we had crowds of 'people' cut out and painted and moved across the screen on a conveyor belt.

All this was something completely new in its time. It was the first film scene in which dramatic effects were heightened by purely visual means. That was what Murnau gave to the cinema: this tireless perfectionism, this uncompromising determination to attain a unique visual intensity, of which the final and sovereign result was *Tabu*.

What we, Murnau's team of collaborators, were afraid of then was that there was nothing new left for us to achieve. But in the course of making *Tartuffe* and *Faust* we came to realize that we were only at a beginning. Every day brought new problems. Often we would have to abandon something we were trying on the set, until long nights of discussion and countless marginal experiments showed us the solution. In those days there were no real cranes in film studios, and for the flight through the air on Mephisto's cloak we first tried Carl Hoffmann's suggestion: a sort of switch-back made of plaster over which the camera travelled on a little cart. But when we saw the rushes, instead of the hoped-for rising and falling effect there were only unusable blurs. Hoffmann was in despair and wanted to give in his notice. Röhrig and I were also very depressed and went to have a drink in the Potsdamer Platz to cheer ourselves up. But when we came out into the street again we both stopped in our tracks at something we saw there: a very low-built truck unloading a car. We looked at each other and smiled without a word, then rushed to the station, where Röhrig telephoned the studio and told them to wait for us. On the train we designed a trolley with a very low platform and heavy solid wheels, such as can still be seen today. Once we had hit on the idea all we had to do was trust to Hoffmann's skill. And so we were able to shoot the flight through the air. We did so in a shed 35 metres long and 20 wide that was specially built for the purpose, for we knew we should need plenty of time for experiment and we didn't want it to get in the way of the other work.

The 'landscape' – plains, rivers, waterfalls, forests, mountains, and cities – was a relief model, with working miniatures of birds and animals of all kinds. We based it on a picture by the German painter Altdorfer: there were pines and larches made of reeds and rushes, glass-wool clouds, cascades, fields of real turf carefully stuck on plaster. When Murnau saw us at work he bent his great height to help us make our little rocks and trees. When he was shown the rushes he sent for champagne, and though he normally never drank, he joined us on this occasion, as happy as a little boy at the future he foresaw. Soon after this Hoffmann invented transparency projection. He set up the apparatus in a primitive sort of manner on the lot near the studio, but the method itself was the same as that used today in special-effects labs.

Though he was not a technician himself, Murnau, a 'Raphael without hands', knew that it was possible to achieve. And all that was done was done simply because he insisted on it, and because he stimulated us into being capable of it. I think his imperturbable calm in the studio was due not only to a sense of discipline, but also because he possessed that passion for 'play' itself which is necessary and essential to any kind of artistic activity. For instance, I'd made a steam apparatus for the heaven scene in the Prologue to *Faust*. Steam was ejected out of several pipes against a background of clouds; arc-lights arranged in a circle lit up the steam to look like rays of light. The archangel was supposed to stand in front and raise his flaming sword. We did it several times, and each time it was perfectly all right, but Murnau was so caught up in the pleasure of doing it that he forgot all about time. The steam had to keep on billowing through the beams of light, until the archangel – Werner Fütterer – was so exhausted he could no longer lift his sword. When Murnau realized what had happened he shook his head and laughed at himself, then gave everyone a break.

I have never known anyone else who enjoyed the strange business of film-making so much as Murnau, although he took his work intensely seriously.

Ufa had wanted to cast *Faust* with actors of international importance. In addition to Faust (Gösta Ekman – Sweden), Mephisto (Emil Jannings), and Marthe (Yvette Guilbert – France), they wanted to have Lillian Gish as Gretchen. But Lillian Gish had made it a condition that the film should be shot by her own cameraman, Charles Rosher.[8]

But Röhrig and I considered that Carl Hoffmann was the only person capable of carrying out our intentions. So Lillian Gish didn't come, and Rosher, who had already sailed for Europe, came only as a spectator. We were appalled at the thought of having to find a Marguerite to equal Lillian Gish.

During the shooting for *Tartuffe* we had needed a close-up of Elmire's legs and feet, and for this we had used an unknown young actress called Camilla Horn. Now we recalled her appearance, and agreed that she was the one we needed for Marguerite. Murnau had her make some tests, rehearsed her, and got both the distributor and the directors of the film company to accept her among the cast of famous international stars. When we'd finished shooting and were leaving the studio, young Camilla Horn complained about the enormous fatigue and constant psychological strain she had suffered while working under the implacable Murnau. She lamented her scraped knees, her eyes red and sore from winds of dust or salt, and the tortures she had been submitted to in the burning scene. She had had to spend hours tied to the stake, with flames leaping round her from twenty lykpodium burners. When she fainted she was not acting.

Even Jannings had to put up with the same sort of thing. For example, he had to stand on an iron grill covered with Mephisto's cloak, while the cloak was blown up to a height of twelve feet by three enormous fans. There, over the model of the town, he had to stand for hours, swathed in feathers and with two vast bat's wings, while the breath of plague hovered over the city. The breath of plague consisted of soot driven by a propeller. This sequence was taken several times, and in the end not only was the actor cursing and swearing but everyone else felt like going on strike too. Murnau was the only person who made no comment. He smiled, gave his ruined white overall to the studio manager and put on a clean one. And all he said was: 'If it's too much for you, don't bother to come.'

[8] Nils Asther was to play the archangel.

I don't think any of the people who worked with him – actors, colleagues, or studio staff – had ever before had to exert themselves as much as Murnau demanded. As Jannings was in the habit of pointing out, he wanted to know about everything, to try everything from every possible angle. And the possibility of other people's fatigue never occurred to him, any more than his own. For him, work itself was a kind of intoxication: he was fascinated and gripped by the actual processes, carried away in spite of himself, like a scientist performing an experiment in a laboratory, or a surgeon during a complicated operation.

4. Murnau, the Camera, and Lighting

In his *Index to the works of F. W. Murnau*, Theodore Huff deplores the fact that because so many of his films are lost, analysis of the development of Murnau's style is impossible. Moreover, he continues, we cannot say whether the 'Murnau touch' should be attributed to Mayer alone or is due, as far as *The Last Laugh* at least is concerned, to a close collaboration between Mayer, Freund, and Jannings. Certainly the evidence is contradictory.

We know we can rule out Jannings. For this it is enough to read what that intelligent and very skilful actor says in his autobiography, *Life and Me*, about the cinema, which he regards as primarily a commercial affair; or to recall how Murnau reacted to his comments on artistic problems.

It is Karl Freund who gives most of the credit for artistic direction and effort to Carl Mayer.[1] Huff's more cautious suggestions also originate in what Freund told him in the United States.

In two of the letters he wrote to me, Freund is quite categorical:

I don't think Murnau ever looked through the view-finder; it didn't much interest him. He left all that to me. He didn't have anything to do with the lighting either, and I must say Carl Mayer used to take much more interest than he did in the framing. I gave Mayer one of our view-finders, which he always used when he was working on a script at home. That's why Mayer's scripts were always full of suggestions for camera angles.

[1] See *A tribute to Carl Mayer, 1894–1944*, Memorial Programme, Scala Theatre, London, 1947.

In another letter he says:

I'm perfectly right about Murnau. He showed little interest in the camera and the lighting. Before shooting started, Mr Herlth used to make sketches for the whole film, general shots, medium shots and close-ups, in which lighting and composition were indicated in detail and then copied into a big book.

'I can't agree with Karl Freund,' Eduard Kubat wrote to me. Kubat worked with Murnau on *Nosferatu* and was studio manager for *Die Austreibung* (1923).

Murnau was a very strong-willed director, and even with colleagues as distinguished as Karl Freund he always put his own personal imprint on the work. What's more, I never saw Carl Mayer there when we were shooting, either in the studio or on location.

Heinrich C. Richter, the designer for *Der Januskopf* and *Der Gang in die Nacht*, confirms what Herlth says:

Murnau concerned himself with lighting effects because he did all he could to make a film a total work of art. He was especially interested in effects that were still novel, like beams coming through a door or headlights piercing darkness.

Freund emphasizes that Mayer always wanted to learn more about the possibilities of the camera. He tells how Mayer would often come to his flat in the middle of the night with some new problem about which he needed technical advice. Long before they were actually filmed, Mayer would experiment with Jannings on new ideas for certain sequences. Freund says there were two and a half months' preparation before shooting began on *The Last Laugh*. During this time, he says, Mayer had at least one discussion with each member of the team – with Murnau, Herlth and Röhrig the designers, Pommer, Jannings – or with Freund himself, who concludes that all the innovations in *The Last Laugh* were the result of this collective work.

There can be no objection to this last remark: German cinema of the golden age was always the result of team work to which everyone made a contribution. But why not, like Herlth, allow an important and decisive part to Murnau too? It is necessary also to compare what Charles Rosher told Kevin Brownlow (see p. 184).

Freund gives Mayer all the credit for the innovations in the use of the moving camera. According to him it was Mayer who asked how it was possible to go without cutting or editing from a close-up of a face to a detailed shot of just the eyes. Freund perhaps does not remember that Guido Seeber had already used the so-called 'unchained' camera for Lupu Pick, in *Sylvester*. In the scenario for the latter film, of course, Mayer had only indicated panoramic or dolly shots for the symbolic *Umwelt*,[2] the immaterial world

---

[2] For *Umwelt*, see Eisner, *The Haunted Screen* (1969), pages 186–93.

Murnau, 1921, by Heinrich Richter

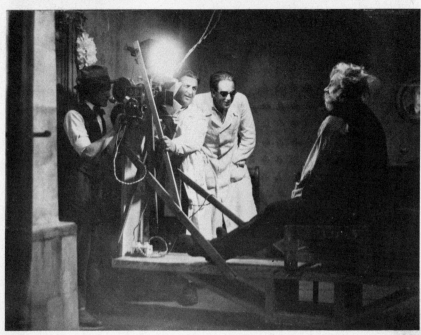

On the set of *The Last Laugh*. Opposite (top) Jannings, Murnau, and Freund; (bottom) setting up the drunken dream with Jannings, see page 81; (above) Freund at camera, Murnau thoughtful next to Jannings

which surrounds the characters without their knowledge; the action proper was limited to more traditional shots. And it was only with *The Last Laugh* that the camera was taken from the trolley and put on a crane, or attached to Freund's chest while he rode a bicycle, and so on.

And then, what are we to think about some of the mobile shots in the dazzling opening scenes of *Faust*, which is based on a script by Hans Kyser, without any collaboration from Mayer at all? Or, even though Mayer wrote the scenario, of the marsh scene in *Sunrise*, which was shot in America while Mayer was in Europe? Herlth has given us the answer as far as *Faust* is concerned.

Was it really Carl Mayer who, for the prologue and epilogue of *Tartuffe*, wanted actors without make-up and 'modern' (what we were soon after to call 'Russian') photography, to contrast with the 'artistic vagueness' that conferred imprecise values on the images of the main action? All Mayer indicates in his script is that the main action should be in a style 'of no precise period' (*zeitlos*). He concedes that the costumes at least may be more or less of the early nineteenth century, but at the same time they too were to be as *zeitlos* as possible. He explains that what he wants is a style without a too definite historical reference, which will bring out the symbolic nature of the play itself. (Murnau and Herlth did not follow Mayer's ideas for the costumes, which in the case of the women are nearer to the eighteenth century than to the time of Molière.)

The prelude was to be in the style of the present day, with a few old-fashioned and provincial touches. But there is no indication in the script that Mayer has decided on different camera styles for different parts of the film.

The atmosphere of some shots seems to have been intensified by the sets and lighting designed by Herlth in agreement with Murnau at points where the script itself is rather vague and unevocative. For example, the scene of the rendezvous in the boudoir, where Tartuffe gets up from the tea-table to see if anyone is spying on him from the hall. Mayer's script, apart from certain panoramic and dolly shots, only provides the terms *gross* for the close shots, *grösser* for nearer ones, and *ganz gross* for the close-ups, and his version of the scene reads simply:

> For: Now:
> He goes
> To the door. To the hall
> Now: He opens
> To peep outside?
> But!
> Insert:
> General shot: The hall looks empty
> Silence everywhere.
> And then!
> Close shot: he shuts the door again.

It will be remembered that in the film the shot of the hall includes part of the curve of the great staircase, and that all is bathed in soft layers of afternoon light, with a few shadows on the floor and on the walls, and a glimpse through the window of the shady gardens beyond. Was it not Murnau and Herlth who brought Mayer's silent empty hall to life? When, before Tartuffe comes to her boudoir, Elmire lets down the muslin curtain in order to make the atmosphere dimmer and more ambiguous for the pretended rendezvous, the window-frame can just be seen through the material. This image too was invented by Murnau and Herlth; there is nothing of all this in Mayer's script.

There is also the marvellous still-life of the tea-table, a shot that reminds us of the sumptuous table in Jean Epstein's *L'Auberge Rouge* (1923). The silver and china are always exquisite in Murnau. He never left the choice of properties to a studio manager; he gave detailed specifications in the script. Lil Dagover told Alexandre Astruc:

Not only had the sets to be executed down to the last detail under his eye and according to his plans, but he used to place each prop with his own hands, so keen was he on 'total creation'.[3]

Such care over detail should certainly indicate an equal concern for every angle of the actual shooting.

It should be remembered that all the dream and nightmare scenes in the scripts were always modified in Murnau's own handwriting; that he adds 'back-lighting' for certain scenes in *Nosferatu* and suggests the rail dividing the shot of the undertaker's mutes; and in other films notes 'angle-shots' or 'reverse angle-shots' or 'lighted candles' or 'strong sunlight'; all evidence of his interest in lighting and framing. Moreover, how else are we to explain the power of many of the shots in both *Faust* and *Sunrise*?

For *Faust* Murnau obtained some astonishing pictures from Carl Hoffmann for the scene of the monk preaching penitence to the revellers. In the foreground he places a gigantic image of the monk, or of enormous columns, thus distancing the drunken procession and giving an effect of extraordinary depth. The same device is found again in many shots in *Sunrise*, for which Rochus Gliese was the designer and Charles Rosher the cameraman. The use of an enormous foreground figure to establish the proportion of the rest of the image seems in fact a characteristic element of Murnau's mature style. He often asked his designers for sketches of such shots. Take for instance an image in the scene of *The Last Laugh* where the aunt brings what is left over from the wedding feast and sees the new porter. In the left of the picture we see part of the back, arm, and broad shoulder of the new porter, framed in the doorway. And in the background, towards the right, very small, the figure of the aunt, dumbfounded. Was this shot indicated in Mayer's script? Other scripts by him give us leave to doubt it.

Of course Mayer does sometimes mention elements intended to serve such purposes. There is, for example, the huge view of the old man's shoes in the prologue of *Tartuffe*:

General shot:	Now she stops
Closer shot:	Looking at the two shoes
Very close shot:	which are pointed, like those of an 'old gentleman'. And then!
Close shot:	Her foot pushes one of them away, with a violent gesture of anger. Then, she opens the door.

In the film we see the pair of shoes for a very long time in the foreground; by contrast the corridor appears very long. And the image thus takes on a

[3] *Cahiers du Cinéma*, 18 December 1952, p. 14.

Perspective: *The Last Laugh*

much more intense meaning: Murnau, delighted with the shot that Mayer and Herlth have made possible, superimposes his rhythm on Mayer's. Mayer needed the close-up in order to reveal the housekeeper's hidden malevolence; for Murnau it was also an additional element in the formal composition.

In *Faust* it was Murnau himself who had the idea of the image of the soles of the feet (the feet of someone struck down by the plague), made to look gigantic because of the angle from which it was shot. Here Murnau the art-historian is perhaps remembering the foreshortening employed by Mantegna or Holbein in their pictures of the recumbent Christ.

Fritz Arno Wagner, cameraman for *Schloss Vogelöd, Nosferatu*, and part of *Der Brennende Acker* (1922), told me that for Murnau the directing of a film depended on the camera angle, the framing of the image, and the lighting. During the shooting of a film he would never say authoritatively, like Fritz Lang, 'Do so and so', but always, very politely: 'How would it be if you tried it like that?' Or sometimes he would suggest gently: 'I'd try it such-and-such a way. What do you think?' Perhaps Freund drew a wrong conclusion from this very discreet approach.

Wagner has also said that Murnau experimented a great deal before shooting. And Robert Baberske, who was assistant cameraman and worked with

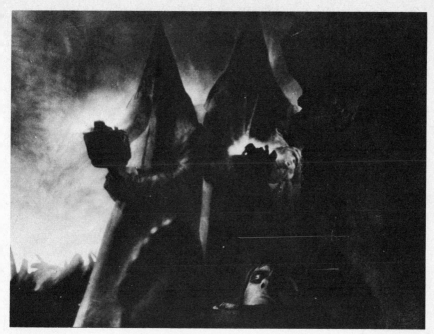

Perspective: *Faust*

Freund on many of Murnau's films, recalls that Murnau always thought over every shot and every lighting effect long before he started actually to make the film. Charles Rosher, cameraman for *Sunrise*, has told me how at Lake Arrowhead and elsewhere Murnau and Gliese used to discuss ideas and then sketches right down to the last detail. Murnau, he added, disapproved of any unnecessary interference:

He would tell me, always holding the sketches in his hands, what he wanted – camera angles and lighting. Then, during the shooting, he would say: 'You know what I want.' He had confidence in me, and as everything had been decided in advance there was no need for him to verify the picture in the view-finder.

In the projection-room, looking at the rushes, he would tell us if anything needed modifying. He was very fond of having the characters followed by the camera. But he preferred dolly-shots to trolley-shots – although the tram journey had all been filmed with a camera on a trolley. And whenever possible we used a camera suspended somewhere above the actors.

Rosher also told me that Murnau liked to film what presented itself by chance, like for example the shadow of wind-stirred leaves on water, the ripple of waves on a lake after a boat has gone by, the glitter of the sun on the lake's surface. 'He had an eye for all light and movement.'

In any case it is impossible to define the part played by each individual in the shooting of a film. Where does improvisation begin in the studio, or on location, and which member of the team originates it? Was it chance that produced the exquisite tracery on the walls in *Tartuffe*, when the footmen carrying candlesticks pause on the landing and the flames cast shadows of the wrought-iron staircase? And what about the similar image in *Sunrise*, shot by another cameraman? The couple are reconciled and embrace each other in church and we see behind them a pattern of shadows cast by an invisible grille of wrought iron.

We must suppose a single intention behind all these varying images.

This is what Mayer gives:

> By the side door of the church:
> Close shot: Close by a wall: the two of them.
> They embrace.
> In tears. Near to each other.

Then the man falls at the woman's feet asking her forgiveness.

> Then she leans right down to him
> With a saintly smile.
> For: as a ray of sunlight now
> Shines through a window above her
> Bathing her head in gold
> She gently draws him to his feet.

Instead of this symbolic lighting Murnau preferred to use the play of shadows, thrown into relief by the light from a window opposite.

We should also remind ourselves of the lattice-work of mist and light that veils any artificiality in the model landscape in the flight through the air in *Faust*, just as the city built on a lot at Foxhills is veiled during the tram journey in *Sunrise*. In all the films of the mature period we find these oscillations of light and shadow on the faces and clothes of the characters, combined with the use of a moving camera: the waverings of a lamp in *Nosferatu*, *Faust* and *Sunrise*; in *Nosferatu* the swinging of the empty hammock; in *The Last Laugh* the sinister swinging of the cloakroom door, and, in the opening of the film, the disintegrating shapes and flashing lights shot from a descending lift. In *Faust* there is, in the titanic prelude, the chaotic maelstrom of shadows from which heavenly light is born, to leap across space until the marvellously orchestrated forms and movements, brightness and darkness, resolve themselves into archangel and demon. And, in the same film, the extraordinary marble mask of the dead mother, which seems to be faintly echoed in *Sunrise*, where we see the white face of the drowning woman drifting on the grey waves of the lake.

The mysterious chiaroscuro, the dim *sfumato*, the opalescent reflections from mirrors and walls of glass, all these are common characteristics of all the classic German films of that time (Eisner, *The Haunted Screen*, 1969). But it was his continual transformation of all nuances and tonal values, his ever-flexible range of graduations, his interlacing, interchanging compositions, his mobile yet limpid luminosity, which gave Murnau's visions their originality.

The outstanding example of a sequence representing crowding impressions is the drunken dream of the porter in *The Last Laugh*, which certainly derived from the experiments made for the nightmare in *Januskopf* or the *fata morgana* in *Phantom*. Herlth tells us that Carl Mayer's suggestions for the dream in *The Last Laugh* had to be modified. Thanks to Baberske we have a picture of them all at work: Jannings sitting on a sort of turntable, while Freund, with the camera fixed to his chest and counterbalanced by batteries hung on his back, flounders about 'like a drunken man'. Murnau and his team intended the shot to have a double significance: was it the porter himself staggering, and his chair whirling about in space? or was it the room starting to spin around him?

Baberske tells a story which seems characteristic, of how Murnau tried to merge artificial constructions with natural elements, a method which Rosher recalls being used for the village in *Sunrise*. Baberske had to sacrifice a lot of sleep in order to film the light of dawn (real) on the back-yard (constructed). The camera was left in place for a whole week, closing on a fade every night, and opening on a fade every morning until what they called *Morgengrau* (i.e. 'dawn of morning') became for them *Morgengraus* (i.e. 'morning horror'). The film shows that they were ultimately successful in capturing the effects Murnau required.

We get another glimpse of them at work in another account of a technical device that Baberske described to me in detail and which Herlth and Freund [4] also mention. Wanting to translate an aural effect into an image, said Baberske, they had built a sort of basket-lift for the camera in the backyard, for the scene where the wedding-guests are downstairs and one of them has started to play the trumpet. As we saw in Chapter 3, Murnau wanted the sound of the trumpet to be heard 'visually' by Jannings, who was up in the dining-room. The camera was installed in the lift together with the cameraman; they were supposed to ascend 'with' the sound, thus giving it a visual equivalent. But the lift would only carry its load down, not up, so they had to take a sort of descending angle shot, which then had to be played backwards. The whole thing was undercranked so as to produce an accelerated movement

---

[4] See Karl Freund, Carl Mayer Memorial Programme, p. 11.

in the finished film, where the movement from the magnified mouth of the trumpet to the room where Jannings hears the sound produces a vertiginous effect anticipating some of those fine space-abolishing shots in Kurosawa.

Baberske says it was Murnau's idea. Freund, although he says 'We used to delight in looking for fresh difficulties, as a sort of challenge to solve problems calling for completely original solutions', seems to suggest that it was Carl Mayer who inspired such visual ingenuities. Unto everyone that hath shall be given. . . . That applies to both Murnau and Mayer. It is not my intention to belittle in any way the poetic greatness and essentially visual gifts of a man like Mayer who, as Charles Rosher said to me, 'inspired the cameraman through his poetic creations'.[5] Nevertheless, I think it is more natural to suppose that the extraordinary and close collaboration between on the one hand people like Mayer, Herlth, Röhrig, Gliese, together with such talented cameramen as Wagner, Freund, Hoffmann, Rosher, and others, and on the other hand a director as perceptive and intuitive as Murnau, was a rare and fruitful opportunity for the art of the cinema at that time, and one of the reasons for the almost ideal fulfilment it achieved.

One factor gives a good deal of matter for speculation. As early as his scenario for *Sylvester*, Mayer speaks of a revolving door:

> The revolving door: It has come to a standstill again.
> But!
> Through the glass, there now becomes visible:
> the hall. . . .

And in the hall there are tall mirrors in which the visitors look at themselves; and page-boys open a glass double door.

The camera pans a little to the right, and Mayer writes:

> And lo!
> The glass door is seen more clearly
> And suggests a room beyond. All splendour and light.

Then he indicates the waiters hurrying to and fro among the tables with their trays.

I have not seen the scenario for *The Last Laugh*, which I believe is still somewhere in the United States. Murnau may have taken it there with him. But is it likely that with such phrases as 'all splendour and light' Mayer could have indicated in that script the dazzling whirl of light and movement we glimpse through the revolving door – an effect that could only have been produced on the set by the combined manipulation of lighting and cameras?

[5] Rosher adds: 'And for this reason the only scenario I ever kept was the scenario of *Sunrise*.'

The Last Laugh: the camera in its improvised elevator

And how was it, if all these mobile and scintillating effects were due to Mayer's script, that Lupu Pick did not produce similar ones in *Sylvester*?

It is best to quote what Murnau himself says about the camera. I have had the good luck to find some notes of his, typed on Decla Bioskop paper and apparently written in answer to a request from one of the big German dailies devoted to the cinema which was bringing out a Christmas number. Here is the text:

With all respect to Father Christmas, I haven't any Utopian wishes to ask him to fulfil: he will never bring the 'marvel', nor the 'perfect' script, nor the 'international star' who doesn't aim at being one, nor a permanent team of actors at the director's disposal for every film. But although such presents are beyond the bounds of possibility, Father Christmas's magic wand could create the instrument which is more important than any fortuitous outside aid: a camera that can move freely in space.

What I mean is one that at any moment can go anywhere, at any speed. A camera that outstrips present film technique and fulfils the cinema's ultimate artistic goal. Only with this essential instrument shall we be able to realize new possibilities, including one of the most promising, the 'architectural' film.

Murnau goes on to explain what he means by this expression:

What I refer to is the fluid architecture of bodies with blood in their veins moving through mobile space; the interplay of lines rising, falling, disappearing; the encounter of surfaces, stimulation and its opposite, calm; construction and collapse; the formation and destruction of a hitherto almost unsuspected life; all this adds up to a symphony made up of the harmony of bodies and the rhythm of space; the *play of pure movement*, vigorous and abundant. All this we shall be able to create when the camera has at last been de-materialized.

To attain this end we don't ask for some complicated new technical apparatus; what we ask for, and this precisely from the artistic point of view, is just the opposite: we want to return to a technical process that will be almost artistically sober and self-sufficient, creating a completely neutral medium which will lend itself freely to every new creation.

That was how Murnau saw the possibilities opened up by a camera that would be free to move about in space, in about 1922 or 1923, when he was working for Decla. He extolled the possibilities of the camera again in January 1928, in an article in the American review, *Theater Magazine*:

Real art is simple, but simplicity requires the greatest art. The camera is the director's sketching pencil. It should be as mobile as possible to catch every passing mood, and it is important that the mechanics of the cinema should not be interposed between the spectator and the picture.

Perhaps Karl Freund's severity towards Murnau can be explained by the latter's disdain for matters of a purely technical nature.

Here is the impartial testimony of a contemporary who can be very critical of Murnau on occasion – the Austrian writer Arnold Höllriegel, who watched Murnau making *Sunrise* in the United States, and who notes in his *Hollywood Bilderbuch* in 1927:

> Murnau is the most consistent of modern directors: he sees the world through the lens of the camera. He comes, like most film directors, from the theatre. But while Lubitsch, for example, has remained fundamentally a man of the theatre ... Murnau has become a new kind of being who thinks directly in photographs. There are other cinema directors, for instance the Swedish Mauritz Stiller, who is a genius ... who also think in images – but they think in images that are dramatic. Whereas Murnau is a kind of modern centaur: he and the camera are joined together to form a single body. He sees the world through quite a different lens from the one in other people's eyes. That is why he insists on an entirely new style, even in the story, eliminating anything that can't be put in front of the camera. ... He says to the world: 'Be photogenic, please!'

Höllriegel finds a certain coldness in Murnau's work. Yet he goes on:

> But who can deny that he seeks for modes of expression corresponding to the new art of the image-machine, and that he seeks for them with the utmost perseverance? A new way is opening up before that great achievement of the future, the art film. F. W. Murnau teaches us to *see* the modern film; others will come and teach us to *feel* it.

Seeing – that is the great faculty that Murnau proclaims in the foreword to his *Theater Magazine* article:

> Screen art ought, through its unique properties, to tell a complete story by means of images alone; the ideal film does not need titles.

It is surely unreasonable, after all this, to say that Murnau was not interested in the possibilities of the camera, in images and in lighting.

And in an interview with some American journalists, published in *Cinéa-Ciné* on 1 April 1927, Murnau repeats the necessity for purely and essentially cinematographic subjects; that the picture is all-important; that there must be a 'theatre for the eye'; that nothing counts so much as the way an object or character is placed in front of the camera and filmed – their relationship to other characters or objects is 'an element in the symphony of the film'.

Frank Hansen, Murnau's loyal assistant on *Four Devils* insists that Murnau used his camera to obtain dramatic effects.

> As everyone knows, he used a mobile camera to intensify a scene or for some special effect. As soon as his films were shown in America our directors tried to outdo one another in the search for original camera angles.

But Murnau said:

> There should be no such thing as 'an interesting camera angle'. The angle in itself has no significance, and if it does not intensify the dramatic effect of the scene it can

even be harmful. When you have the opportunity of seeing the rushes of a film every day, you are sometimes very enthusiastic at the time about certain shots that seem very clever. But afterwards, when you see the film as a whole, with all those so-called interesting camera-angles, you realize they damage the action: they only lower, instead of intensifying, the dramatic interest of the story, because they are merely 'interesting' without having any dramatic value.

Hansen goes on:

Murnau made photography into an art that conceals art, where every detail was so technically perfect that you didn't even notice it.

In an article, 'La Caméra, personnage de drame',[6] Marcel Carné refers to Murnau's visionary mastery. He shows how in *The Last Laugh* the camera glided and rose, hovered and manoeuvred – in short, became a 'character in the action'. He talks of the lift scene where the hall, seen from above, looks like an immense space in which 'the relief is brought out by movement'. He recalls the flight through the air in *Faust*, and the panic at the fair, which the camera seems actually to sweep away. He describes how on the misty marsh in *Sunrise* 'the mobile camera gives the impression that a second person is following the hero'. We must remember that this is one director speaking of another. But Carné's unhesitating attribution of the magic of the omnipresent camera to Murnau is surely justified, *since each of the three films he speaks of was shot by a different cameraman.*

Frank Hansen said:

Murnau was everywhere and did everything himself when he was making a film.

The preparation used to take up all his time for a year beforehand. All this while he would keep aloof from any distraction, working with the author every day and discussing with him every detail of the action and the script. His general contribution was at least fifty per cent.

He used to live each part, experiment with every possibility of the plot, draw up a mental picture of the sets, and perfect each detail of the whole with the greatest care, always asking himself what was the best way of presenting it by means of the camera lens. His knowledge of all aspects of the theatre and of art in general enabled him to initiate sets himself, and to direct in person the work of the designer. For he was his own designer, his own artistic director, and even his own studio manager. *He was his own cameraman, he knew how to manage the lighting* and do his own editing. He himself used to suggest the main elements of the score to the composer.

He knew exactly what he wanted. He wanted perfection, and each finished film was the result of meticulous care. He brought to the cinema a culture, a knowledge of production, a sense of artistic beauty and of lighting which until today have known no equal.

In an interview in *Cahiers du Cinéma* (August 1961) Edgar G. Ulmer, who collaborated on *Die Finanzen der Grossherzogs* and the shooting of *Sunrise*,

[6] *Anthologie du Cinéma*, introduced by Marcel Lapierre, Paris 1946, pp. 233 ff.

Sunrise

said that Murnau used to like to be quite free to concentrate exclusively on the plastic composition of each shot.[7] Ulmer praises his extraordinary visual imagination: 'At the beginning of his career people used to say *Murnau had a camera instead of a head.*' And he goes on: 'What was marvellous about Murnau was that he was always trying to do something new ... *he knew all the secrets of optics.*' In an interview Ulmer also talked to me about Murnau's mania for perfection.

He was a great purist who worked under a sort of hypnosis; that is to say, each time it was as if he hypnotized himself afresh.

He always saw a film as a whole. Those about him would be arguing fiercely over some technical question, and he would listen, though we were never quite sure he had understood the theoretical problems involved. Then he would say calmly: 'Let's try it.'

Afterwards, when we were looking at the rushes, he would explain what was

[7] Ulmer says, as the others have done, that Murnau's films were always made by a team of two or three collaborators; that he always wrote the script with the author and made his own shooting-script; and that for *The Last Laugh* he explained to Jannings what to do right down to the smallest gesture.

wrong, what we ought to do differently, and above all how to set about it. We might have to start all over again, and often we used to get exasperated, and ask him why he hadn't said all this before we started shooting. He answered curtly: 'I'm not a painter or a technician. If I were I shouldn't need you.'[8] He had to *see* the sequence first before he could tell us what needed to be changed. And if we answered that we didn't think the result had been too bad, he would answer cuttingly: 'Good is not good enough'. It was the sort of leitmotiv of his art.

Ulmer went on to describe how for *Die Finanzen der Grossherzogs* Murnau insisted that Rochus Gliese do a drawing for each shot. Gliese had an idea for the lighting which Murnau adopted with enthusiasm: this was to paint effects of light or shade on the sets themselves, in such a way that they could be effaced if necessary and replaced by different effects for another shot (a somewhat more sophisticated version of the method used for *Caligari*).

Ulmer also spoke of various visits by Murnau to Sweden, even several years before the tests Ekman did for *Faust*. In Sweden, as in Switzerland, Murnau had seen Debrie's metal cameras. (In Germany they were at that time made of wood.) Thanks to these cameras he had become familiar with certain more advanced techniques, and when he made *Nosferatu*, the idea of using negative for the phantom forest came to him from Sjöström's *Phantom Carriage*, which had been made in 1920. Above all he had a love-hatred for Mauritz Stiller, whose *Herr Arne's Treasure* he couldn't help admiring. And so Murnau, the descendant of ancient Swedish ancestors, exposed himself to the influence of the classic Swedish cinema at its source.

But neither these immediate influences, nor the admirable team of technicians and creative designers, are enough by themselves to explain the singular perfection of his work.

[8] See the similar answer reported by Robert Herlth, p. 60.

5. Two Rediscovered Films

Der Gang in die Nacht

Taking into consideration the few films lost from Fritz Lang's early period, and the complete preservation of the work of Georg Wilhelm Pabst, the loss of all the films of Murnau's youth from 1919 until *Schloss Vogelöd*, and after that, with the exception of *Nosferatu*, until *Die Finanzen des Grossherzogs* (1923), seems a great disaster.

Fortunately Henri Langlois spotted the name *Der Gang in die Nacht* among a pile of boxes of negatives in the Staatliches Filmarchiv in East Berlin, and, at the request of the Cinémathèque Française, a print was made.

The plot of *Der Gang in die Nacht* is somewhat melodramatic, based on *The Victor* by Harriet Bloch, who wrote for the Danish cinema. A doctor, Eigil Boerne, is engaged to a girl called Hélène who is very distant in manner and doesn't press him to marry her only because she doesn't want to harm his career. To celebrate her birthday he takes her to a cabaret, and there Lily, a young dancer, pretends to sprain her ankle in order to try to overcome his indifference towards her. He goes to attend to her in her dressing-room, and falls victim to her charm.

Believing that Hélène is cold and lacking in real feeling, he asks her to forget him. He then renounces his professional ambitions, marries Lily, and goes to live with her as a country doctor in a little fishing village. There they meet a young painter who has gone blind. Boerne performs an operation to restore his sight, and in spite of the presentiments of Lily, who is instinctively afraid of having him there, takes the patient into his home to await the results of the operation. Boerne does not understand his wife's anxiety, and hearing that Hélène has fallen seriously ill as a result of the ending of their engagement, he returns to town for a few hours. He does not manage to see Hélène, but when he gets back Lily tells him that the painter is her lover. He leaves in anger.

Several years pass. Boerne has become a famous oculist, but he is still disillusioned and unhappy. One day Lily comes to his consulting-room: the painter has gone blind again and she wants Boerne to cure him once more. Boerne thinks of his ruined life and of Hélène's suffering, and says harshly that he would cure the painter only if Lily did not exist. Overcome with emotion, he faints. When he comes round she has gone. He realizes something terrible is going to happen and runs after her, but arrives too late. Lily has committed suicide so that Boerne will cure her lover, and perhaps also to prove to him that she was capable of real love. The blind painter forgives Boerne because the doctor had made it possible for him to see Lily. Now that she is dead he doesn't want to be cured, and remains in his darkness. Next day Professor Boerne is found dead in his study.

For the first time, in my opinion, a contemporary German critic wrote something worthy of the great director. Willy Haas, who later scripted for *Der Brennende Acker*, wrote movingly in the *Film Kurier* of 14 December 1920, about *Der Gang in die Nacht*. It reminded him, he wrote, of some Ibsen productions by Otto Brahm,[1] or Tchekhov productions by Stanislavski.

He speaks of a certain ineffable musical quality in the film: A man and a woman sit facing each other at a table under a soft gas light. In the cosy warm room they breathe deep and begin to fall in love, while outside the rain lashes down and the wind rages.[2] Or the jilted girl lies on a divan, tired and ill and preparing to renounce her own happiness, and gropes under a cushion to find a scrap of newspaper with some trivial item about the man who was her fiancé. In short, here were the subtleties of a real *Kammerspiel*: Haas writes that it is impossible to say where the art of the author ends and that of the director and actors begins, for the whole thing is perfect. Carl Mayer's evocative script, at once simple and exquisitely subtle, shows him to be a great poet. Willy Haas talks of headlights gliding over rain-wet asphalt in the dark city, of rough seas, a dazzling sunrise, almost imperceptible gestures, facial expressions so eloquent that they reveal the soul within. It is impossible, he says, to speak specifically of Murnau's contribution as director: it is to be seen everywhere in all the great qualities of the film.

[1] A naturalistic theatre producer, Max Reinhardt's predecessor at the Deutsches Theater.
[2] This scene is missing from the surviving version of the film.

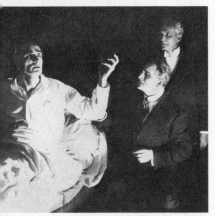

Der Gang in die Nacht

Der Gang in die Nacht

Was *Gang in die Nacht* Murnau's first masterpiece, or is Haas simply the first critic to have perceived Murnau's quality?

An advertisement in the *Film Kurier* of 30 December 1920 describes *Gang in die Nacht* as 'a sort of milestone in the art of the cinema'. For the first time, it says, a film has aimed at being a *Kammerspiel*, imbued with atmosphere, with *Stimmung*, with a small number of characters and a strong plot full of tension and subtle psychological detail.

When Murnau started work officially as a director at Decla Bioskop, in July 1921, on the resignation of Robert Wiene, Willy Haas wrote about the extreme sobriety and distinction of his character and his aristocratic austerity with regard to decorative effects. Haas saw these qualities as inextricably linked with the restraint and subtlety with which he directed the actors themselves. He referred to Murnau as the 'designer', to distinguish him from other film directors. His characters were like designs or drawings set down on paper with discreet but absolute assurance. His rigorous patrician objectivity and contempt for all superficial trickery reminded Haas once more of Otto Brahm, the last great theatrical director in north Germany.

What is left of the *Kammerspiel* that aroused so much enthusiasm in Haas?

The surviving copy of *Gang in die Nacht* has lost all its titles, and we know that Mayer and Murnau used a lot of titles at that time. Though they later insisted that a real film didn't need them and ought to say everything by means of images, they had a weakness, at the beginning of their careers, for 'poetic' texts. The titles were often in the form of arbitrary interludes inserted between images which were designed to develop psychological suspense, but which were themselves expansions of almost static situations. Such titles carried a great deal of the 'emotional' weight of the *Kammerspiel*. Also, some slowness and deliberation in the images themselves may be due to the fact that other essential parts besides the titles are missing.

The script confirms that some passages were conveyed by titles, diaries, or letters. For instance, Mayer suggests the reticence of Hélène's behaviour by making her write, in her diary:

The more promisingly he approaches his goal, the more restrained is my passion for him; he knows nothing of this, for I am always afraid lest my love distract him from his path.

In the script Boerne doesn't rush after Lily to save her – he is just found dead in his office. In his hand is a letter from the painter:

Friend, I do not accuse you. None of us is guilty. But don't try to cure me again. You gave me the gift of light once. I was able to look at her. Now I go back into my darkness.

In the film as we have it the blind man was probably supposed to say these words in a title before Boerne rushes away in desperation after learning of Lily's suicide.

Among other scenes which the script shows to be missing from the film are some of Boerne's decisive visit to the dancer. Only the first sequence remains:

In front of a fashionable hotel. It is raining steadily. The traffic is reflected in the flagstones. Porters. Pageboys. Visitors. Cabs. Cars. A porter opens the door of a car. Boerne. He goes towards the entrance.

The following passage is inserted into Boerne's interview with Lily:

The square in front of the hotel. The volume of traffic keeps increasing. Twilight fell [sic]. Cars. Cabs. Light. People. Lights flash. And the rain goes on falling, heavily.

Then Boerne talks about himself. A rather ordinary scene is made more subtle by the cross-cutting.

The external world penetrates into the scenes in the villa by the sea, thus helping us to understand Lily's behaviour, and showing her fears about the painter's presence in a much more cinematographic manner:

The villa by the sea. The sky grows overcast and dark. The wind starts to rage in the distance. The windows of the villa are hastily shut, The storm begins.

Lily knows that the bandages are to be removed from the patient's eyes at six o'clock. And the face of a clock mingles symbolically with her apprehension. As in *Sylvester* the tumult of nature provides an echo to the human drama. When Lily is waiting for Boerne to come back from a visit to one of his patients, Mayer writes:

Sky and house. The house very tiny. The sky immense. The sea shrieks [i.e. since this is a silent film, is very rough]. The air is dark. Strident, jagged lightning. Passage inside the house leading to the cellar: Lily is coming down the stairs. She slips along the corridor, groping her way. Now she stops. Listening at a door. Her breathing is impeded.

Dark, low-ceilinged room. The stranger lies there silent and stiff. The blind man. Motionless.

Lily still stands there. Listening. Shuddering. Trembling. Then she turns. She almost runs away, up the stairs.

Storm. Trees writhing in the storm.

In the script Lily searches feverishly for her dancing dress, puts it on, and starts to twirl round in a frenzy. Cross cut with the sea and the face of the clock. All this is missing from the film as we know it.

Hélène's behaviour after Boerne abandons her is also seen in a much more filmic manner, in an atmosphere of *Kammerspiel*:

Atmosphere of evening. An express train goes by.

The quiet street. An open carriage with Hélène sitting in it. Boerne's house. The carriage stops. She stares at the house without moving. All the shutters are closed. Hélène remains there as if gazing at a tomb. Pause. Then the carriage moves off.

This film seems much more dated now than, for example, *Schloss Vogelöd*. Of course there are some subtle lighting effects, and the furniture already shows Murnau's taste in and for elegant interiors. The shaded hotel entrance, with colonnades standing out against the surrounding chiaroscuro, is characteristic of his style. Young women, sitting dreaming by curtains which reveal transparently the shape of the window frame, create a typically nostalgic atmosphere.

Sometimes the depth of focus forms a sort of mysterious back-cloth to the psychological relationships between the actors. A certain hesitation in the gestures, a slowing down of action, suddenly ennobles the naïve and clumsy melodrama which served Carl Mayer as the basis of his plot. But the young director is not happy in his actors, particularly the famous Olaf Fønss, who is stiff and foppish and grimaces horribly to indicate anger or passion.

As for Conrad Veidt, he is dark and inflexible, and acts like Cesare in

Der Gang in die Nacht

Caligari, apart from wringing his hands like Orlac.[3] This Expressionist style clashes with Gudrun Bruun's naturalistic and unconvincingly sprightly interpretation of Lily. Only Erna Morena as Hélène is really at home in this *Kammerspiel*, the tragic mask of her face recalling that of Asta Nielsen.

There is just one passage which truly reveals Murnau's art: that in which Fønss, overwhelmed by Lily's betrayal, buries his face in the grass. At this moment he forgets his former pompous and exaggerated style, and the tumult in his heart is echoed by the fury of the storm.

At a commemoration of the thirtieth anniversary of Murnau's death, presented by the Cinémathèque Française at the Academy of Fine Arts in Berlin, Gerhard Lamprecht pointed out that *Der Gang in die Nacht* recalled the Danish films of 1915–16, and that Murnau must have been influenced, perhaps unconsciously, by the method of directing actors then prevalent. This would explain a style which is astonishingly old-fashioned for the beginning of the twenties.

But what is equally striking is the love of landscape and the feeling for

[3] *Orlacs Haende*, by Richard Oswald, was not made until 1924.

nature, closer to the Swedish than to the Danish cinema. Twice, and in a different way each time, Murnau shows a boat sailing through the dusk. The surface of the water and the shore combine to form in each case a perfect image, full of rhythm and movement, and vibrant with atmosphere.

Even setting aside our changed modern conception of acting, it is hardly possible today to express a judgment on a film which may have lost its original rhythm through surviving only in an incomplete form.

According to Ernst Jaeger, Murnau later said, 'My old films are unbearable'.[4] Perhaps this film is to be regarded rather as a still somewhat hesitant step towards the achievements of *Der Brennende Acker* and *Phantom*.

Phantom

Phantom was found recently in the Moscow Film Archive, in a version that seems more complete than was often the case with copies sold for foreign countries: films were shortened, especially German ones when it was thought that their plots were too slow.

After the unanimous success of *Der Brennende Acker* one is a little surprised at the much less enthusiastic response to *Phantom*. Murnau had made the mistake of taking on a work by the national poet, Gerhard Hauptmann, a sort of nineteenth-century Goethe. His producers compounded the error by releasing the film during the solemn celebration throughout Germany of the great man's sixtieth birthday.

Hauptmann himself was indulgent enough. In a sober programme with a cover similar to that of the published novel, which like many of the novels adapted by Murnau had previously appeared in the *Berliner Illustrierte Zeitung*, the poet spoke of the cinema in general as 'spiritual nourishment for the people', though he did also compare the enormous consumption of films to that of bread and potatoes. But these somewhat general and conventional considerations contain not one word about the film in question; Hauptmann doesn't take up any position, or make any attempt to defend any artistic point of view. The same is true of Thea von Harbou, who merely refers in her usual inflated manner to the tragic quality of 'spiritual events'.

But on 14 November 1922, in the *Berliner Tageblatt*, the chief paper of the Berlin democrats, a second-rate critic really let himself go. During the various pompous speeches before the showing of the film, someone had been foolish enough to suggest that whereas a literary work was made of words alone, a film, which had images at its disposal, could show the lives of people directly. But according to the *Berliner Tageblatt* critic, Thea von Harbou had only

[4] See *Der Neue Film* for a series of articles called 'Nicht zur Veröffentlichung' ('Not for Publication'). Wiesbaden, 1954.

created picture-postcard stuff; even the best pictures are still not 'interior landscapes'; even the most ingenious photography does not come near the psychological subtlety of a writer like Dostoievski; and even good actors cannot salvage the film. Only its technical side strikes him as sometimes excellent.

Not a word about Murnau. The critic savagely attacks film people 'who in their enthusiasm pat their fat bellies pathetically'. There could be no better sign of the contempt of non-trade papers at that time for the unknown art of the cinema.

If only Murnau had worked with someone like Carl Mayer on the film! Even such an un-literary trade journal as *Kinematograph* said, on 19 November 1922, that the adaptation by Thea von Harbou, 'a sentimental and pretentious author', was as superficial as one might expect, and that she got bogged down in detail in a typically feminine manner. However, the article went on, Murnau, 'a subtle poet, though German and therefore ponderous', had skilfully abridged or got round the most longwinded passages. Thanks to his delicate technique, which was supported by excellent photography and marvellous sets, the adaptation was in the end harmonious and subtle. Murnau knew how to reproduce an atmosphere and bring out psychological truths.

Other German film journals were of the opinion that even a director as sensitive and perceptive as Murnau could do nothing against such a superficial adaptation as Thea von Harbou's. One provincial paper only praised the brevity and precision of her titles, as well as the beauty of the softly dimming images in the dream sequences.

The much-duped copy I saw in the Wiesbaden Film Institute has very little of the varied and delicate light and shade Murnau usually put into his films. But even in this rather dark copy his feeling for depth of focus is still evident. In many shots windows are used as backgrounds in order to introduce space and air. Before writing his life story and confession, Lorenz Lubota looks out into a garden of fruit trees in flower. The bookbinder's shop has big panes of glass looking out on the narrow studio streets of the little town. And there is an audacious shot when Lubota goes to the Harlan's house to ask for Veronika's hand: the camera looks down with Mrs Harlan from a landing to where he waits below in a large hall full of the antique furniture Murnau was always so fond of showing.

All the sorrowful weight and tension of the *Kammerspiel* film is here; we feel the vibrations between the characters. Under Murnau's direction Alfred Abel manages to convey the somnambulistic vagueness of someone who has lost himself and become a mere puppet in the hands of a crook. Frieda Richard as Lubota's mother foreshadows Mutter Krause or the mother in

Phantom: Lubota and his aunt

Such is Life. The two more realistic characters, Wigottschinsky the crook and the Baroness, are sketched in a few deftly humorous strokes.

But, as in *The Last Laugh*, all the characters except the principal are left somewhat vague, as if Murnau were only interested in his unheroic hero and his frustration and degradation.

We see little of the softly dimming dream sequences referred to by the critics and described by Hermann Warm (opposite). Perhaps some distributor thought they slowed down the action, and so cut them. Only once now does dream take over from reality: as Lubota creeps furtively down the street to his aunt's house at night, the houses seem to crush him and the dark shadows of their gables claw at him ferociously. Little however remains of the scene where Lubota, sitting in the bar with the Baroness's daughter, suddenly feels everything spinning about him.[5] We can only briefly notice a shot where their table appears to be descending at the edge of the screen; while twice we see quick cuts of a rather broad spiral staircase wheeling around – the first

[5] In the script this scene of the spinning table appeared when Lubota meets the Baroness and her daughter for the first time. By transferring it to the moment when Lubota dances with the daughter, Murnau uses it to greater dramatic and psychological effect.

time with a dim figure pursuing another, and the second with a single figure running down the steps.[5] The scene of Lubota's first perception of the wretchedness of his home is now scarcely visible. The dream image of Veronika meeting Lubota before the town hall in the company of several gentlemen in top hats and dress coats, come to pay homage to him as a famous poet, is at best a poor shadow of the dream sequence in *The Last Laugh*. Veronika's white spectral carriage floats only briefly across the screen, and there is only a momentary shot of Lorenz in pursuit of it to recall the drawing in the script.

Even allowing for some errors in editing (amended when the film was shown by the Cinémathèque Française), and the tedium of the titles, the film – for so long a lost legend – is in the event disappointing, certainly lacking the richness of *Nosferatu* and the maturity of Murnau's later work.

[Hermann Warm has given this account of the trick techniques used for the nightmares in *Phantom*.]

People often wonder how we managed to produce certain nightmare visions, like that of the 'tottering day' in *Phantom*. Of course we had to use trick effects that entailed very elaborate techniques.

I went with Murnau to Breslau to see if the actual places that Hauptmann had described in his novel could give us any inspiration for the sets. But this didn't help much, and we realized we should have to find other sources of inspiration for the exteriors that were to be constructed in the studios at Babelsberg.

For the street in the 'tottering day' sequence, in which I wanted to avoid realism, I made use of a vague memory of a street in Breslau. The left side of the street was actually built, with houses of cheap material. Between the houses were quite large spaces, which were invisible because they were hidden by hoardings. In this way I gave the impression of a long street of uninterrupted façades: it had to be a long street because the coach with the white horses was supposed to gallop along it.

The right side of the street was faked. The gabled fronts of the houses were made of plywood and mounted on sloping rails so that they could be made to move faster and faster. Behind all this, still on the right, was a ramp with very powerful arcs, so that the moving houses could throw their shadows on the opposite side of the street, where the buildings were motionless and bathed in livid moonlight. In this way we succeeded in making it look as if the shadows of the houses were pursuing the young man as he ran after the carriage.

The other trick effect was even more interesting. It concerned the scene where the young man goes into a bar and feels everything spinning round him. The set for the bar was oval. On one side there were semi-circular boxes opening on to the dance-floor. In one of these boxes the young man sat at a table. Now this box was in fact reproduced in another part of the studio, over a trap and in the midst of a scaffolding of beams. It was actually a big round platform two metres in diameter, fixed on a wheel which turned on the same axle as another wheel beneath. The lower wheel was attached to *another* platform, and on this platform, which was fixed, a man lay on his back and moved the upper wheel round faster and faster with his feet. The upper wheel moved the upper platform round, with the young man sitting at his table.

But this was not enough. We wanted to give the impression not only of a whirlpool, but also of a fall. So three steel bands, four centimetres wide and one millimetre thick, were attached to the fixed lower platform, and passed over three rollers up among the beams. At their other extremity these steel bands were attached to a third and narrower platform on which were placed weights of fifty kilos totalling less than the weight supported by the moving platform. The platform with the weights on was on a slide, and could be stopped by the application of a brake.

Thanks to this complicated machinery we could make the big platform with the young man and the table turn round faster and faster. We could also make it shoot downwards into the darkness through a sort of funnel formed by the other boxes, which made a curve three-quarters open towards the camera. A fade at the end made the shadows even deeper and gave only a glimpse of the final phase of the fall. The platform could descend $6\frac{1}{4}$ metres, and to break its fall we used a brake and also sprung buffers.

Curiously enough the review of *Phantom* by Herbert Jhering in the *Börsen Courier* (14 November 1922) speaks about three different scenes which we see today very much shortened: the shadowy collapse of the houses, the spinning around of the staircases (which Warm does not mention) and the sinking down, not the spinning, of the table.

6. Schloss Vogelöd

This film still exists, although, as in the case of *Der Gang in die Nacht*, the titles are missing. Their absence makes the film rather difficult to understand in some places, for although a later Mayer script such as *The Last Laugh* had no need of titles, *Schloss Vogelöd* has a complicated plot adapted from a semi-highbrow, semi-commercial novel, and much necessary explanation was consigned to the numerous titles. They were numerous indeed: the script includes no less than a hundred and sixty-five, though judging by the spaces for titles in the surviving copy, Murnau reduced them by almost half.[1]

It is therefore necessary to lay some stress on what is the real content of this film, especially as Theodore Huff, in his *Index*, provides only vague and sometimes inaccurate glimpses. He says it is a horror film; this is an error. He says too that it is plainly influenced by the Swedish school, and is notable for atmosphere and impressionistic sets which projected the lonely feelings of a young couple living in a deserted castle. The conjecture about the Swedish influence is safe enough; but the error of thinking Vogelöd is a *deserted* castle seems to have arisen out of a too literal translation, and hence misinterpretation, of the name – literally – 'bird's desert'.

The same is true also of Kracauer's comments, which Huff quotes:

... he knowingly used faces to reveal emotional undercurrents and orchestrate suspense. This early film moreover testified to Murnau's unique faculty of obliterating

[1] Eighty-six titles are indicated in the copy in the Cinémathèque Française.

the boundaries between the real and the unreal. Reality in his films was surrounded by a halo of dreams and presentiments, and a tangible person might suddenly impress the audience as a mere apparition.[2]

These fine phrases would apply better to *Phantom* or *Nosferatu*. The two dreams in *Schloss Vogelöd* are treated merely comically, and there is neither any unreality in the film nor any close-ups of faces to show emotion. At this period emotion was expressed rather through attitude and gesture.[3]

Here is a summary of the film.[4]

It is autumn. In the castle of Vogelöd the owner, his young wife, and his hunting companions await the arrival of the beautiful Baroness von Saffer-städt and her husband; her first husband, Count Peter Paul Oetsch, died three years previously in mysterious circumstances which still remain unexplained. The guests debate in whispers whether it was not the Count's own brother, Johann Oetsch, who shot him.

Then this brother himself arrives uninvited at the castle. Everyone feels uneasy. The guests avoid him, and the Baroness is horrified and wants to leave at once. But she decides to stay in order to see Father Faramund, a distant relative of her first husband, who is due to arrive soon from Rome.

The next day the guests go hunting, with the exception of the Count. It is a fine day, and he says he prefers to hunt in the rain. And indeed, when the hunting party is forced to return by a sudden downpour, the intruder leaves the castle, ostensibly to go hunting himself.

This strange behaviour makes the guests all the more uneasy. That evening a carriage arrives; it is Father Faramund, who is taken straight to the Baroness, who says she wants to confess. The confession is given in flash-back: it shows the Baroness's first marriage, four years ago, which was at first a very happy one. Then her husband went away on a journey, and when he came back appeared to be entirely changed. He buried himself in ancient books and lived like a sort of saint or mystic, neglecting his young wife and telling her that real happiness could only be found in renunciation. Frustrated and consumed by sensuality and a passion that no longer met with any response, she saw evil in everything and thought only of committing it. It was while she was in this mood of rebellion that she met the Baron.

At this point in her confession the Baroness falters and cannot go on. She sends Father Faramund away, and a servant shows him to his room. He asks

---

[2] *From Caligari to Hitler*, op. cit., p. 78.

[3] There are close-ups in *Caligari*, of course, for example the one of Cesare opening his eyes. But the real close-up as created by the German *Kammerspielfilm*, making visible every emotion, came after *Schloss Vogelöd*.

[4] This summary was made by Henri Langlois and myself after I had examined the film and read the fragments of titles written in ink on the leaders. It was later compared with the rediscovered scenario and found to be correct.

Schloss Vogelöd

the servant to give his excuses to the master of the house for not seeing him until the morning.

In the kitchen the evening meal is being prepared. A comic interlude: the cook finds the scullion tasting the cream and boxes his ears.

Night falls. The guests, tired after the chase, are asleep. But the Baroness cannot sleep. She rings for a servant and sends for Father Faramund. The servant knocks at his door but there is no answer. The master of the house and the other guests are roused, the door is opened with a pass-key, but Faramund is not there! The porter swears he hasn't let anyone out.

The friar's mysterious disappearance increases everyone's apprehension, and even troubles the sleep of a 'nervous gentleman' who barricades himself in his room and has a nightmare in which the claw of a phantom bird gets hold of him and drags him towards the window!

The scullion is more fortunate: he dreams that the cook falls fast asleep where he stands, as in 'The Sleeping Beauty', so that the boy is free to eat anything he fancies.

Morning comes, but still no Father Faramund. Unable to bear the oppressive atmosphere, the 'nervous gentleman' and another guest leave the castle.

Schloss Vogelöd: the confession

Only one man fails to share the general unease: the man whom everyone suspects. Perhaps he has done away with Father Faramund too? He looks them all insolently up and down, and even lets fall the embarrassing word 'murder' to the Baron, a sombre taciturn man, who gets up angrily and goes to his room.

Before all the company the young Baroness, on the brink of hysterics, suddenly accuses her former brother-in-law of murdering her first husband. He looks at her for a long while without saying a word, then goes out.

The guests look at one another in dismay: what will happen next?

But suddenly Father Faramund reappears as mysteriously as he disappeared. The Baroness goes on with her confession: 'It was Baron Safferstädt who, thinking he would be the instrument of my desire to do evil, shot my husband.'

The pace quickens. Father Faramund goes to the Baron, whom he finds in a state of collapse and who confesses how anguished he has been since he committed the murder. Then Faramund removes his spectacles, false beard, and wig: it is Count Johann Oetsch disguised as a monk!

Still dressed as a Capuchin friar he comes down the stairs, the guests watching in stupefaction from the hall below. The sound of a revolver shot is heard in the distance: the Baron has expiated his crime.

The Baroness embraces her friend and hostess for the last time, saying as she goes: 'He at least is not suffering any more.' A title and a picture of the peaceful water suggest that she has gone to throw herself in the lake.

The peace of evening falls. The rain has stopped . . . the universal oppression gives way to relief.

A carriage arrives, the door-bell rings. The porter opens: the real Father Faramund has arrived.

Only the efforts of Murnau, Carl Mayer, Hermann Warm, and Fritz Arno Wagner could have succeeded – as indeed they did – in creating out of this somewhat confused story an authentic, oppressive, anguish-ridden atmosphere.

But the castle, far from 'deserted', and full of hunting trophies, is rather like the one in Stroheim's *Honeymoon*. Mayer says a faint wisp of smoke comes up out of the chairs when the guests sit down; this already creates a sort of *Stimmung*.

But at bottom all these gentlemen are rather tedious in their costumes of the period and with their slicked-down old-fashioned hair. And for characters in a Murnau film they are all very ugly!

The flash-back scenes are quite a different matter. Here the sets are noble and varied, and the images luminous and mysterious. The handsome Count, Peter Paul Oetsch, sits in his study buried in his books, while the Baroness tries in vain to embrace him. A Rembrandtesque light shines through the velvety darkness. In the script, Mayer had written:

A study. Standard lamp. Lighting effect.

Murnau and his team did the rest.

The most impressive image is of a long, narrow, high-ceilinged room. The light pierces downward from two tall windows into the blackness; two shadowy figures face each other, leaning against opposite walls, withdrawn into the dark.

Mayer had indicated:

A very long, high room. Afternoon. Almost general shot: room in antique style. Severe. Practically no furniture.
Only the walls!

And:

The Baroness. Crouched against a wall. Frozen with horror. Struggling not to cry out. She remains thus. Panting horribly. And the Baron. A long way away. Crouched against the other wall. His anguished face turned upwards. Thus he remains like her, not moving.

This is the scene that follows the Baron's confession to the young woman that he has murdered her husband. It is one of the most beautiful pictures Murnau ever created.

In his review in *Film Kurier*, 8 April 1921, Willy Haas says:

> There is a scene in this film introduced by the title 'The confession'. In a large lofty room stand a murderer who has killed for love, and his beloved; and they both remain there motionless like statues. Such a thing has rarely been seen in the whole existence of the cinema. . . .

Haas refers again to the infinite restraint exercised in *Schloss Vogelöd*:

> Murnau's artistic tendency is to moderate strong gestures into others more noble and subtle. This makes him more successful than any other director in conveying intimate dialogue, the completely silent exchanges of the heart, as in the scene of the confession, where the emotion is expressed through the extraordinary tension of the bodies.

There are some very beautiful landscapes in the main part of the film – shrubs lashed by the rain, a carriage driving through the evening like a shadow, reminding one of the coach in *Nosferatu*. Mayer was keen on showing the castle, either lit up or in darkness, with the rain falling on it. For this Murnau used a model, and inserted several shots of it among interior scenes. He and Mayer were to use a similar juxtaposition for Orgon's house in *Tartuffe*.

The very conventional and formal visual treatment of the crowd scenes involving the guests seems to be intentional.[5] Perhaps Murnau wanted some grey tones in his drama to match the rain outside. At least more intimate scenes, like that in the boudoir between the Baroness and her hostess – though the characters act in a way that is curiously passionate, even tormented – have much warmer values and a much more subtle *Stimmung*.

At all events it was certainly with deliberate intention that Murnau refrained from giving any really supernatural atmosphere to the 'nervous gentleman's' nightmare. We are a long way here from the nightmare in *Januskopf*. Murnau is making fun of the character's timidity, and the part is played by Julius Falkenstein, a well-known comic actor of the German cinema.

Neither is there any of the fascination that emanates from the dream in *Phantom*, or any resemblance even to the dream in *The Last Laugh*, in the little scullion's 'wish-fulfilment' dream. In these two dream sequences in

---

[5] The same contrast can be seen in *Die Finanzen des Grossherzogs*, where everything is bathed in sunshine except the scenes in the capital, which are deliberately nebulous and dull.

Schloss Vogelöd we are face to face with the 'other' Murnau, the Murnau of *Die Finanzen des Grossherzogs*, the rather naïve epilogue to *The Last Laugh*, or the absurd Luna Park gags in *Sunrise*. As all his friends tell us, Murnau could be shy, sensitive, and melancholy. But he could also suddenly be as gay and mischievous as a schoolboy. Such is the double face of *Schloss Vogelöd*.

7. The Riddle of Nosferatu

An issue of *Bühne und Film* in 1922 [1] – which incidentally includes a photograph of Ernst Hofmann as 'The Blue Boy', with no mention of the fact that it is from Murnau's film *Der Knabe in Blau* – is devoted to publicity for *Nosferatu* just before its first showing:

Nosferatu – who cannot die!
A million fancies strike you when you hear the name: Nosferatu!

$$N_R O_A S_T F_U E$$

does not die!
What do you expect of the first showing of this great work?
Aren't you afraid? – Men must die. But legend has it that a vampire, Nosferatu, 'der Untote' (the Undead), lives on men's blood! You want to see a symphony of horror? You may expect more. Be careful. Nosferatu is not just fun, not something to be taken lightly. Once more: beware.

Then comes a summary of the story, with illustrations, of which one seems to be a production photograph. It shows Nosferatu, without his coffin, resting on a bench in the little town square which in fact he only passes through in the film. After this there is an article on 'Vampires' by Albin Grau, the designer of the film. Is the story he tells pure invention? It is winter, 1916, in Serbia.

[1] No. 21, 3rd year.

An old peasant with whom Grau, who was then in the army, is billeted, tells him and the other soldiers how his father, who died without receiving the sacraments, haunted the village in the form of a vampire. He shows them an official document which says that a man named Morowitch was exhumed at Progatza in 1884. The body showed no signs of decomposition, but the teeth were strangely long and sharp, and protruded from the mouth. The Lord's Prayer was said over the body, and a stake driven through its heart. And the 'undead', then known in Serbia as a *Nosferatu*, gave a groan and died. . . .

Grau embroiders this tale in the approved German manner: it is midnight, the room is full of menacing shadows, a blizzard rages outside, the wind howls down the chimney and the log in the grate blazes up. The soldiers all listen nervously, with bated breath.

Then, years later, travelling in the Tatra mountains looking for exteriors for *Nosferatu*, Grau claims to have met by chance, in the old alchemists' city of Prague, one of the other soldiers who had been there that strange night in Serbia. They talked about it and Grau told the other about the film. His friend said he would come to see it 'even if I were at the other end of the world.'

Grau ends his article: 'And Prana Films will not forget him!' So perhaps it was all just publicity pure and simple.

This does not mean that Grau might not, even so, have provided the title and the idea for *Nosferatu*: the film, though based (without authorization) on Bram Stoker's *Dracula*, is not very close to the novel. (Grau, it incidentally appears, was at that time an ardent spiritualist.)

As we possess the final shooting script of *Nosferatu* we can now more or less elucidate the riddle posed by the two copies of the film preserved in the Cinémathèque Française.[2]

One of these is sub-titled in German, the other in French. The German is clearly a contemporary copy from the original negative. It has fine illustrated sub-titles with half-shaded pictures by Albin Grau, the designer of the film. These pictures are similar to the five included in the original programme, which were also drawn by Grau. The lettering of the subtitles is lanky and tortuous, like that in a contemporary copy of *Caligari*.

Subtle tones and values confer on both landscapes and interiors a relief which is further enhanced by the lighting. There are beautiful views of jagged clouds scudding across the sky, or leaves driven along a path by the wind, as the sinister second night falls over the castle. A phrase in the script refers to this:

A ghostly twilight falls, visible between fantastic trunks of trees.

[2] See *Cahiers du Cinéma*, No. 79, January 1958, p. 22: Lotte H. Eisner, '*L'énigme des deux Nosferatus*'.

Perhaps Murnau, when he was in the Carpathians, photographed some views of clouds against the evening sky, images not indicated in the script but which he came across by chance.

In this German version there is also more varied cross-cutting than in the French copy; these shots are likewise to be found in the script. The shots of Ellen sleepwalking, as the monster comes in to her husband's room in the castle, are placed a little earlier than in the French copy, and thus render the suspense more unbearable. Then, in the 'race against death', as one of the German titles has it, Nosferatu's journey by sea and Hutter's by land, the incidents at Ellen's house and those concerning Knock, succeed one another in a sort of parallel *montage* that seems to have been invented by Murnau, who as we have seen suggested this succession of rapid images in manuscript notes added on Galeen's script.[3]

But the German copy lacks some very effective shots which exist in the copy with French, un-illustrated titles: the diabolically heaped-up coffins on the cart in the courtyard of the castle, the still-swinging hammock of the dead sailor, the curtains that suddenly shift, twice, like a warning of imminent danger. These passages occur in the script.

What is the explanation of the thousand additional metres of film in the German copy, which contains two long passages, which are not hinted at in the script and which we find curiously unlikeable? As Hutter journeys in haste towards the enchanted castle a German title says he 'passes by merry feasts'. And then come longwinded and commonplace sequences of peasants dancing and banqueting at a long table. There is no trace of Murnau's style in these scenes of would-be folk-lore of a kind that recurred so often in later Ufa films.

There are other puzzling scenes, too, like that of some young peasant girls roaring with laughter at a village conjuror whose hen lays a constant stream of eggs.[4]

Another strange sequence shows an interminably long mass said for a victim of the plague by a very handsome young priest assisted by some even more attractive choirboys, a passage which seems to prefigure parts of *Faust*. (The scene might be somewhat more comprehensible if the mass were for the captain of the ship.) There is nothing of any of this either in Galeen's script or in Murnau's annotations.

[3] Frank Hansen says in a letter: 'Murnau was the first to use *rapid montage*. I don't know whether he alone devised the process, but quarter and half frame *montage* (four image and two image) were first used by Murnau in his German films.' (Hansen does not realize that Gance and Epstein used the same process independently of each other at about this time, in *La Roue* (1922) and *Cœur Fidèle* (1923).)

[4] The same passage, though in a shortened form, occurs in a copy preserved in the Spanish Cinémathèque.

Nosferatu: Act I

Nosferatu: Acts I and II

Nosferatu: Acts II–IV

Fritz Arno Wagner, the great cameraman of *Nosferatu*, whom I consulted about these two passages, wrote to me a few months before his death in an accident:

The original was not very long, so it is quite possible that certain parts were added afterwards. Plenty of material was shot. But I don't know anything about the scene of the conjuror and the eggs. Nor did I ever shoot the mass for the dead; it must have been added ready-made. Moreover I've never seen this lengthened and changed copy, and I can vouch for the fact that Murnau himself never knew this second version.

How is one to account, then, for these two passages, in which, needless to say, none of the real characters in the film appears? The first passage is far too crude to have been taken from one of the lost 'peasant-films' of Murnau.

As to the other changes, I had previously thought that some over-zealous distributor, or perhaps even the producing company itself, Prana Films, made use of some of the footage Murnau shot but rejected in the interests of rhythm and balance, without consulting the director. This would explain the long-drawn-out finale in the German copy, showing, in a series of images irrelevant to the main structure of the film, the general restoration of peace after the disappearance of the monster. Some of these pictures certainly were shot during Murnau's visit to the Carpathians; he probably filmed them on the off-chance they might be useful, but used only some of them for his final version. There is no suggestion of this finale in the script, which ends with Ellen's death; and the French copy only has a few scenes of peaceful aftermath and some quite relevant shots of the now-ruined castle.

Both the French and Spanish copies give us the fine sequence of the opening-up of one of the coffins in the harbour, at night. Here the German copy inserts a scene of a sailor playing the accordion, though there is no mention of this in the script. Both the additional shots, however, have the same mysterious chiaroscuro as the rest of the passage. Perhaps Murnau himself shot these scenes, but afterwards rejected them as detracting from the dramatic effect of the coffin scene.

If there was doubt about these two long passages, other variations appeared equally apocryphal. For instance, in the German version Ellen, instead of sacrificing herself and dying in order to save the city from the vampire, comes to life again. This surprising happy ending was achieved by simply transferring a sequence showing the couple living quietly and happily together from the beginning to the end of the film. The script, the summary in *Bühne und Film*, the reviews in the film journals, and the original programme all confirm that Ellen dies: she gives her life in exchange for the disappearance of the vampire, whom she keeps with her till sunrise.

The French copy faithfully follows the script, which inserts symbolic images of a carnivorous plant and a cuttlefish in the sequence where Knock, in the asylum, awaits the arrival of the monster, sucking the blood of flies and triumphantly displaying a spider which is attacking an insect caught in its web. The German copy, in which the sequence of the happy young couple has been removed from the beginning, opens the film with these symbolic sequences.

The German copy is also deprived of the dramatic effect of the famous vampire-book. In his room at the inn, Hutter merely reads the Bible, instead of, as in the script and in the French version, finding the sinister volume which at this stage only makes him laugh. Nor, in the German version, does he again find the book in his room at the castle, before the arrival of the monster. Yet Galeen says in the script:

Did the inn-keeper's wife put it there? [i.e. in his knapsack]

And the French copy uses the incident to increase the suspense. In the German copy it is Ellen whom we see reading the vampire-book, with no indication of where it came from.

The riddle of the variant versions of *Nosferatu* was solved when Gerhard Lamprecht, the well-known film historian and director, sent me a censor's certificate dated 14 November 1930. The certificate refers to a film pretentiously entitled *Die Zwoelfte Stunde* (The Twelfth Hour), with the subtitle *Eine Nacht des Grauens* (A Night of Horror). An unknown company called 'Deutsch Film Produktion' is given as producer, and, curiously, no director is mentioned. On the other hand, the 'artistic adaptation' is by a Dr Waldemar Roger, also unknown! The film had been sound-synchronized by the method Organon G.m.b.H. Polyphon Grammophon Konzern.

The actors are given new names, and an extra member has been added to the cast: Hans Behal, who plays the handsome and rather equivocal young priest.[5] The censor asked that he should be cut out of the film, together with the Mass for the Dead sequence and the choir at the end, all on religious grounds!

The German copy is therefore this 'artistic adaptation'. Deutsch Film Produktion must have bought the very fine original negative of *Nosferatu*, together with the unused shots, from Prana Film, the actual producing company. To lengthen the film Dr Waldemar Roger simply added the peasant scenes (did he find them ready-made, perhaps, at Ufa?) and then perhaps shot and cut in the sequence of the Mass for the Dead. Instead of using the original music written by Hans Erdmann to accompany the

[5] This passage has a rather disconcerting resemblance to a famous literary forgery: the apocryphal short story of 'The Priest and the Choirboy' long attributed to Oscar Wilde.

silent film, he commissioned Georg Fliebiger, another unknown, to write a new score.

The plastic beauty of the German copy is explained by the use of the original negative. The fine supernatural drawings that accompany the titles also come from the negative.

Of course it is this same Dr Waldemar Roger who resuscitates Ellen for the happy ending, and edits in the vampire flowers and animals at the beginning.

This 'artistic' distortion of the original film was almost certainly done without Murnau's knowledge when he was busy with other things in the United States. Hence the German version which is more than three reels longer than the French copy, which correctly corresponds to the script.

Let us consider that long narrow street, typical of a north German city, with regular houses on either side, along which a procession of undertaker's mutes advances, with dreadful slowness, carrying the narrow coffins of the plague-stricken – all seen in an angle shot looking down from a window, whose glazing-bars run right across the picture.

The script has:

> In the distance, a strange procession is wandering across the street. One coffin after another carried by survivors.

Galeen has a man who staggers as he walks at the head of this procession. Murnau rightly cut out this figure, which would have been a distraction. But for the window he notes: *with frame*. So this unexpected and astonishing glazing-bar must have been Murnau's own invention – the rail replacing the frame during the shooting so as not to clutter the picture. Twice during this scene the German version inserts shots of bells tolling. This may heighten the atmosphere, but it is neither in the script nor in the French copy. There were similar bells in *Sunrise*, but so there were in many other German films, and even in Stroheim's.

In this street scene Murnau reveals his skill at making his subject materialize from the farthest depths of a shot. He uses the same method when the vampire advances towards the scared young man at nightfall, and when Nosferatu, then still Count Orlok, suddenly appears out of the shadows of the doorway. The long room in the castle where Hutter wakes to find a tempting meal set out on his first morning recalls the setting for the confession scene in *Schloss Vogelöd*. Only Phil Mori, in *Bianco e Nero*,[6] has pointed out the 'systematic use of the depth of focus' which I have also discussed in *The Haunted Screen*.[7]

[6] *Bianco e Nero*, April 1951.
[7] *The Haunted Screen*, 1969, pp. 103–4.

Antragsteller: }
Hersteller: } **Deutsch-Film-Produktion, Berlin SW 48**

Friedrichstraße 233

Haupttitel: **Die zwölfte Stunde. Eine Nacht des Grauens.**

Künstlerische Bearbeitung: Dr. Waldemar Roger.
Akustisches Verfahren: Organon G. m. b. H., im
Polyphon-Grammophon- Konzern. (Schutzmarke.)

P e r s o n e n :

Fürst Wollkoff . . . Max Schreck
Karsten,
    ein Häusermakler . . Alexander Granach
Kundberg,
    sein Angestellter . . Gustav von Wangenheim
Margitta, dessen Frau Greta Schroeder

(Top left) Max Schreck as Nosferatu; (top right) Expressionist make-up: Heinrich George in
Platz, a play by Fritz von Unruh; (below) censor's certificate for the sound reissue of *Nosferatu*

Fritz Arno Wagner kindly sent me a picture postcard of Oravsky castle (Oravsky Zamok), which was built near the river Orava in Slovakia in the thirteenth century, high up on a curiously hollowed-out rock. This postcard reveals that the strange castle we see in the distance when Hutter has crossed the bridge and entered the grim country of the phantoms, is not, as I had previously thought, a model.[8]

As always, Murnau found visual means of suggesting unreality. For the sequence of the mad drive of the demon coach, Galeen merely suggested *Märchenwald* – fairy-tale forest. Murnau notes: 'wild chase through a white forest'. This shows that the idea of using the negative was his. Nor does Galeen suggest, either for this sequence or for that of the 'sinisterly rapid' heaping up of the coffins in the courtyard, the use of stop-action. Perhaps Murnau or Wagner only perfected this method during the actual shooting.

Nosferatu, though it has now become a classic, was for a long time unappreciated. As late as 1946 Theodore Huff wrote that it was rather crude and too 'Teutonic', that the acting was laboured, and that since the film had been produced on a shoestring – and not by American economic standards – the trick photography was ludicrous rather than impressive.

One cannot disagree with Huff's strictures on the actors. Ruth Landshoff, for example, who plays the ship-owner's sister, was not even a professional actress, but a girl Murnau had noticed in Grunewald, on her way to school. Beautiful and refined, she reminded him of a picture by Kaulbach, and he went to great lengths to meet her mother and ask permission for her to take part in the film during the holidays. Wangenheim, who played Hutter, and Greta Schroeder, one of Wegener's wives, who played Ellen, were never great actors. And whatever the visitor to the studio during *Schloss Vogelöd* may have said,[9] Murnau had not yet acquired the masterly technique with actors that was to be evident in his more mature works.

There remain Max Schreck as the vampire and Granach as Knock. No American horror film has anything like the sobriety of *Nosferatu*, in which the ludicrous is always avoided by means of that rigorous abstraction which is inherited from the finest development of Expressionism. If Granach sometimes overdoes the facial contortions, it is because he was always naturally exuberant. But Murnau managed to make out of Max Schreck, a normally

---

[8] Wagner wrote to me that the exteriors were shot in the Upper Tatras in Czechoslovakia, near Zakopane, Propad, and Smokovec; also at Wismar (including the loading of the coffins), Rostock, and especially Lübeck. The interiors were built by Albin Grau at the Jofa studios at Berlin-Johannistal. Wangenheim, who was mistaken on this point, speaks of the Staaken studios near Berlin.

[9] See pp. 34–35.

undistinguished actor, a tragically ambiguous character, whom André Gide called 'dashing, venturesome, and even very pleasingly bold', and whom the audience sees vanish at cockcrow as much with regret as with relief.[10]

But Gide complains of the film's Germanic heaviness and sums it up as a failure. It was impossible that he should like what remained fundamentally a romantic abstraction, very far removed from his own French Protestant severity.

Nevertheless *Nosferatu* was a long way from the facile horrors of *Frankenstein* or *Dracula*.

[10] André Gide: *Journal*, 27 February 1928. Vol. III of the Justin O'Brien translation, Knopf, New York; Secker and Warburg, London; 1949.

8. The Lost Films

Little is now known about the lost films of Murnau, among which the loss of *Der Brennende Acker* is particularly regrettable.

Apart from such scripts as have been found, for instance that for *Der Januskopf*, and the scenario of *Satanas*, I have been able to consult various original programmes. But one cannot place too much reliance on the brief summaries these contain. They are often written in very primitive and sentimental publicity jargon by press officers. The same applies to most other contemporary evidence – the puffs in the trade papers, or the rare paragraphs accorded to the cinema by Berlin dailies or periodicals, which at that time had little respect for the seventh art.

But in spite of all this I have tried to reconstruct at least the plot of the lost films, in the secret hope that somehow, somewhere, some of them may eventually be found, though by now they may no longer have their original titles attached to them.

The crudeness of some of the subjects Murnau used is nowadays astonishing. He was obliged for *Der Gang in die Nacht* to make use of one of the many scenarios that the declining Nordisk Film company had thrown on the German market.

On the other hand it seems to have been from choice that he based *Schloss Vogelöd* on a novel by a third-rate writer, Rudolf Stratz, which appeared, like other stories used by Murnau, in the *Berliner Illustrierte Zeitung*, a popular

Der Knabe in Blau

weekly published by Ullstein. And *Die Finanzen des Grossherzogs* was taken from a very ordinary novel by an undistinguished Swedish author, Frank Heller.

Even *Sunrise*, a very fine film, came from another third-rate author, this time a sort of German Paul Bourget who was fashionable in middle-class drawing-rooms at the end of the nineteenth century: Hermann Sudermann, later nicknamed 'Sudelmann' (i.e. 'dauber').

Fortunately Murnau always found himself distinguished adapters even for undistinguished material. The subject was a matter of indifference to him so long as the adaptation was really cinematic. As early as 1922, in an interview, he strongly condemned the habit of basing films on novels or plays.[1] And years later, in the United States, he said in another interview[2] that one had to eliminate everything that was not pure cinema, to get rid of everything trivial or superfluous and all the tricks, gags, expedients, and clichés that had nothing to do with film and 'belonged to books or the stage'.

Der Knabe in Blau (1919)

Here, according to Mme Hedda Hofmann, widow of Ernst Hofmann, is the plot of Murnau's first film, *Der Knabe in Blau* (1919), inspired by Gainsborough's 'Blue Boy'. Murnau used the famous portrait in the film, but substituted for the original face that of his young and handsome protagonist.

Thomas von Weerth, last survivor of an old noble family, lives in poverty and retirement with an old servant in a romantic broken-down castle surrounded by water.

He often contemplates the portrait of one of his ancestors, with whom he feels a mysterious bond. Is he the re-incarnation of this young man in blue, who wears on his breast the famous 'emerald of death' that has always brought bad luck to his family? To avoid the curse, another of his forebears hid the jewel somewhere in the castle, and Thomas, haunted by the portrait, searches everywhere for the emerald, but in vain. One evening he falls asleep and the boy in blue steps out of the picture and leads him to the hiding-place.

When he wakes von Weerth finds the emerald in the place indicated to him in the dream, and takes no notice when his old servant begs him to throw it away.

At this point some travelling players arrive at the castle and the young master falls in love with a beautiful gypsy girl who, with the aid of the leader of the troupe, gets him completely in her power. They strip him of everything: the emerald is stolen, the castle burns down, the portrait is destroyed. Thomas

---

[1] See article by Fritz Olimski, *Film Kurier*, 11 September 1922.
[2] *Cinéa-Ciné*, April 1927.

falls ill but is saved by the pure love of a pretty actress, and awakens to life again thanks to her disinterested devotion.

It is possible that this film was never shown as a main feature, and so never attracted the attention of the press. There seems to be no mention of it at all by contemporary critics.

Satanas (1919)

Satanas (1919) is a film in three episodes, each taking place at a different period in a different place; and was clearly influenced by Griffith's *Intolerance.* Perhaps Murnau's film in turn influenced another which was also composed of three episodes – Fritz Lang's *Der Müde Tod* (*Destiny*) (1921), which also has an episode in Venice. Again, the Egyptian episode of *Satanas* may well have influenced Lubitsch's *Das Weib des Pharao* (1921); both films were designed by Ernst Stern.

A more complicated question is the relationship between the modern episode of *Satanas* and the third story in Carl Theodor Dreyer's *Blade af Satans Bog* (*Leaves from Satan's Book*), which was begun in 1918 but not completed until 1921.

The first part of *Satanas* is entitled 'The Tyrant'. Amenhotep, Pharaoh of Egypt, is in love with a young slave harpist, Nouri. He appoints as inspector of his gardens a young man called Jorab, who Nouri pretends is her brother but with whom she is really in love. Jorab, however, can only think of a girl he saw once by a well when he was still only a shepherd.

The hermit of Elu, the only man who has been able to interpret a dream which the Pharaoh has had, refuses all the treasures Amenhotep offers him as a reward, asking only to be allowed to attend one of his courts of justice. When he sees the King pardon an adulteress he is unimpressed by his clemency but says that before dawn Amenhotep will have the chance to show if he is really a wise judge.

Nouri asks the hermit to help her find the woman who as a child had saved her mother from being unnjustly stoned to death. For she promised her mother to devote herself to this benefactress, who will be recognized by means of a brooch bearing the likeness of the goddess Pha. The hermit tells Nouri to ask Pharaoh for the key which he wears round his neck: this will open seven doors, and behind the seventh she will find the woman she is seeking. Then the hermit takes Jorab through the seven doors to the room of Phahi, the Pharaoh's neglected young wife who turns out to be the woman Jorab loves.

Nouri's cries when she finds Phahi and Jorab in each other's arms bring the Pharaoh to the scene, and the adulterers are sentenced to be executed before dawn. Left alone with them, Nouri recognizes Phahi from her brooch as the woman who saved her mother. Then she covers Phahi with the royal cloak the

King has given her, not to save Phahi but so that she herself may die with Jorab. The executioners take her and the young man away, and at dawn Pharaoh finds only Phahi there, half mad with grief. She begs him to tell her her lover's name so that she may die with it on her lips.

The hermit changes into a vast angel of death, Lucifer, who goes through the palace crushing beneath his scorn the mediocrity of mortals.

The second episode is called 'The Prince', and is taken from Victor Hugo's romantic melodrama *Lucrèce Borgia*.

The third episode takes place about 1917. Hans Conrad, the son of very poor German parents, is a law student in Zurich. He becomes friendly with some Russian refugees, in particular one Ivan Grodski. When the Russian Revolution breaks out, Hans, hoping to become the champion of the oppressed, sets off with Grodski for the small town in Germany where he was born. There the revolutionary crowd choose him as their leader and seize the castle.

At first Hans opposes all violence, but Grodski makes him sign orders that become more and more brutal. He seeks consolation with an unknown girl called Irene whom he has met by chance, and who is equally ignorant of his identity.

Gradually he becomes drunk with power. A plot is hatched against him, and Irene, who is the daughter of the former keeper of the castle, takes on the job of killing the despot, as she knows of a secret passage leading to his room. But the plot is betrayed, Hans posts guards at the entrance to the tunnel, and though he is horrified when they catch Irene, he coldly gives the order for her execution. Grodski looks on him with scorn for supposing himself a great man. He becomes gigantic, and Hans, a poor mortal, goes mad and recognizes Grodski as Satan.

Murnau made little change to Robert Wiene's somewhat far-fetched scenario for this film. The principal alteration was the use of Satan to open and close a curtain before and after each episode. Probably this was a reminiscence of the theatre. Murnau used this curtain again for the sequence in *Faust* where Mephisto spies on the scene of the seduction of the Duchess of Parma.

In the revolution sequence Murnau changed some rather conventional images suggested by Wiene and gave more life to the struggle of the barricades.

The original programme for *Satanas* shows that a sort of Goethean 'heavenly prologue' was added, in which Lucifer, the fallen angel, deplores his lost halo. God promises him salvation if he can find a single human being capable of bringing good out of evil. Lucifer goes off through time and space to seek his salvation, but in vain.

There were certain things in the scenario that must have appealed to Murnau's innate feeling for lighting: the dense tobacco smoke and steam from the samovar, for instance, in the little room where the Russian refugees meet.

Satanas: the Egyptian episode

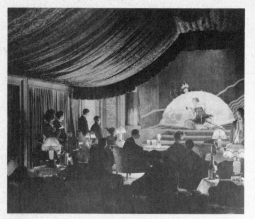

Der Bucklige und die Tänzerin

As one of them talks of the oppressed people in his native country, an out-of-focus image of a poor cottage appears superimposed over his face, with moujiks toiling away like beasts inside. Against another face is shown a hovel with Silesian weavers; then a close-up of Hans's face fades to a view of the shabby room in which his parents live.

If it were not that *Illustrierte Film Kurier* prints extremely banal photographs for other films that we know to be excellent, we might conclude from those it gives for *Satanas* that this was a very undistinguished film.

The pictures illustrating the Egyptian episode have none of the Babylonian splendours of *Intolerance*; and it hardly seems likely that the Venice created by Ernst Stern, Max Reinhardt's favourite designer, could really have been so old-fashioned, theatrical, and cardboardy as the picture of the inn in the second episode might lead us to suppose. 'The director, Murnau, has succeeded perfectly on the visual side; he can create scenes of striking beauty', wrote a contemporary critic,[3] though he objected to the number of titles which he thought tended to counteract the *Stimmung* of the pictures themselves. Murnau only realized gradually that a story had to be told through images alone.

It is significant that the name of Robert Wiene, who had produced many films before *Caligari*, carried more weight at this time than that of the still unknown Murnau. The *Film Kurier* refers to the 'cinematic direction' of Wiene, and just mentions Murnau in passing, after having praised Stern's sumptuous sets and the marvellous photography of Karl Freund. The same critic mentions some incredible näiveties in the first episode, and makes fun both of the poison scenes in the second and the clumsy and childish revolutionary scenes in the third. He also criticizes Murnau for not having chosen suitable actors for certain parts.

Der Bucklige und die Tänzerin (1919–20)

Der Bucklige und die Tänzerin, made in 1919 and shown for the first time in July 1920, has no connection – although Theodore Huff thought it had – with *Sumurun*, a pantomime by Max Reinhardt which Ernst Lubitsch made as a film in 1920.

Wilton, a hunchback who has always suffered because his infirmity makes him repulsive to women, has come back a very rich man from Java, where he discovered a diamond mine. At a fashionable cabaret he meets Gina, a dancer, who has just quarrelled with Smith, her wealthy middle-aged lover. On the rebound, Gina accepts presents from the hunchback, who has learned in Java strange secrets about cosmetics and perfumes. She even seems to take an

---

[3] *Lichtbildbühne*, 31 January 1920.

interest in his adventurous life, and Wilton takes her tears of sympathy for proofs of love. But she is reconciled with Smith and they become engaged, and Gina no longer comes to see Wilton in his strange and sumptuous apartment. When she has used up all the beauty elixirs he has given her and comes and asks him for more, he mixes a subtle poison with the oils and unguents, so that anyone who kisses her will die, while she herself is unknowingly immunized by an antidote.

Smith, the first victim, dies in mysterious convulsions. Gina begins to suspect Wilton when a young baron, Percy, with whom she is passionately in love, begins to show the same symptoms.

She rushes to Wilton's house. He, mad with passion, kisses her, but when he tries to raise the antidote to his lips she snatches it away from him to save Percy. Wilton runs after her, falls down the stairs, stretches out his arm towards her, and embraces only emptiness.

The script shows that Mayer and Murnau were still leaving the titles to take care of the dénouement. The Doctor explains the hunchback's mysterious death with the words:

> Thus the poor wretch mixed an unknown poison into his harmless beauty lotions. You yourself had been immunized against its fatal effects by the antidote you had already drunk.

A contemporary review of the film praises its fine images, but says they are not always related to the action which is sometimes unconvincing, and far surpassed by Robert Neppach's masterly sets.[4] Again the film is described as 'created' by Carl Mayer and 'directed' by F. W. Murnau. Carl Mayer, the scenarist of *Caligari*, is considered more important than the director, just as was Wiene in the case of *Satanas*. The non-trade Berlin dailies also only mentioned Mayer. The *Berliner Börsen Courier* alone was a little more explicit, and said it considered that the story, though quite strong in itself, might have been very interesting indeed if it had been treated in the style of *Caligari*. Murnau's direction, it said, rendered to film that which was film's, 'without making any essential artistic concessions'.

The critic of *Film Kurier* was more appreciative of certain beauties in the film and of Murnau's direction: in Mayer's curious script, often dangerously close to commonplace eroticism, he sees occasional glimpses of mystic depths worthy of Edgar Allan Poe or Gustav Meyrink.

Of Murnau he writes:

> I have never seen a production in which the characters are bathed in such atmosphere; it has a kind of psychic perfume like the scents the hunchback brought from Java.

[4] *Film Kurier*, 3 February 1920.

Sehnsucht

Was this the first film to establish the *Stimmung* of the *Kammerspielfilm* so dear to Mayer and Murnau? The *8 Uhr Abendblatt* speaks of a distinguished psychological study, and the review in *Film Kurier*, itself written in a curiously Expressionist style, makes the film sound very interesting, and illustrates it with a photograph of a lavish set in mysterious chiaroscuro, enhanced by a carefully studied depth of focus.

Der Januskopf (1920)

It is strange that none of the Berlin critics seems to have recognized Stevenson's *Dr Jekyll and Mr Hyde* in *Der Januskopf* (its sub-title, 'On the Borders of Reality', is very characteristic of the tendencies in all Murnau's work). The film tells the grim story of Dr Warren, a rich London doctor, who can change himself whenever he wishes into the dreadful Mr O'Connor.

An article in *Film Kurier* for 27 August 1920 says that Hans Janowitz claims to have adapted the film from an English original: 'That is possible. In that case the English original must contain elements we have already encountered in E. A. Poe and Oscar Wilde, as also in *Der Student von Prag* and to a certain extent in *Trilby*.' This critic, though he seems to know nothing about Stevenson, goes on to talk about the spiritual duality of Faust.

Janowitz's scenario used the same names as in Stevenson, and if Murnau decided to change them it must have been for the same reason as *Dracula* became *Nosferatu*: in a Germany isolated from the rest of the world it wasn't considered necessary to buy the adaptation rights.

While *Kinematograph* praises Conrad Veidt's talent and doesn't even mention Murnau's production, *Film Kurier*, on the other hand, finds it excellent. Its only reservation is that certain high-brow passages might have been shortened; in particular, the critic thinks that the crowd scenes by the obelisk in the nightmare sequence (which, judging by Murnau's annotations of Janowitz's script, must have been very weird)[5] were superfluous and even slowed down the action(!).

Sehnsucht (1920)[6]

Is *Sehnsucht* the same film as *Bajazzo*? Their credits are identical, though the titles are different. The newspapers of the day give no help in the matter. The film was passed by the censors on 18 October 1920; its sub-title was 'Die Leidensgeschichte eines Künstlers' (The Story of the Suffering of an Artist). Gussy Holl remembers that it was about the unhappy love of a Russian dancer, Conrad Veidt, for a grand duchess played by herself. She still remembers with horror the ginger wig Murnau made her wear. 'He had a strange weakness for getting up his heroines in wigs, as he did with Camilla Horn in *Faust* and Janet Gaynor in *Sunrise*.'

Here is the plot of *Sehnsucht*:[7] A young Russian student in Geneva (the publicity calls him an artist, and even sometimes a dancer; perhaps this is what he was studying!) gets himself sent on a mission by the Nihilists so that he can return to his native country at someone else's expense. In Russia he meets and falls in love with a girl. He is arrested, but manages to escape. But he cannot find his beloved, and he searches for her everywhere until at last he learns that she died while he was in prison.

It is just possible that the student might have become a famous dancer, but whatever had the grand duchess to do with all this saga of love and renunciation?

[5] See Chapter 2, pp. 28ff.

[6] Gussy Holl, Veidt's first wife and the widow of Emil Jannings, has told me about a film called *Wahnsinn*, shown in October 1919, which Murnau is supposed to have made before *Sehnsucht*. 'This film was not only called *Madness*, it *was* madness as well, and I can't remember anything about the story,' she said. But the author of the film, Margarete Lindau Schultz, told me that although she had founded a production company with Veidt and Murnau, the film was directed entirely by Conrad Veidt. An advertisement in the *Lichtbildbühne* confirms this.

[7] According to the censor's certificate kindly communicated by Rudolf Leutner-Vienne.

Programme illustrations for *Abend ... Nacht ... Morgen*

Marizza, genannt die Schmuggler-Madonna

Abend . . . Nacht . . . Morgen (1920)

To judge by the programme, the plot of *Abend . . . Nacht . . . Morgen* was horribly banal. We do not know what Murnau's visual gifts may have added to this American-style detective story by Rudolf Schneider, an unknown author from Munich. (Even in *Der Bucklige und die Tänzerin* the characters had American names.)

Maud, a young demi-mondaine, is kept by a millionaire called Chester who overwhelms her with presents. Brilburn, Maud's brother (Conrad Veidt all in black as he was in the role of the blind painter in *Der Gang in die Nacht*, and so still very close to the character of Cesare in *Caligari*), is a ne'er-do-well who gets money from his sister. He makes Maud ask her friend for a beautiful pearl necklace in a jeweller's window, so that he, Brilburn, will be able to get his hands on it. As the necklace is very expensive, Chester says he will think about it. When he eventually goes back to the shop to buy the pearls he meets his friend Prince, who is a gambling addict. They drive to their club, and Chester shows the necklace to his friends.

Prince, who is heavily in debt, breaks into Chester's house during the night to steal the necklace. In order to find out where it is, he deliberately breaks a vase, then hides behind a curtain. Chester, having heard the noise, comes in and opens the safe to make sure the pearls are still there. Prince knocks him down and hangs him from the chandelier. Smoking a cigarette, he types a suicide note, then goes off with the necklace. Next Brilburn breaks into the house to steal the necklace. He sees the man hanging and, horrified, cuts him down and runs away, having first unwittingly dropped his dagger and torn a button off his coat.

Prince hides the necklace in a heap of coal in a yard, throwing a lump of coal away to make room for the jewel-case. Some policemen come and find Brilburn unconscious near the yard, and take him to the police-station as a drunk; he has been knocked unconscious by the lump of coal in fact.

Ward, the great detective, investigates. Chester has been revived, so there is no question of suicide. It is also clear that two people were on the scene of the crime, each independently of the other. A cigarette-end of an expensive type leads Ward to Prince, who gets himself tied up in explanations. The dagger and the button make Brilburn suspect number two. But thanks to the piece of coal that hit Brilburn, Ward finds the place where the necklace is hidden. All he has to do is wait until Prince, who decides to run away, comes to look for the necklace in the coal-yard.

Was this simply a stylistic exercise for Murnau, to get his hand in? Dupont too made *Detektivfilme*, which were then very fashionable. 'This film,' said *Film Kurier*, 'sometimes seems to be an unconscious satire on detective pictures. But in this film of Conrad Veidt's there is suspense and a certain structural logic.' None of the critics mentions Murnau; one of them goes so far as to say it would be best if the director's name were not mentioned.[8] Could Murnau have been so embarrassed at having made a film on such a subject that he asked not to be mentioned?

Marizza, Genannt die Schmuggler-Madonna (1920–1)

In the case of *Marizza, genannt die Schmuggler-Madonna*, the photographs and illustrations in the programme indicate a great care for chiaroscuro and depth of focus.

Marizza toils in old Yelina's scanty potato-field. She is beautiful and all the men desire her, especially Haslinger the gendarme, enemy of the smugglers. Yelina forces Marizza to play up to the customs men, like Carmen, in order to help get contraband through. Marizza is tired of this life, and gets a job on the farm of Mme Avricolos and her two sons, Christo, an impulsive and dynamic young man, and Antonino, a student, dreamy and shy. Mme Avricolos, an aristocrat who has come down in the world, tries to do business with Pietro Scarzella, a rich but unscrupulous merchant who exploits the peasants and finances the smugglers.

Sadja, Pietro's daughter, a gentle delicate girl, loves Christo, and her father wants her to marry him especially since Christo has lost a lot of money through bad harvests. But one night Mme Avricolos cannot sleep and, going into Christo's room to talk about this marriage, finds Marizza, whom she turns out of the house. Christo promises to marry Sadja, and Marizza, thus abandoned by him, flees across the frontier with Antonino, the dreamer, who loves her.

Mme Avricolos gets the smugglers to look for them: Mirko Vasics, their leader, wants to get Marizza back to help them with their affairs again. Grischuk, one of the band, has seen them: they are starving and wretched, Antonino playing the fiddle at inns, and Marizza going round with her baby in her arms, collecting money from the customers.

When Marizza starts to flirt with Haslinger again, to help Mirko, Antonino is crazy with jealousy and threatens the gendarme with his dagger. To save Antonino, Marizza kills Haslinger.

But Antonino accuses himself of the murder. Mirko denounces Pietro as being behind the smuggling, and Pietro is arrested. The soldiers begin to surround and set fire to the smugglers' cottages. Marizza, who has left her child in Yelina's cabin, is told by Sadja that it is on fire. She rushes into the flames to save the child, and at the last minute both are saved from the flames by Christo.

'Thanks to Janowitz's skilful adaptation and Murnau's excellent mise en scène, this complicated story becomes quite a comprehensible film,' wrote a

---

[8] *Film und Presse*, 2 October 1920.

critic in the *Lichtbildbuhne* of 21 January 1922 'which isn't at all boring.' Karl Freund's camera work was admired greatly. It was the first of Murnau's series of peasant films, the prelude to *Der Brennende Acker*, *Die Austreibung*, and *Sunrise*.

Der Brennende Acker (1922)

In *Der Brennende Acker* Rog, an old peasant, dies leaving his farm to his two sons. As in *Marizza* the two young men are very different in character. Peter is active and very attached to the land of his ancestors. But Johannes, a dreamer, doesn't want to be a peasant, and gets a job as secretary on the vast estate of the Count of Rudenberg. Here two young women fall in love with him: Helga, the Count's second wife, and Gerda, the Count's daughter by his first marriage, who is more or less betrothed to Baron von Lellevell. In Johannes' own village a young peasant girl called Maria longs for his return.

The old Count dies, leaving his wife only one piece of land, called 'the Devil's Field': it has its name apparently because one of the Count's forebears excavated beneath it to look for treasure which according to old documents was buried there, only to perish in a mysterious explosion as he descended with a torch.

The old Count had consulted an expert, who told him that the field contained a rich source of oil. Johannes, having overheard this conversation is obsessed with the hope of getting rich and hastily marries Helga, the Count's widow, although he does not love her.

Johannes, whose one thought is the field, neglects his young wife. One night his hopes about the oil are confirmed and he rushes to town to get the necessary money to exploit it. He refuses to take simply the millions that are offered him, insisting as well on being made managing director of the new company he intends to form.

Meanwhile Helga has gone to see Peter and begs to sell him the cursed land that deprives her of her husband's love. Peter, out of politeness, offers her twelve hundred crowns in cash. This seems more than the land is worth, and Helga accepts it and goes off happily to give it to her husband. Johannes is furious: he tells her he has always known the land was worth millions, and that she has spoiled everything by selling it.

Helga, in despair, and realizing that Johannes only married her for interested motives, goes back to Peter to beg him to cancel the deed of sale, then drags herself across the snow-covered fields and throws herself into the river.

Peter, in disgust, tears up the deed of sale and flings the pieces in Johannes' face.

Drilling begins and they find oil. But Johannes, because of his guilt over Helga's death, takes no interest in the work.

Der Brennende Acker

At this point Gerda, who, angry at Johannes' marrying her step-mother, has gone away and married Lellevell, hurries back. She has misunderstood Helga's suicide, and thinks Johannes loves *her*. But Johannes impatiently tells her that he never loved either of them, and that his only motive was ambition.

Gerda in revenge sets fire to the oil-well, which goes up in flames. She dies in the fire. Johannes understands at last that his ambition was vain, and goes back to the village, to the land, to begin a new life with Maria.

German and foreign critics alike pronounced this film perfect. Everyone talked about the poetic charm of the snowy landscapes, and the marvellous lighting that reached its peak in the fire at the oil-well at night, surrounded by snow. Contemporary illustrations enable us to see the harmony of the peasant interiors with their light-coloured walls and dark beams, balanced by the window-frames. We can see the wonderful depth of focus in the low black-and-white tiled room at the farm, which forms a complete contrast with the huge airy room at the castle, light and rich and decorated with delicate mouldings.

Within these atmospheric interiors the characters were arranged with enormous skill according to value and tone, even when they were in movement. They had to convey at one and the same time these 'tonal chords' and 'dramatic chords in space', as Murnau said in one of his articles. But above everything else was the authenticity of all the complex psychological incident – what a French review called a sincerity 'faithful to life and reality'.

A little over two reels of *Der Brennende Acker* – the last part of the film – were found by the Staatliches Filmarchiv of East Berlin. They represent the end of the film and are in rather bad condition and somewhat shortened. Compared to Willy Haas's script they appear to be mere fragments. These sequences are enough to demonstrate Murnau's lighting sense, his love of depth of focus, and even *Stimmung* in a peasant setting. Nevertheless, even with these fragments one feels that the film must have been deeper, subtler, with more nuance of mood and more resonance in the relationships between its characters. Around the heroes of Murnau's great films there hover unspoken emotions, in a kind of musical nostalgia, but these feelings are quite absent here. The lonely, wintry landscape and the famous explosion of the oil fire seem less thrilling and astounding than they must have been in the original.

Haas's script, incidentally, is less laboured than Thea Harbou's script for *Phantom*. It is both sober and poetic.

At the beginning Murnau himself intensifies the atmosphere with a note:

Night. Flurry of snow. Tiled roof. A tile falls in the storm and shatters on the roof. The weather-vane twirls this way and that, jackdaws flying round it. Night. Storm.

Haas uses the storm to give depth to a situation:

The countess Marina enters timidly. The light wavers in the draughts.

Close shot:	a window is blown violently to and fro, breaking a pot with a palm growing in it. The glass becomes covered with frost.

Haas is aiming at *Kammerspiel*, and is always suggesting the characters' psychological reactions:

	Grischka.[9] She sees Bosko approach.
Close shot:	A gleam of happiness lights up her face. Instinctively she takes a step towards him, beginning to stretch out her arms. Then she hesitates, for Bosko hasn't seen her.
Panning shot:	(the camera follows her until he and she are both in the picture)
	She says in a voice that trembles:
	The minister has gone to see someone who is ill.
Close shot:	Bosko has heard her voice, turns his head towards her, sees her, lowers his head (this is the sole indication to suggest: 'Heavens, is she still alive?'), then goes slowly towards her and out of the frame.

For the scene where Bosko sets out for the city to see the financiers about the oil, to his wife's surprise, Haas, who was simpler than Murnau, has:

Bosko: You are surprised to see me up so early. Marie's eyes open wider: he is lying. 'I must catch the train for Warsaw this morning, the lawyer wants to talk to me. About your legacy.'

Murnau, more dramatically, suggests:

A room. Bosko hastily opens a case and starts to throw in his things. Marina appears in the doorway, anxious and not understanding: she runs to him, throws her arms round him, tells him she loves him and asks him where he is going. He answers frenziedly, he is delirious with happiness: 'The field, the field,' and hurries out. Marina, dazed, stands there silent.

Haas has a moving scene where Marina throws herself in the river:

Marina going through the snow. She sees her shadow falling in front of her, and like a sleepwalker lifts her arms and starts to dance, as if she were dancing with her shadow. She spins round faster and faster,[10] staggering as if she were trying to escape from herself. Then she falls exhausted, remains lying there motionless for a moment, then drags herself on.

[9] The script uses the old Polish names, which Murnau later changed.

[10] When I first saw this film in East Berlin something still remained of this scene. The new copy made from the old nitrate, which had deteriorated badly, omits it.

While Haas's sobriety attains a certain lyricism, Murnau seeks more dramatic tensions. This is how he sees the beginning of the explosion at the oil wells:

> Grischka. Foreboding. Anxiety.
> Steeple. Village church. Bells swinging.
> Now no more moon, but a glow as from a distant fire.
> Grischka staggers back from the window.
> Village street. Lighted windows.
> The financiers get into the car. How red the horizon is! But they get in indifferently.

Die Austreibung (1923)

The last of the lost films, *Die Austreibung* (The Expulsion), a 'peasant *Kammerspielfilm*' based on a play by Gerhard Hauptmann's brother Karl, is about the ancient conflict between fidelity to the land that has belonged to one's ancestors and the desire or need to abandon it.

An old man called Steyer lives peacefully with his wife, his son, and his son's daughter Aenne on an isolated farm up in the Riesengebirge, a range of mountains in Silesia. The son, against the wishes of his parents, marries as his second wife a girl called Ludmilla from a village in the valley. She only marries him as a means of escape from poverty; all the village knows that she deceives him with Lauer the hunter, who was too poor to marry her.

One day Steyer meets Lauer outside the house, but Ludmilla tells him that the hunter is courting Aenne. She wants him to sell the farm and buy an inn in the village so that she will be nearer her lover.

The farm means a lot to Steyer, but when Ludmilla says they will be happier in the village and she cannot bear the isolation any longer, he agrees to sell it, in the hope that this will make her more cheerful and affectionate. That evening, to show everyone how happy they are together, he takes her dancing in the village. Steyer starts drinking, signs a deed of sale on the farm, and wants to betroth Aenne to Lauer. Then he suddenly repents of having sold the farm and goes off to get the notary to cancel the sale.

Ludmilla asks Lauer to see her home, but on the way there is a sudden snowstorm and he persuades her to take shelter in his house. Her husband will never be able to find them in this blizzard. But Steyer, looking everywhere for his wife, follows their footsteps in the snow. When he finds the tracks lead to Lauer's house, he hurls himself on the hunter and knocks him down. Ludmilla faints.

Next morning the storm is over. Steyer's old mother and father have packed up their things ready to go. They have no wish to stay on the farm now that it has been sold to a stranger.

The critics were kinder to Murnau's version of Karl Hauptmann's play than they had been to the script of *Phantom*. As in the case of *Der Brennende Acker*, there was much praise for the beautiful natural snowy landscapes, the atmospheric interiors, and Karl Freund's night photography.

The *Kinematograph* of 28 October 1923, however, said Murnau used too many titles and too heavy a pace.

He tries to prepare the *Stimmung*, and enhance it in accordance with the nature of the *Kammerspiel*, by alternating general shots and close-ups, but this often produces the opposite of the desired effect. Nevertheless it goes without saying that this is a film of distinction, in which one senses a love of art, a gift for conjuring up visual atmosphere, and the desire to create a means of artistic expression.

The critic adds that the film will never be a great commercial success.

In spite of the success of *Der Brennende Acker*, Murnau was still unknown to the general public. On 11 September 1922 *Film Kurier* wrote, reasonably enough:

It would be an exaggeration to count Murnau straightaway as one of our great film directors: the general public scarcely knows his name, and we shall have to wait to see if he ever can become a popular idol. But since his very first films he has attracted the attention of specialists, and of that part of the public that looks for quality in the cinema. It was an event when he demonstrated a year ago in *Der Gang in die Nacht* how nature can be brought to life by the subtle and diverse gradations of a *Stimmung*. In *Nosferatu* he showed a remarkable virtuosity in handling the language of the moving image; no one could remain unmoved by the impressions he created. . . . And it was another event when he brought out *Der Brennende Acker*, in which for the first time we saw the Swedes' marvellous sense of psychological intimacy fully recreated in a German film. . . .

At all events, with Murnau we are dealing with a strong personality. He is no opportunist hungry for success at any price, but a contemplative artist, always seeking a way of enriching the German cinema, which has clearly come to an impasse and lost its way.

Murnau is an exception in our film world, even in his personal appearance. You don't often meet a blond Friesian among our directors.

Such are the few traces we have been able to find of all these lost films. We know some of them must have been magnificent. What about the others?

Before making criticisms based on what little evidence survives, we might remember a letter that Murnau wrote to Pommer on 21 January 1925:[11]

People may like or dislike my films. I am always glad of valid criticism that comes from a serious source and that can be discussed objectively. But I have been deeply hurt to be the object not of that sort of criticism but of a judgment which, though it

[11] See p. 40.

Die Austreibung

On location for *Die Austreibung*

sets about it in a devious manner, aims quite obviously at reducing my work to nothing.

Let us hope that one day we shall find some of Murnau's lost films. They may contain some surprises.

Unrealized Projects

It is not widely known that Murnau collaborated with Rochus Gliese on a scenario signed Peter Murgli, the surname being a combination of their own two names. This was *Comödie des Herzens* (1923), based on a novel by Sophie Hochstätter. The author herself could not produce a satisfactory adaptation, so Gliese and Murnau took it on.

As for *Orkan*, a film announced by Decla in 1922, which Murnau intended to base on Wagner's 'Flying Dutchman', Gliese has told me that it was he and not Murnau whom Pommer chose as director. The project was abandoned because it was anticipated by a Danish film on the same subject. (Greta Schroeder, one of Paul Wegener's wives and the heroine of *Nosferatu*, has confirmed to me that Murnau really was going to make *Orkan*, and had even spoken to Wegener about it.)

In June 1927 Murnau wrote from his villa in Grunewald to Winfield Sheehan at Fox Films, asking him to offer Einar Nickelsen, author of *Frozen Justice*, 3,000 dollars for the adaptation rights of his second book, *John Dale*. The story, he said, was 'powerful and dense, and took place against a similar background to the first.'

When Murnau returned to Berlin from America, he was given a ceremonial reception by his colleagues and the publicist Stefan Grossmann, on 13 April 1927. He thought he would be staying in Germany long enough to be able to produce some films himself, and intended the first of these to be *Zwischen Neun und Neun* (*From Nine to Nine*), based on the novel by Leon Perutz. He had to give up the idea, however, because of his contract with Fox.

But it was a project that meant a great deal to him. Herlth says:

Murnau had already set up models of the sets. He wanted places and objects to take part as essential dramatic elements in the action. That is, he wanted to push Expressionism, which had only found graphic form in *Caligari* through its décor, to limits that had never before been reached.

Among Murnau's papers in his brother's possession I have found the synopsis of *From Nine to Nine*, written in English by Francis Marion. The story deals with a man psychologically bound to the movement of a clock. He goes furtively through the crowd, slumps down on a park bench, and watches children eating. A dog jumps up at him and grabs the sandwich he has just bought in mysterious circumstances; he dare not show his hands, and hides them under his coat. He is hungry, but when a pedlar selling cakes comes up he doesn't buy anything. Finally he goes into a café and orders a meal, asking at the same time for some magazines; he hides behind these in order to eat. The owner of the café is afraid he hasn't enough light, and pulls the curtains. The sun bursts in, a policeman approaches, and the man flees without having swallowed a single mouthful.

A siren sounds; it is noon, and the man goes to see a friend, Steffie, who makes wax dolls. He tells her his terrible secret: he is wearing handcuffs, for he is an escaped prisoner. For two days and nights he has hidden, without food or drink. All this is because he is madly in love with Sonja Hartmann. Stanislaus Demba, for that is his name, is a penniless student, and stole some valuable old books because he had promised to take Sonja to Venice and wanted to prevent her going with Weiner, a commercial traveller. When he tried to sell the stolen books, the bookseller called the police.

Steffie, who loves Demba though he doesn't know it, promises to get a key to undo the handcuffs. She takes an impression of the lock with the wax she uses for her dolls, intending to get the key made by a locksmith who is in love with her; she will tell him she has lost the key to her diary.

Demba goes to see Sonja in her factory. She is frightened when he draws her to him, thinking she feels a weapon, and promises not to go to Venice with Weiner but to wait until he, Demba, brings her the tickets. Demba goes back to his room and asks his room-mate to lend him two hundred crowns for the tickets. Oscar has only six crowns, but tells Demba there is a postal order for two hundred waiting for him. Demba knows this, but he dare not sign for the money.

The locksmith, who has accidentally dropped the impression into the fire, gets Steffie's diary from her mother in order to make a new key. Demba goes to a family where he gives lessons and asks for an advance; he drops the money out of his pocket, and a policeman picks it up to give it back to him. But he dare not take it, and tells the policeman it is not his. It is five o'clock, and still he has no money! Steffie offers him her week's pay, and he goes to a gambling-den to make more, while she goes to fetch the key. He gets a friend to play for him, and wins enough for his purpose. But before he can claim his winnings, a man shouts that his watch has been stolen. Everyone must be searched. Demba refuses, and runs away without the money.

It is raining, and night is falling. Women are leaving the factory, and from a distance Demba sees Sonja meeting Weiner. Demba is prevented by his handcuffs from reaching them through the crowd: Sonja and Weiner go off in a cab. Demba runs after them. As in *Phantom*, people turn round and laugh. At last he catches up with the cabman, who is in the rank outside the café Hibernia.

He hears Sonja laughing in one of the private rooms, and throws himself against the door. It opens, Sonja cries, 'He's got a revolver!', and Weiner, afraid, begs Demba not to kill him – it is all Sonja's fault. Sonja, disgusted, insults Weiner and throws the tickets for Venice in his face. She wants to be reconciled with Demba, but he sees her for the first time as she really is. He pulls himself away with a bitter smile, and leaves.

He goes to find Steffie; he now realizes she loves him. They go up to her room. He rests his head in her lap and dreams. They both dream, like the lovers in *Sunrise*, that they are walking hand in hand through a field of flowers. Suddenly they are roused by heavy footsteps and a knock at the door. 'Police!' Steffie at last remembers the key, but cannot unlock the handcuffs.

Demba tells her to go and open the door, and when she goes out he opens the window and jumps into the void. As he falls he seems to see his past life, the clouds part at last to reveal the gates of a mysterious paradise, the light grows suddenly bright. Steffie comes to meet him. But the darkness engulfs him again, and he cries out her name.

Demba lies below, wrapped in the peace of death; the handcuffs have been broken in his fall. Steffie is strangely calm: for a few moments she has been happy. A policeman gives her a piece of paper: the bookseller from whom Demba stole the books has withdrawn the charge and the watch lost in the gambling-den has been found. The police had come to tell Demba that he was free.

An afternoon in spring; Steffie kneels in prayer at Demba's grave. Sonja goes by; she bends down, picks a flower that is growing on the grave, and puts it in Weiner's button-hole.

Such is the main outline of the synopsis. It is not hard to see why the subject, with its curious atmosphere of mingled reality and dream in which objects play a dominant dramatic role, must have appealed to Murnau.[12]

---

[12] It is interesting to learn, from Madame Denise Vernac, Erich von Stroheim's companion, that Stroheim also tried to obtain the rights of *Zwischen Neun und Neun*.

Die Finanzen des Grossherzogs: crew and actors

9. The 'Realist' Murnau

'Actually, from 1924 on, there was a current of realism in Germany which took social observation as its object. *Kammerspiel* and metaphysics were soon swept away. . . .' This is the opinion of Raymond Borde and Freddy Buache,[1] who see *The Last Laugh* as a definitely realist film.

And yet is not *The Last Laugh* the *Kammerspielfilm* par excellence? Are the extremely stylized characters that surround Jannings to be taken as 'keyfaces' in the style of George Grosz?

The antinomy between the *Kammerspiel*, with its psychological interest, and the Expressionist vision, which excludes all psychology, gives a certain hybrid quality to Carl Mayer's scripts. He was at one and the same time an Expressionist writer and a poet of the *Kammerspiel*.

And to this is added another ambiguity: Murnau's own predilection for oscillating between reality and unreality. His alternative title for *Der Januskopf* was 'Am Rande der Wirklichkeit' (On the Margin of Reality). Later he wrote:

I like the kind of reality of things, but not without fantasy; they must dovetail. Is that not so with life, with human reactions and emotions? We have our thoughts and also our deeds: James Joyce demonstrates this very well in his works. He first depicts a

---

[1] Raymond Borde, Freddy Buache, Francis Courtade, Marcel Tariol: *Le cinéma réaliste allemand*, Lausanne, 1959. Documents published by the Swiss Cinémathèque.

character's thoughts and then balances it with action. After all, the mind is the motive behind the deed.[2]

Do we owe the realist element in *The Last Laugh* – the comical fairy tale of the epilogue – to Mayer or to Murnau? Or in fact to Jannings, as he himself claims in his memoirs, *Das Leben und Ich?*

Jannings says that the last three films Murnau made in Germany were linked by a sort of 'internal relationship' and that the external action is therefore limited to a minimum. The inner development of the characters, 'guided by the sure and provident hands of Murnau', was much more important than the plot. But Jannings considered the schematization of the characters in *The Last Laugh* 'exaggerated'; in his view they were reduced to caricature. To lessen this extreme and 'negative' abstraction, and because 'the character of the porter had not been given sufficient relief to become a tragic figure', Jannings says that he asked for a happy ending.

It is clear that Mayer, who in *Tartuffe* used for symbolic purposes a framework that was intended to be 'realistic', was carried further in this direction by 'modern' camera-work. On the other hand, Murnau himself seems to have been responsible for some of the gags in the Luna Park sequences of *Sunrise*; these effects, though based on vague stylized suggestions by Mayer, acquired a more striking authenticity of their own.

Die Finanzen des Grossherzogs

'One was curious to see,' wrote a German journalist when *Die Finanzen des Grossherzogs* came out, 'how Murnau, so committed to gloomy themes, would tackle so agreeable a subject. He changes himself into a story-teller with a feeling for the use of ironical images. Here one discovers a hitherto unknown side of Murnau. . . .'

The Murnau he speaks of is certainly unfamiliar, but is he the Murnau we most admire? Afterwards Murnau hated talking about the film – this 'realist fantasy' that contemporary German critics found graceful and full of tension and gay charm.[3] As in *Nosferatu* the exteriors are real. They were shot in Yugoslavia, at Ragusa, Spallato, Cattaro, and on the island of Arbe. Murnau had chartered a sailing-boat; and a plane, and even a battleship, had been put at his disposal.

It is strange that the director who had discovered such moving natural images for *Nosferatu* should have been satisfied little more than a year later with a few dull snapshots of rocks or a conventional picture-postcard sea. The dreary landscape gives no hint of the dazzling Mediterranean sun. The

[2] *Theater Magazine*, January 1928.
[3] Ernst Jaeger in *Der Neue Film*.

Die Finanzen des Grossherzogs

brilliant mother-of-pearl city of Split, with its ancient ruins which still throb with life, becomes no more than a grey background. The film seems to hurry quite by chance through the splendid temple ruins. Everything appears dim. What has happened to 'the luminous layer of southern sun and adventures bright with local colour, the charm of semi-tropical landscape' for which contemporary critics praised the camera-work of Karl Freund?[4]

This is confirmed by a letter written to me by Eugen Sharin, now in New York, who at the time when Murnau was preparing to shoot *Die Finanzen des Grossherzogs* was a young Yugoslavian student. Murnau took him on as interpreter when he was looking for exteriors. Mr Sharin writes:

The film was full of light and sunshine when I presented it at its première in Zagreb. For the palace Murnau had wanted to use the Grand Hotel on the island of Rab. But modern details like telephone wires made it unsuitable for a fairy-tale, so the palace was rebuilt on the set. Murnau had been very taken with the lacy open belfries he had seen all over Spallato (now Split), and asked his designer, Rochus Gliese, to put one on the roof of the palace! Before the actual shooting Murnau took much pleasure in photographing the boat performing all sorts of manoeuvres at sea. I still remember one lovely long shot of the boat in full sail, which the whole audience applauded at the première at the Ufa Palast am Zoo in Berlin. There was also a shot of a locomotive seeming to head straight for the camera in a swirl of smoke and steam: the silent pictorial effect seemed to visualize the sound perfectly.

It may simply be that our present mutilated copy of the film, taken from a bad dupe, has lost all those shots which showed the play of light, shots which depended, even in black-and-white, on the juxtaposition of a very blue sea and a marvellously clear sky. Perhaps they were eliminated subsequently because they didn't add anything to the childish story about a comic-opera grand duchy: a trumpery revolution – hatched by three malcontents and a shady financier who wants to transform this artificial paradise into a more profitable sulphur-mine – threatens the life of the insipid grand duke, who prefers a life of idleness for himself and his subjects. The film is based on a mediocre and conventionally anti-Semitic novel which contemporary German critics considered subtle, elegant, and full of wit and humour.[5] According to such critics

---

[4] 'The film was made in bright sunshine in Dalmatia,' Gerhard Lamprecht wrote to me. 'And the castle, which was built at Babelsberg, was also shot in brilliant sun, as Rochus Gliese confirms. Only the shots of the car chase were made by deliberate contrast in hazy shadow. It was a film that was only meant to entertain. Murnau could be very gay, you know, and had an excellent sense of humour when he wished. . . .'

[5] Murnau was a close friend of the Ehrenbaums (see page 17), who treated him as their own son, and Robert Plumpe Murnau tells me he always hated racialism. In the same way, when he was working in a neighbouring studio, he used to make fun of the chauvinism of Cserepy, who was making *Fridericus Rex*. In the case of *Die Finanzen des Grossherzogs*, every trace of anti-Semitism has disappeared from the film version of the novel.

Die Finanzen des Grossherzogs

Thea von Harbou had managed to create a skilful and logical story out of what seems to us now a ludicrous ragbag: the Grand Duke, threatened with being hanged from his own throne, is saved at the last moment by the Grand Duchess Olga of Russia, who is in love with him and willing to pay all his debts. A letter from this lady, which apparently has been stolen, and is considered compromising, passes from one to another of the conspirators as in a Mack Sennett farce. The *deus ex machina*, a kind of twentieth-century Eulenspiegel (according to the German critics) is an amiable adventurer of the Arsène Lupin variety, who has little to do with the plot and is played in an affected manner by Alfred Abel. Nor does Murnau know quite what to do with the commercial-traveller charm of Harry Liedtke as the Grand Duke.

Even at the time (at least according to one reviewer), the film, which had been criticized for some over-long explanations at the beginning, must have been heavily cut.[6]

Only one shot now survives which seems really characteristic of Murnau: a street-lamp burning and traced like filigree against a cloudy sky. And some-

[6] For the longueurs see *Film Kurier*, 8 January 1924; and for the cuts, *Kinematograph*, 13 January 1924.

times, occasionally, in a street scene, the skilful orchestration of the traffic anticipates *The Last Laugh* or *Sunrise*; or there may be an exciting play of light and shade over the passengers in a car.

Of the two shots that the critics most praised, one is a distinct precursor of one of the finest images in *Sunrise*: a train with the lamps switched on rushing out of a lighted station. The other is where the Grand Duchess Olga, fleeing from her brother and his agents, pauses, and sees in her mind's eye her desolate hotel room, which spurs her on to resume her flight. The idea would have been more effectively expressed by means of an out-of-focus image such as was used in *Phantom*. But a certain authenticity in the architecture, the discreet sumptuousness of the Babelsberg sets, and deep-focus effects here and there, still allow us a glimpse of the care Murnau bestowed on this minor film.

Perhaps it is simply the congenital inability of German directors to bring off light comedy that makes this film such heavy going. It has none of the winged irony of Stroheim in *The Merry Widow*, nor even the frivolity of Lubitsch in *Trouble in Paradise*. The scene in which Harry Liedtke throws coins in the water for boys to dive after has none of the homosexual sensuality of some of the shots in *Tabu*. Yet this often latent tendency in Murnau is more noticeable in *Die Finanzen des Grossherzogs* than in any other of his films. The only girl – the Grand Duchess Olga, played by pretty Mady Christians – is treated with indifference, except in the sequences where she is disguised as an old frump to escape detection by her brother. The critics of the day were on the wrong track when they praised her talent for burlesque.

In an interview in *Film Kurier* in 1922 Murnau had spoken with enthusiasm of only two kinds of film: the supernatural and the *Kammerspielfilm*. Very clearly he could not feel at home in comedy, and his usual discretion vanished when faced with an imbroglio from which his audience expected broad farce. There can be no other explanation of the low level of all the acting in *Die Finanzen des Grossherzogs*.

In 1919 a critic of *Satanas* had said Murnau had not managed to get appropriate performances out of his actors.[7] Yet in 1921 a visitor to the studio where he was shooting *Schloss Vogelöd* was struck with an exactly opposite impression.

In an interview published in *Film Kurier* in 1922, Murnau said:

> The film is nearly always finished before one has had time to get the actors to forget the bad habit of 'giving a performance'. If only our actors could learn to act like the Swedes. German actors don't get any artistic satisfaction out of their work nowadays. They are too business-like, and in too much of a hurry to go from one film to the next.

[7] *Film Kurier*, January 1920.

One is always encountering Murnau's preoccupation with restraint and understatement rather than overstatement. Ramon Novarro, who never actually worked with Murnau, says that Murnau taught him that an actor ought to stop 'acting' sometimes, in those sequences where the drama reaches its height, because the audience has already reached the required degree of tension. Murnau told him of the trouble he had had with Jannings in *The Last Laugh*, when he returns to his room after his deception has been exposed. Murnau wanted him to do nothing but just flop into his chair; Jannings wanted to burst into tears. Murnau said that would be terrible: 'You're too exhausted to cry.' Jannings insisted, and Murnau let him do it both ways.

Then, when they had seen the rushes in the projection room, Jannings got up and put his arms round Murnau, who, naturally, had been right.

'Murnau knew how acting ought to be,' says Frank Hansen.

He could analyse feelings as well as show how they should be conveyed. The actors and actresses in his films had a profound inner life, and he could get the best out of them, even those who were mannered or over-stylized. He created characters who came to life and were not mere stereotypes.

Why then was the acting so stiff and false in *Die Finanzen des Grossherzogs*? The history of Murnau's style, like that of his life, contains many riddles.

10. The Last German Films

There remain the three last films which Murnau made in Germany, films whose variety of style and mood is often puzzling. They are briefly dealt with here in a single chapter since I have already treated them extensively in *The Haunted Screen*: my aim is only to offer a reminder or, for those who have not read the earlier book, a resumé.

The Last Laugh

The original German title, *Der Letzte Mann* – like the French title *Le Dernier des Hommes* – is perhaps more complex and adequate than the title in this country, *The Last Laugh*. This seems a little to anticipate the comic happy ending that has been thrust arbitrarily on to the film, rather as a comic afterpiece used to be appended to the performance of a tragedy.

The petty tragedy – the story of a hotel porter, proud of his livery and of the respect of the courtyard in which he lives and where the neighbours treat him like a general, who feels utterly degraded when, becoming too old and weak for his job, he has to change his 'uniform' for the white jacket of the lavatory attendant – could only be a German story. For it could only happen in a country where the uniform (as it was at the time the film was made) was more than God.

Lupu Pick was to have directed the film, but he fell out with his favourite writer Carl Mayer. Pick would most likely have deepened this petit-bourgeois tragedy by means of weighty symbolism, as he had done in his film *Sylvester*.

Murnau's films had always possessed a *Kammerspiel-Stimmung* at once more vibrant and more diffused than Pick's, a kind of anxiety floating around the characters, as in *Phantom*; as if the ground below their hesitant feet was never quite sure, as if Destiny might tear away from them every last feeling of security.

Lupu Pick's *enfesselte Kamera* – which Pick himself had only used for the symbolic *Umwelt* at its most expressively abstract – gave Murnau, on the contrary, the possibility of finding visual counterparts to the most intimate reactions of the soul, as well as great variety in the angles and perspectives. While in *Sylvester* the rhythm of the *Umwelt* dominates ordinary everyday events, dwarfing them, the world as it is seen by the porter is within his grasp and in proportion to him: those people who devoutly salute his uniform, the shrews who revile the degraded man by their monstrous laughter, the insensitive manager, the phantom merrymakers who order taxis and dine copiously. They exist only around him, anonymous and abstract, giving relief to his tragedy, seen through his eyes, the camera from time to time indeed ceasing to explore his actions, and becoming subjective.

By means of camera angles, the man in his glory, splendid and bemedalled, seems always bigger than the people he meets on his way to the hotel, and among the guests at the wedding he seems in higher relief, bigger in volume, while the others dissolve in the background. After he has been stripped of his uniform, he becomes a poor wretched thing with bandy legs, crumpled trousers, a worn-out jacket. Murnau shows him, with his livery gone, bewildered, looking up at the hotel in a curiously diagonal position, splayed like an Expressionist actor across the screen, in front of the same wall which he used to pass each morning, in the splendour of his pride.

In such a way the images become expressions of the reactions of souls. Images taken from a low angle emphasize his chest and his pompous importance, in the manner of Soviet films. Pictures taken from high up make the poor wretch in the washroom seem more and more seedy.

Apart from this, as seen in Chapter 3, pages 62–67, the film is characterized by daring angles, trolley shots, and dolly shots. When Freund, seated on a bicycle, comes down in a lift, and rides out as far as the revolving doors of the hotel lobby, in order to record the dazzling impressions of light in motion and the motion of lights, it makes a vigorous opening to the film in which the bustle and transformation of events and appearances becomes quite palpable.

The buttons on the forfeited uniform glitter seductively as it hangs in the cupboard. The circle of light from the nightwatchman's lamp glides along the walls to reveal finally the poor wretch who is taking back the stolen livery, since his neighbour has discovered his petty crime.

The Last Laugh

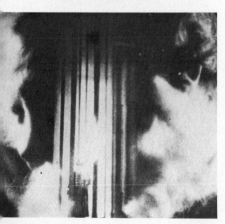

The Last Laugh

Light and movement, puddles of water in which the light from lanterns bathes, a shiny wet street, windows which light up in the dark façade like the white squares on a chess board. A black and oily raincoat, wetted by the rain, on which the light from an electric bulb is reflected; the rain running down the window of a motor car. And everywhere glass surfaces which glitter, opalescent mirrors. All this is what Carl Mayer summed up, for *Sylvester*, in a single expression, 'in Licht und Glanz', which means, more or less, 'luminous and resplendent'. Visually and dramatically Murnau goes much further, breaking out of the strict framework of the bourgeois *Kammerspiel.*

Then the dream of desire when the porter is drunk, with its ironic, fantastic, essentially *Expressionist* characteristics. Multiple, vague spectres which try vainly to lift an enormous trunk. A phantom lift glides through the storeys of an unreal building. The porter's head is split by the banging of the revolving door, with which is mingled the banging of the door of the washroom. And when he wakes, the porter sees his neighbour carrying a coffee pot, in double image, and the face of another woman on the landing, distorted like an anamorphosis.

It is perhaps in contrast with such passages that one feels most strongly the platitude of the banal happy ending, the modern commercial fairy tale, where Murnau becomes as gross as his German audiences. This is the authentic tasteless glossiness of the Ufa style. It is, of course, all brilliantly done: the bustle of the waiters carrying their plates, the travelling shot across the succulent dishes, the beautiful *mondaine* who swallows her oysters, and all the gluttonous figures busily stuffing themselves: all are caught in their pseudo-elegance and in absurd detail. But how we regret the silent and more appropriate ending, of the poor weary old man gently wrapped in the coat of his friend, the nightwatchman.

Tartuffe

Light and movement equally play a role in *Tartuffe*, as when the bigot hurries down the stairs for his nocturnal rendezvous with Elmire, and we see only a ray of light on the ground before the door shuts like a trap. Light again when Dorine, the buxom serving-girl, leans over the banisters, then descends with her flickering candle before entering the lighted room of Orgon, in order to bring him to Elmire's door.

Movement here too — but the movements of the camera are more attenuated, more subtle, more musical than in *The Last Laugh*. The camera is less in search of depth, but rather moves *across* the screen.

It is the apogee of surfaces and tones. There is an echo of Watteau sometimes, when the camera explores the pearly neck and shoulders of Lil Dagover. When she bends forward, a voluptuous decolleté seems to be offering itself. We seem to hear the rustle of a silken dress as we see its reflecting surface.

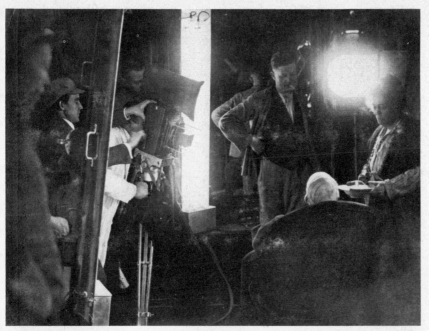

Tartuffe: prologue, lighting and sketch

Then in the presence of the plump and jolly Dorine, an atmosphere of Chardin seems intermingled. A cast-iron balustrade throws a lace of shadow upon the wall when footmen walk up the stairway, carrying lighted candelabra. Or by the tea-table, Elmire lowers a curtain, and the shadow of the window-frame shows softly through the thin material.

The flounces of a crinoline glide like a Mozart melody down the curves of the grand staircase, which is alive with the movement of intrigues. Doors open and shut in the choreography of comedy, hiding, discovering people, dominating the turns of the drama.

Stern, threatening in its rigidity, the black silhouette of Tartuffe cuts across all these delicate tones. At first the action seems to have a certain Prussian ponderousness, of the genre of *Minna von Barnhelm*; but little by little we discover characteristics which are very different from this, even if it never achieves quite the lightness of a Molière comedy.

In *A Film Artist: A Tribute to Carl Mayer* (Memorial Programme, London 1947), Karl Freund writes that Mayer

was extremely sensitive to the broad range of camera styles. He exploited contrasting camera styles in *Tartuffe* – by demanding a cruelly realistic and un-made-up style for the modern sequences, and an unreal, diffuse, Watteau-esque style for the *Tartuffe* sequences.

We know that the images of *Tartuffe* had been presented as if through a gauze, delicately; and we know, since we have been able to read the original scenario, that this effect was more due to Murnau than to Carl Mayer. In contrast to these diffused reflections and shadings, the framing action, the *Rahmenhandlung* which Mayer described in his script only as *zeitlos*, seems to us heavy, jaded, and bourgeois. However, this prologue and epilogue, treated realistically, with faces without make-up in the Soviet manner, and with bold camerawork which shows up every wrinkle, every decayed tooth, every vulgar and nasty trait, brought something quite new to the tradition of German cinema, and looked forward to the social films of the future.

It is not simply these daring images and un-made-up faces which make us accept the ludicrous and clumsy story of the greedy housekeeper who seeks possession of the inheritance of an old dotard whom she slowly poisons. Nor the nephew with the sleek and effete face (recalling Murnau's homosexual tendencies), who is only too easily forgettable.

'It was in the modern sequence of *Tartuffe* that sets, for the first time were lifted from the floor and ramped for the sake of the camera,' Freund further tells us. Thus in this film we have already those tricked perspectives achieved by raising the ground level, which would give Murnau's camera its full verve in *Sunrise*.

Faust: Camilla Horn; Murnau on the set

Faust

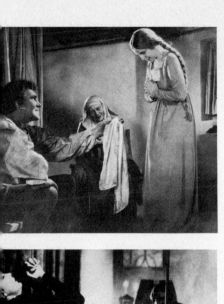

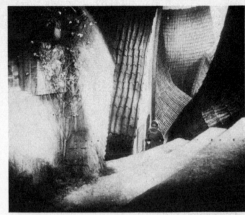

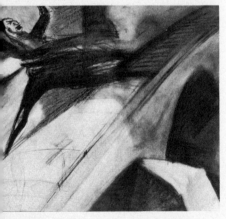

Faust: the last picture is a sketch by Röhrig

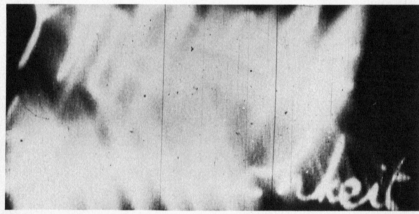

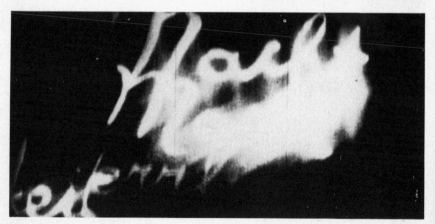

Faust's pact with the devil

Faust

Light and movement: all Murnau's experiments and discoveries in these two previous films came to full fruition in *Faust*.

The beginning and the end are fugues of light, orchestrated with incomparable mastery. The clash between the explosive brightness of the archangel and the darkness which surrounds the devil, in this 'heavenly prologue' is a piercing vision, apogee of the art of the silent film. The gentle sunlight which seems to colour the sky at the end becomes the counterpoint which brings promise of redemption.

The visual magic marks everything. Smoky atmospheres wrap around the little medieval town like a great devil cloak, bringing noxious exhalations of plague. Faust rises up on the screen, powerful, looming out of the mists; the light is diffused when his now immense face leans forward in big close-up. Or Faust throws his useless books on to the fire which seems to fill the whole room. Suddenly the pages of the book of witchcraft blaze with an infernal flame. Finally, delivered into darkness, Faust tries vainly to break through the wall of light which blazes out of the door of the cathedral which he can no longer enter.

Light and movement: the huddled town itself, with its complex stairs and alleys, provokes movement: men in cloaks carry coffins, the crowd crushes on the steps to bring their sick to Faust. Children come to the church like equivocal Botticelli angels, carrying lilies in their innocent hands.

The journey through the skies on the cloak of Mephisto whirls through gliding landscapes, the mists making the models seem entirely authentic. Gretchen's cry of anguish, represented in a series of superimpositions, comes to us across the mountains and valleys, achieving a sort of three-dimensional effect. This plastic quality, this *volume* gives the film its power: the costumes, still more the heads and the bodies of people sometimes acquire this same three-dimensional effect through their modelling.

In all these Rembrandtesque tonalities there are few Expressionist elements, apart from some expressively steep roofs and gables, which the designers Herlth and Röhrig invented. And when Mephisto becomes a devil once again, and cries out for murder, he spreads himself diagonally across the screen like the complete Expressionist actor.

Arno Richter has provided this note on some of the special effects in *Faust*:

When we were making *Faust* (on which I worked as Robert Herlth's assistant), all those not immediately concerned in the work were refused admission to the studio. This even applied to the great Erich Pommer, then one of the great pundits of Ufa. Murnau wouldn't even let him come to the daily rushes. So from that point of view everything was peaceful in the studio, but the ardour we put into our work involved us in many arguments and discussions.

Sometimes too the studio would be full of stifling smoke: old film was being burnt in the doorway in order to create a denser atmosphere, and without the slightest concern about fire!

Properties were of enormous importance to Murnau. I can see him now, sitting in Faust's laboratory, tearing pages out of the magic book that Faust was supposed to throw on the fire. The pages had to appear to be turned as if by an invisible hand or some diabolic breath, and they weren't turning fast enough.

We also had to keep renewing the sheets of parchment for Faust's pact with the devil, which had to be written in letters of fire. Just before each take the parchment had the letters printed on it with a sort of stamp which applied threads of asbestos and a liquid which ignited spontaneously and immediately. This shot was taken over and over again for a whole day: the sheets of parchment kept catching light too soon or burning too fast. They were heaped up in hundreds outside the studio. But Murnau persevered until at last he got the pact with the devil successfully filmed.

The Last Laugh: the original theme for the porter's uniform, written for the author by Giuseppe Becce

11. Sunrise – the American Début

'I accepted the offer from Hollywood because I think one can always learn and because America gives me new opportunities to develop my artistic aims. My film *Sunrise* shows what I mean.' Murnau wrote this explanation for a sort of German portrait-gallery, *Artists of the cinema by themselves*, in 1928.

The success of *The Last Laugh* awakened interest in America, and in July 1926 Murnau went to the United States. William Fox went round everywhere introducing him as the 'German genius'.

According to *Motion Picture Magazine* for August 1926 Hollywood simply raved about *The Last Laugh*. They searched their souls for adjectives to express their amazed admiration. It was the almost universal decision of Hollywood that this was the greatest picture ever made. Yet it was not a successful picture.

In its frenzy of praise, Hollywood overlooked one vital fact: movie fans are not much interested in plots about old men. D. W. Griffith once expressed this in a more picturesque way: 'You often see people stop on the street to pet a dog: but it's always a pup!'

In November 1926 *Motion Picture Magazine* wrote:

F. W. Murnau, famous German director, has just arrived in Hollywood with a great fanfare of trumpets. The film colony is wining him and dining him and making an all-around hullabaloo in general.

The funny part of all that is, that the same F. W. Murnau was in Hollywood no less than two years ago. And he had under his arm the now famous picture *The Last*

Laugh. But there was no brass band to meet him at the train, and there were no dinners given in his honor.

But now the eyes of all Hollywood and all America were on Murnau. He was monarch of all he surveyed, and it was as absolute dictator, with more than ample money at his disposal, that he began the preparatory work for *Sunrise*. William Fox expected him to produce a film that was, in the words of Arnold Höllriegel, 'infinitely cultured, symbolic, in short completely European'.

The plot of *Sunrise* comes from one of Hermann Sudermann's *Lithuanian Stories*, 'The Journey to Tilsit'. Ansass, a young peasant, is bewitched by a sexually appealing servant, and neglects his young wife Indre, 'lovely and pale as a madonna'. His father-in-law makes him dismiss the servant, but every night the young man goes to meet her under the willows by the river, on the edge of the marshes. The couple decide to get rid of the wife by drowning her. Ansass pretends to be reconciled with her and takes her on a journey to Tilsit. They go there by boat, and the girl is nervous all the way, suspecting that he wants to kill her. In the story, which differs here from the film, he doesn't make any attempt to threaten her on the outward journey. Once in Tilsit he sees how everyone else reacts to the charm and beauty of his wife and realizes how desirable she is. They are reconciled. Both naïvely admire the city, go on the roundabout like a couple of children, and set off home again by moonlight, happy and in love. But they are tired and fall asleep, and the river has dangerous currents. In the morning the villagers, anxious at their failure to return, go to look for them. They find the girl floating in the river, tied to a bunch of reeds which, on the servant-girl's advice, the man took with him to save himself when he deliberately capsized the boat, which in the original plan he was supposed to do. But the reverse has happened: the wife is still alive, the husband having drowned in the process of saving her. A posthumous child will be born of their night on the river.

Mayer and Murnau transformed the story. They transposed it to the shores of a lake, and the servant-girl became a city vamp. There is a real attempt at murder on the voyage to town, which gives Mayer and Murnau the opportunity to reveal very subtly the relationship between the young couple, and the slow renewal of their happiness. And there is a happy ending, with the husband and wife both surviving, and the vamp going off again to the city.

We ought not to be surprised that in the poll organized in Brussels in 1958 for the 'twelve best films' of all time, *The Last Laugh* appears in the list and not *Sunrise*. *Sunrise* is much less well-known.

And yet it is Murnau's most powerful and advanced film, far surpassing *The Last Laugh*. The study of Carl Mayer's script only reinforces the

Sunrise

Sunrise

impression made by the film itself. All the skill Murnau had developed in Germany in the years from 1919 to 1926 are here made manifest in the most dazzling manner: his marvellous sense of camera, lighting, and tone-values, his mastery of the composition and rhythmic ordering of images. And his gift for creating atmosphere as well as revealing the complexities of character.

Never again until *Tabu*, his last masterpiece, did Murnau enjoy as much liberty in making a film.

Whereas in the other scenarios Murnau had adopted Mayer's style and singular manner of expression, for *Sunrise* he emancipated himself. The script contains much more specific descriptions of shots than Mayer's, and notes for lighting. And it is written in sober, prosaic German quite different even from that which Murnau used for his annotations of Kyser's *Faust*. It would take too long to make a page-by-page analysis of what Mayer contributed and what Murnau. I shall merely point out in the appropriate places how the play of light and shade and the depth of focus were the result of Murnau's direction.

In *Sunrise* light and movement are once more supreme. It is full of moving lights and flashing movements. When the young peasant huddles anxiously on the back of a tram, the jolting of the vehicle is expressed by bright flashes reflected through the glass on to his face and neck. There is nothing of this in Mayer's script.

At night, streaks of light bob about on the windows of a long, low peasant room, waking 'the woman from the city'; they shine, disappear, glide from one window to another, trace a fleeting pattern on a wall, or cast a sudden vivid shadow of the window-frame. The woman runs to the window to look at the growing crowd of milling lanterns; her strained face is now lit up and now in shadow.

Mayer merely notes that while the vamp is asleep a light, as if from lanterns outside, suddenly appears in the room and multiplies. But Murnau was able to vary and intensify what Mayer only suggests.

Crouched like a wildcat in a tree looking down on a sunken lane, the woman watches the coming and going of the lanterns. The wind stirs the leaves and throws a tracery of shadows on her face. There is no mention of these velvety shadows in Mayer.

There are also slower and more intense examples of the play of light. When the couple, reconciled, are sailing home, a gentle, silky moonlight shines down on the wind-rippled surface of the lake. On a raft somewhere someone has lit a bonfire; dark silhouettes can be seen dancing in front of it, and behind them luminous clouds of smoke. The pictures recall a scene from Goya.

Then comes the storm. The moon is hidden behind the clouds, the wind blows the ship's light to and fro, with an effect which recalls the deserted cabin of the ghost ship in *Nosferatu*, where Murnau showed the play of reflections from the lamp but not the lamp itself.

Darkness and light clash with each other on the lake, as boats comb the night looking for the woman in the water, casting shining beams on the black waves. In his notes here, as in *Tabu*, Murnau detailed exactly how all the boats should move for each shot.

Suddenly, in close-up, the velvet-black waves become grey and all the tonal values change; a boat's light shows us a patch of murky water. A few rushes drift by like bones, half submerged, then we see a bunch of them, disintegrating, showing apparently that all hope of the victim's survival must be abandoned; we have already seen the young woman float by unconscious, like the poor drowned girl in Bertolt Brecht's beautiful poem, her pale face almost submerged. Mayer mentions only the light from the boat; it is Murnau who added the extraordinary plastic values.

There is a skilful balance of black and white in the church scene,[1] where a beam of dust-laden light falls from the high window to the right, an effect which is repeated in the peasant room as well as in many other German films. Mayer gives a 'dämmerlichternder Altar', an altar half-twilit, half-shining, and leaves it to Murnau to translate this to the screen.

Everywhere there are vast stretches of glass shimmering with soft warm gleams, falling away in shadow, sometimes out of focus. A travel poster is followed by a glassed-in railway station through which can be seen the fronts of buildings and the traffic coming and going in the square.[2] In Mayer's scenario there is no travel poster; he just mentions 'tall windows' through which we see the square of a big town, with a mist rising from the road – an effect which Murnau saves for later on when the couple arrive on the tram.

In the film people go by in the street beyond the windows of a café. Inside, the light dimmed by a double glass partition, there is a sort of hothouse twilight, in which the unhappy couple are crouched over their table. Mayer describes the interior of the café thus:

> rear shot:
> Against tall windows:
> Tables.
> Customers.
> Smoke.

[1] Murnau composed and orchestrated all the tonalities: the girls in white dresses, the men in black suits; in the same way, the contrast between the woman in the white frock and the man with dark thoughts, darkly dressed.

[2] For this quite short sequence Gliese made a model for the camera about 20 yards high, overlooking the square. In front of this 'tower' he suspended two model train rails in such a way that, between them, the camera could photograph two platforms with passengers. The platforms, which were life-size, were built 12 yards above the square. The entrance to Luna Park was also a giant model suspended in front of a tall 'tower' that served as a platform for the camera.

The smoke is his method of condensing an atmosphere. He also mentions a glass-covered rack with cakes on it. But the passers-by in the background are Murnau's invention.

In the scene in the huge hair-dressing salon – a scene not in Mayer's script – there are bright stretches of shining glass, and the atmosphere is nearer to realism. It was no accident that Murnau placed Janet Gaynor near a metal globe used for heating towels: it casts a subtle light over her pale face. The palette of graduated tones is extended still farther when she looks at herself in an opalescent mirror.

There are more glass surfaces in the photographer's studio, where a reversed image of the couple is reflected in the plate of the camera. But the most complex of all these effects comes in the scene in a big restaurant in Luna Park, where shining, transparent glass surfaces reveal couples dancing beyond them, illuminated by a thousand lights (see page 87). Murnau was fond of moving backgrounds. Beyond the young peasant trying his skill shying balls at the fair, we see a South Sea island girl doing a belly-dance. Then the camera suddenly shifts to show the huge glass wall of the dance-hall.

People have made too much of 'depth of focus' in the work of Gregg Toland with Orson Welles. Like Stroheim in *Foolish Wives*, Murnau juggles with such effects; the light seems to weave long spaces. When the depths become blurred or imprecise it is intentional and not because of technical inability. Charles Rosher, chief cameraman for *Sunrise*, told me:

I worked with a wide-focus lens of 35 to 55 mm for the scenes in the big café. All the sets had floors that sloped slightly upwards as they receded, and the ceilings had artificial perspectives: the bulbs hanging from them were bigger in the foreground than in the background. We even had dwarfs, men and women, on the terrace. Of course all this produced an amazing sense of depth.[3]

Murnau never tired of varied and multiple backgrounds. When the lovers are sitting in the restaurant with the couples beyond them dancing on the other side of the glass, they toast their happiness with wine. Then suddenly, though they do not turn round, the background starts to spin over their heads like an enormous disc. Then shining mists billow up behind them and grow opaque. The dancers have turned into shapes that fly on invisible trapezes, their silhouettes darting through space, already prefiguring *The Four Devils*. The lovers, drunk with happiness, feel as light and weightless as the airy acrobats.

[3] In the same way, as Gliese informs me in a letter, in the scene of the switchback, the compartments in the foreground were life-size and occupied by adults, while those in the middle-ground were smaller, with children as passengers; in the very background were model compartments occupied by dolls.

Murnau limited himself to an incompletely defined maelstrom of out-of-focus shots. Mayer had suggested in his script:

By a trick-shot the violins in the orchestra seem to have grown blissfully vague:
Shot of the couple: They are sitting down. Close, in front of the camera.
         Their eyes blissfully half-closed.
         While the whole background grows blissfully
         gently blurred.
         And then!
         Are these ladders from heaven descending over it?
         Yes!
         And angels glide down them.
         With violins, and more violins.
         Hovering over the garden.
         Circling round over the couple
         Gently playing their violins.
         As behind them a meadow
         Seems to be superimposed on the background.
         With flowers nodding in a blissful breeze.
         Happy seconds thus.
         And more.

Murnau avoided the picture-postcard bands of angels and replaced them with dark, indistinct figures.

Sometimes the art-historian in Murnau chose to arrange the objects in a shot like a painter composing a still-life.

In the foreground, for example, he has a huge hanging lamp cut in half by the frame of the picture. An old peasant and his wife sit at the table eating their soup. In the far background a door opens and the 'woman from the city' appears, quite tiny, coming to have her shoes polished. The remarkable depth of field is increased by the size of the lamp in the foreground. There is nothing of this in Mayer; it was Murnau who noted:

close-up, with lantern in the foreground.

A similar composition is used for the light from the boat illuminating the passing reeds. In this case Mayer suggested only one shot, a close-up of the reeds scattered on the surface of the water. Murnau divided the sequence into seven different shots.

At another point in the film Murnau has Charles Rosher photograph the crowd in Luna Park with a giant statue in the foreground; this shot recalls many Soviet films. In the corner of another shot a tall fountain plays so as to set off the rearground activity.

There is no doubt that the use of huge figures in the foreground is due to

Sketch by Gliese

Murnau and not to Mayer. One note by Murnau in the script of *Sunrise* says that for a shot of Coronado Beach there must be a diving-board with someone on it in the foreground. This accounts for the Hollywood bathing beauty who forms a sort of gigantic figurehead to the beach scenes.

Another example of a deep focus effect is where the husband wakes out of his nightmares to see the door open in the background, and there, beyond it, in the bright rectangle of morning, his wife scattering corn to the chickens. Mayer here suggests only a panning shot.

A kaleidoscope begins to spin round: it is the entrance to Luna Park, in the stylized over-elaborate design of the later twenties, when interiors still retained traces of *art nouveau*. We might see many faults of taste here, as in the garden scene in *Metropolis*, if Murnau had not bathed all the buildings in ripples of light, and compensated for the conventionality of the forms with constant movement on every side.

Inside the park itself gondolas and trains fly through the air, are poised on giddy slopes or fantastic bridges. The eye is intoxicated with turning, whirling shapes. A thousand electric lights blaze against the darkness. A rocket slowly explodes into bunches of silver grapes.

A dust wind blows up, the forerunner of a storm: grey clouds appear, dark shapes scurry, hats are blown off. Then the rain comes down in torrents, driving everyone before it.

Charles Rosher tells how Murnau organized this storm in advance in every detail. But someone must have pressed a button too soon, for the rain machine started up before everything else and the whole set was flooded. 'That doesn't matter,' said Sol Wurtzel, of Fox, 'we can do without the sequence where the dust heralds the storm.' But Murnau, whom William Fox had given *carte blanche* to spend all that he needed to make a spectacular,[4] was implacable: he must have a dust storm first!

'But we've got three thousand extras waiting,' cried Wurtzel.

'Let them go home and come back in three days, when the sets and stands are dry,' answered Murnau. And he wouldn't budge. It cost Fox an enormous amount of money. Three days later the wind machine started on cue, and they calmly shot the clouds of dust Murnau had to have before his rain sequence.

The blocks of houses are not at all like the smooth, streamlined architecture of Ufa films like *Asphalt*. A luminous floating dust can be seen through the windows when the tram arrives in town. All the façades are bathed in light, which takes away the artificial look of staff or papier mâché.

A square emerges, growing larger, and the vague outlines of distant houses weave an intricate background. Sometimes double exposures, out-of-focus shots, superimpositions, or an 'unchained camera' taking panning or dolly shots, gave to the artificial city built in the waste land of Foxhills, just outside the studios, the air of some dream land, swallowing up the peasant couple in a jungle of cars and crowds. But Murnau knew how to organize this chaos: cars sweep right by the little woman, almost touching her. Her husband joins her. They reappear out of the mêlée, and other cars surge up behind them just as close as before.

In the same way, when they are on the pavement, people walk about, behind and in front of them – not like extras, but like real passers-by in the middle of real traffic.

An innate love of nature led Murnau to choose some beautiful angle shots of Lake Arrowhead taken near the shore. Of course the village itself, which looks completely German, was built from scratch. In certain shots the steep and narrow gables erected by Gliese still retain some traces of Expressionist inspiration.

[4] On 7 September 1926, William Fox wrote to Murnau that Sheehan and Sol Wurtzel were enthusiastic about the progress with the shooting of *Sunrise*. He was glad to see that Murnau was equally enthusiastic, and thought the film would be his masterpiece. The other side of the coin is shown by a letter in which Gliese says that the production company was not always too pleased when he and Murnau had expensive sets and models built for very short passages. 'Our producer,' he goes on, 'took the precaution of staying with the company in New York for nine months, to undo the damage we did by overspending our budget. Otherwise we wouldn't have been able to finish the film.'

The village and the city

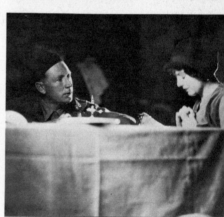

On the set of *Sunrise*

The vamp

But this village, although it was built more or less as if it had been in the studio, had its own life in the midst of surrounding nature. Thus Rosher, at Murnau's request, had to get up and go out in a boat for a week at four or five in the morning to try to film the rising sun coming out of the clouds and lighting up the roofs, the gables, and the steeple: all this was for the sake of the film's symbolic end. But the attempt failed, or was only made successful by means of a piece of trick-photography done in the studio with the sil-houette of the village placed in front of a transparency.

Studio and nature complemented and harmonized with each other. Mists wreathed a landscape which had been built on the set. An artificial moon rose over the real marshes; the camera, expressively mobile, revealed pools of water, and squelchy soil with deep footmarks and thick clumps of rushes growing out of it at the bottom of the picture.

After the wreck of the boat, filmed on a reservoir on the lot, the fog rose over the real lake, and the light of the moon looked as if it had been superimposed. Where does reality begin? [5]

[5] Gliese says the marsh was filmed in the studio. These vivid sequences, which are in the script, were shot with a camera on a rail fixed to the ceiling and which could be adjusted in

The transition made by a panning shot from the real forest to the artificial city is amazing. It was an inspired piece of trick photography to which the skills of both Murnau and Gliese contributed. Höllriegel, the Austrian journalist, was there:

> Within this short distance Gliese had recreated every kind of landscape, from fields and meadows, through an industrial area and the sparse gardens of the suburbs to the city itself. All this provided the landscape through which the couple travelled in the tram to the city, followed by the camera. The designer rode on the tram and, with the help of the view-finder, decided on the pictures and angles to use. Only what was strictly necessary was constructed, and the sets never went beyond what the camera itself required.

Everything was built in terms of the camera lens, using artificial perspective and *trompe-l'œil*, even for the goods in the shop-windows. Yet as the tram moves through the constructed landscape, the artificial becomes one with the real lake and its limpid shores: we seem to see only a single shot and a single landscape.

Murnau repeats the symbol of

> the song of man and woman that can make itself heard anywhere, in every age, in every place, wherever the sun rises or sets, in the bustle of the town or under a country sky, there where life is ever the same, sometimes bitter, sometimes sweet, full of laughter and tears, sins and forgiveness.[6]

Thus in the peasant room a warm light falls from the window, casting the shadow of the frame on the victim on the bed – in the symbolic form of a cross – an image not indicated in Mayer's scenario.

The silent film could not make use of interior monologue which (in the manner of O'Neill's *Strange Interlude*) is so useful in sound film, and there could be no such thing as the actual voice of temptation. Psychological depths were sometimes suggested by means of superimposed images. Thus the temptations of the city appear superimposed over the picture of the lovers as they lie near the edge of the marsh. The first panning shots here, which interpret suggestions in Mayer's script, and are themselves a reminiscence of all the supernatural visions in Murnau's former films, remind us of the fluidity of the dream scene in the hotel hall in *The Last Laugh*.

Another example is the blurred vision of the plotted murder, in which in slow motion the vague figure of a man throws a shape out of the boat. Murnau

---

height. Two artificial moons had to be used. An astonishingly authentic atmosphere was produced by means of a big painted blow-up and moveable transparencies.

[6] A typical passage of Carl Mayer, from his preface. His 'anonymous' designation of the characters – 'the man', 'the woman', 'the woman from the city' – in the titles are the last traces of the Expressionism of the *Kammerspielfilm*. Murnau gives them the names they have in Sudermann's story.

uses blurred images and slow motion to indicate thought which has not yet become action.[7]

In the morning the man wants to escape from the spell that binds him. But the temptress appears superimposed first on one side, then on the other, whispering in his ear, kissing him (this sequence is in Mayer's script). Then she appears in enormous profile at the top right of the image, dominating the weak and undecided lover; while suddenly, to the left, appear two gigantic images of her bewitching eyes. This touch was added by Murnau.

Murnau has often been criticized for an inability to suggest physical love between a man and a woman. *Variety*, in fact, was given to Dupont to direct, as being too 'sexy' for Murnau. But the eroticism of the marsh scenes in *Sunrise* is undeniable. The music of the superimposed jazz band corresponds to the rhythm of the girl's body as it twists, turns faster and faster, and yields, in an almost Expressionist manner, in the man's embrace.[8]

Nothing could be more subtly erotic than the high-heeled shoe that gets stuck in the marshy soil, and the perfect curve of leg when Margaret Livingstone, the vamp (a wonderful artist who sometimes recalls Louise Brooks), bends down to pick the rushes. And was it really just a concession to Hollywood tradition to show her at the beginning of the film in a black lace slip? Mayer and Murnau have her smoking a cigarette in her room, with the cloud of smoke enveloping her voluptuously.

Although this is a silent film, sound becomes perceptible everywhere through the power of the images and the eloquence and precision of the acting.

The husband, sole survivor of the shipwreck, kneels by the bed of his lost wife and buries his face in the covers. He is overwhelmed with sorrow – a typical attitude for one of Carl Mayer's heroes. We can feel the weight of an oppressive silence. Then suddenly the silence is pierced by the temptress, whistling. But now it recalls the cause of his wife's death, and enrages him. He wants to strangle the temptress. He appears, menacingly, in the doorway, and the vamp takes flight, with the man in pursuit. But now comes the open mouth of the maid shouting, 'She's alive! She's alive!', and the cries seem to fly through the air to him. He rushes to the house. This translation of cries into a visual effect is also used when the man calls the woman's name first on the rocks and then in the boat.

[7] This interior vision of the drowning was shot in speeded-up motion in the studio. Gliese writes that the boat was suspended from a crane invisible to the camera and hanging from the rafters of the studio; two acrobats doubled for the actors, and the woman fell into a net out of camera range.

[8] See Dorothy B. Jones's excellent essay, written from a point of view both psychoanalytical and filmic, in *The Quarterly of Film, Radio and Television*, Spring 1955, University of California Press.

We also see a reverse angle shot of bells pealing wildly, or a close-up of the enormous hand of Gibson Gowland, the hero of Stroheim's *Greed*, pressing on a klaxon as a dream meadow appears round the couple while they embrace at a road intersection crowded with cars.

The conventional beginning of the film, with the arrival of the ferry carrying summer visitors, is rather disappointing, as are various superimposed images representing the temptations of the city, which have the smooth and soapy appearance of those Ufa films which Murnau had always despised.

Rochus Gliese mentions a rather significant incident in connection with these scenes. A huge tree had been cut down in the forest, floated down, and re-erected by means of a crane on the landing-stage. In the process it had lost all its leaves, so thousands of artificial ones had to be brought via the only road that led to Lake Arrowhead, which was often completely blocked to other traffic by the lorries from the studio. Three hundred Mexicans were employed to put the new leaves on the tree, but when they had finished and the extras were all on the ship and shooting was about to begin, Murnau realized that the second lot of foliage had all withered in the heat of the sun. So the Mexican workmen had to be brought back, the scaffolding put up again, the withered leaves picked off one by one, and replaced with others that resisted the sun better. By the time this had been done and the scaffolding finally taken down again, the operation had taken nearly a fortnight! Meanwhile the extras strolled about, all expenses paid.

All this trouble for scenes that now one hardly notices!

There are also some rather laborious gags, though one involving a cheeky man in the hairdressing salon and another with a woman with epaulettes are details worthy of Chaplin. But the actual scene at the hairdresser's, and the comic sequences at the photographer's, and above all the chase after the pig in Luna Park, seem very ill-assorted with the tragic developments of the plot.[9] These comic episodes are not in Carl Mayer's script. Did Murnau invent them?

Carl Mayer did not write the scene in the hairdresser's, but he did write a rather superfluous scene where the husband is buying his wife a lace mantilla that they have previously seen in a shop window: the assistant pays the wife compliments as she tries it on and looks at herself in the glass. Mayer also wrote the scene at the photographer's, though there is nothing comic in it: the

---

[9] Another laboured and superfluous scene, which occurs in Mayer's script, has the old fisherman telling how he saved the girl. After the fine flashback pictures of the rescue, the maid embraces him and his shrewish wife objects. This is not in Mayer's script. The peasants' dance makes one think with regret of the dance of the lovers in *Tabu*, before the inhabitants of the 'civilized' island: the *Sunrise* scene is clearly used only as a pretext for the excellent gag about the epaulettes.

photographer doesn't want to accept payment, saying that the girl's beauty is sufficient reward. All these sequences are used by Mayer merely to show the young peasant realizing the attractions of the wife he had been about to sacrifice for another woman, less beautiful: these scenes are more or less the counterpart of the passage in Sudermann's story where people sitting at tables near the couple talk about the young peasant girl's 'madonna-like' beauty.

One might have supposed that it was the Fox gag-men who had invented all these comedy scenes, if Murnau hadn't crossed out some rather stylized and abstract suggestions by Mayer for the crowd and the roundabout in Luna Park, and put in the margin a suggestion for the peasants' dance. He also added that it should come 'after Ansass has caught the pig', which is the only evidence that the pig episode was added in the United States during the shooting of the film.

A letter from William Fox to Murnau on 27 December 1927 on the subject of *The Four Devils*, which was to be the next film, may throw some light on this point. He says:

I look forward to receiving your complete scenario.
I hope it will contain pathos, thrills, well-timed and well-calculated comedy situations intermingled with the other emotions which I am certain every large picture requires.

Was Murnau obliged to 'intermingle' the Luna Park gags in *Sunrise*?

At the opposite pole from comedy was the true and profound *Kammerspiel*, as only Mayer and Murnau could create it. Under Murnau's direction Janet Gaynor and George O'Brien were truly transformed into German peasants.

Murnau made O'Brien act 'with his back', as Dupont made Jannings in *Variety*. He walks heavily, his shoulders hunched up, leaning forward as he goes towards the house dragging the dog behind him.

The girl waiting for him in the boat half rises, irresolute and anxious, as if to run away. Then she stops worrying and sits down again, smiling at her fears.

In the middle of the lake O'Brien stops rowing and goes towards her. His back, which looks immense and threatening, is towards the camera. He advances on the girl at the tiller like some bestial Caliban. In Mayer's script he just draws himself up and gives her a terrible look, but does not move. On the other hand, his slow walk, his dull-witted manner and slow reflexes look as if they were inspired by a passage by Carl Mayer. Rosher says Murnau had twenty pounds of lead put in O'Brien's shoes to make him shamble along like a gorilla.

Janet Gaynor is transformed into a sort of German Gretchen. Was it the memory of Camilla Horn in *Faust* which made Murnau give her a blonde wig which often looks like a rather peculiar cap? Perhaps it was rather to distinguish her from the vamp, Margaret Livingstone, whose hair was done in a fashionable flapper's fringe. Louise Brooks tells me that at that time both actresses in fact had curly red hair.

There is a touching image of Janet Gaynor after she has been saved and is lying in bed with her blonde hair, for the first time untidy and tangled, damply framing her sad face. She looks almost like Lillian Gish in *Way Down East*.

This film, in which each image speaks and each face reflects its innermost thoughts, had no need for sub-titles. If Murnau put them in it was simply for the sake of the American audience. Wherever possible he links them to the pictures, to the superimposed images of the city, to the surface of the water, where the letters seem to sink one by one into the depths of the lake.[10]

In January 1928, in an article in *Theater Magazine* which reads like an interview, Murnau said:

> I hope to be able to make the next picture without any titles whatever. *The Last Laugh* had only one. One way of eliminating titles is by showing two antagonistic thoughts as parallels; for example by wishing to convey the wealth of a certain person as being extreme, I would show alongside of him a greatly impoverished character. Symbolism would obviate titles.[11]

Looked at from this point of view, some passages in *Sunrise* where Murnau makes use of Mayer's extreme symbolism become more comprehensible, and the unrealistic ending seems more effective.

Since the original French edition of this book appeared, Kevin Brownlow has published an interview with Charles Rosher in *The Parade's Gone By*;[12] and I am very grateful to him for permission to quote those sections which refer to Rosher's collaboration with Murnau:

> After Doug and Mary got married, I was with them in Europe and Doug went with me to the Ufa studios in Berlin. I did special tests of their stars to demonstrate glamour lighting. They always lit them with heavy, dramatic lighting and deep shadows. Erich Pommer was there then, and he put me under contract for a year, with Mary's consent. I acted as consultant on F. W. Murnau's *Faust*. I didn't do anything on the picture, but Murnau expected to go to America, and he kept asking, 'How would they do this in Hollywood?'

[10] Rosher filmed the sub-titles in reverse, using a special process by which the gelatine had to stay wet all night without hardening. It was this which made the letters look fluid, as if merging into the water itself.

[11] As was done in *The Last Laugh*, with the rich customer and the wretched cloakroom attendant.

[12] Kevin Brownlow: *The Parade's Gone By*. Alfred K. Knopf, New York, and Secker and Warburg, London, 1968.

Carl Hoffman photographed *Faust* and I learned a great deal from him. I took several ideas back, including the dolly suspended from railway tracks in the ceiling, which I adapted for *Sunrise*, Murnau's first American picture.

That was a very difficult film, *Sunrise*. We had many problems. My assistant was excellent, and very helpful — Stewart Thompson, later cameraman for Bing Crosby. For some scenes, such as the swamp sequence, the camera went in a complete circle. This created enormous lighting problems. We built a railway line in the roof, suspended a little platform from it, which could be raised or lowered by motors. My friend and associate, Karl Struss, operated the camera on this scene. It was a big undertaking; practically every shot was on the move. The German designers built an enormous set on the Fox lot, with false-perspective buildings. Real streetcars were brought in, and streetcar rails laid.

For the forest scene, a mile-long track was built out at Lake Arrowhead; the end of the track came right in to the city. All of it was specially built, including the streetcar, which was mounted on an automobile chassis. On those big scenes, such as the fairground and the café, I think I used more lights than had ever been used before. . . .

I found it difficult to get Murnau to look through the camera. 'I'll tell you if I like it in the projection room,' he used to say. I would have continued to work with Murnau on *Four Devils*, but I had to go back to Mary Pickford. I very much wanted to continue with Murnau; I was with him a few hours before he died in a car accident. We were very close friends.

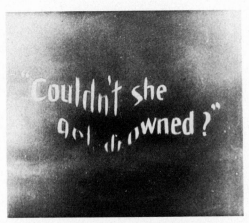

'Couldn't she get drowned?'

12. Compromise in Hollywood?

On Tuesday, 29 November 1927, at the Carthay Circle Theater, there took place the gala of 'Mr. F. W. Murnau's astounding directorial triumph', *Sunrise*. According to the sumptuous invitation card the film was to have a 'masterly' presentation, with an overture and score composed by Mr Carli Elinor and played by his famous orchestra. There was also to be a 'colossal atmospheric prologue, conceived and staged by Mr Jack Laughlin'. Mr William Farnum was the grand master of ceremonies, and the invitation had only been sent to a 'very select group' for 'the greatest of all film social events'. The less fortunate had to pay five dollars, war-tax included.

Sunrise had already been shown to some leading critics. Robert Sherwood said in *Life*:

Although my admiration for Ernst Lubitsch is great – some would say 'excessive' – the title of the World's Greatest Director, according to my personal rating, is no longer held by him. It is applied to F. W. Murnau. *Sunrise*, to my mind, is the most important picture in the history of the movies.

The *New York American* said

For years after most of the cinema successes of today are forgotten, *Sunrise* will be re-issued wherever movies are shown.

And yet after this triumph Murnau had to resign himself to making his next film under completely different conditions. Was it because the small-town audiences hadn't shared the critics' enthusiasm?

The Four Devils (1928)

On 22 December 1927 Murnau wrote to William Fox that he intended to start *The Four Devils* on 3 January 1928. He said he was delighted with Hermann Bang's story, because it was about young, beautiful, wholesome people, which enabled him to introduce and train a group of new talents who hadn't yet had their heads turned by stardom.[1] He would be able to make the film for a reasonable sum because he wouldn't need 'exorbitant' sets as in *Sunrise*. Moreover, because of the uncertainty of the Californian weather, all the shooting would be done in the studio. On 27 December William Fox replied:

I felt sure that you would make the film at a reasonable cost. The selection of your cast is of such a character that, as you say, I am sure they are unspoiled and you will be able to mould them, to make them children of your brain and manikins in your hand to do with them as you please and as you will.[2]

According to *Motion Picture Magazine*, when Murnau got back from a visit to Germany, he accompanied Ringling, Barnum and Bailey's circus on a tour through Virginia in order to study his subject.

The negative of *The Four Devils* still survives in the Fox archives, but in the absence of a print I have been obliged to rely on pre-war memories of seeing the film in Germany. However, thanks to George Pratt of George Eastman House, I have been able to examine a script translated into English and not annotated by Murnau, which still bears traces of Mayer's complicated and poetic phraseology. This is now preserved in the George Eastman House archives, in Rochester.

As in Hermann Bang's novel there is a prelude in which Cecchi, the manager of a travelling circus, ill-treats first two, then four children. This prelude contains few lighting effects, but one of them is unforgettable. Cecchi, completely drunk in his caravan, makes the kind old clown play cards with him. He wakens the children and frightens them, out of pure malice; and a struggle to the death begins between him and the clown. The script here merely mentions a lighted lamp. But, in the film, for a long time Murnau shows only the giant shadows on the wall above the four terrified children.[3]

---

[1] The 'new and unspoiled talents' that Murnau already had in mind were Janet Gaynor, Charles Morton, Barry Norton (who was later in *The Mother and the Boy* and *What Price Glory?*), and his discovery Dorothy Kitchen, who was later replaced by Nancy Drexel.

[2] See p. 183 for Fox's feelings about 'thrills' and comedy scenes.

[3] Frank Hansen says Murnau expanded the original story of the script through his imagination. It was his way of continually involving you in the action, and it had to be done in the twinkling of an eye. This was how he got the idea of the sequence of the huge shadows struggling above the frightened children. When he looked at the rushes he probably realized that the shadows alone gave the idea of menace, so departed from the indications in the script.

The clown wins and goes off with the children to begin a new life. When we meet them again it is in Paris, in winter, and they have become famous acrobats. Carl Mayer had assembled all the elements Murnau needed for the fluid mobility of his lighting:

Evening. A large city covered with snow
through which come –
dazzling, moving, crossing, whirling electric
light signs – which we see on shadowy façades
and roofs
half finished words, names of hotels
Places of amusement
Through which appears the motif:
'THE FOUR...........'
'GREAT SENSATION........'
'LEAP...OF...DEATH...CIRCUS'
'......DOME!!!'
   A large billboard advertisement
      Depicting four people swinging on four
      trapezes. This is rather dim at first but
      is suddenly brighter as the powerful lamps
      of passing motor cars play across it.
out of all these
elements shapes it-
self
      The brilliantly lit façade of a large circus.
      And we see, in large burning letters, the
      dominating legend:
'THE FOUR DEVILS!'
'GREATEST SENSATION!'
'THE LEAP OF DEATH IN'
'THE DOME OF THE CIRCUS!!!'

Then all dissolves, giving place to a close-up of the head of a galloping horse, its mane streaming in the wind. And, as if through the horse's eyes, we see many other horses galloping. It is still through the horse's eyes (the camera was attached to its head) that we see the milling audience, with its thousand faces, floating in misty darkness. And up above four glittering trapezes wait. . . .

Music. The players look towards the conductor, their faces faintly illuminated. The audience has vanished in a semi-darkness which comes down like a light mist. When the Four Devils come on, each standing astride two white horses, Mayer takes care not to show us their act right away. At first all we see is the reaction of the audience. The faces of the audience show delight.

The Four Devils

Their bodies sway rhythmically, as if in time to something to which their eyes are all raised. The ease and freedom of the acrobats' performance is conveyed through the behaviour of the spectators. Other members of the circus gather backstage and approach the curtains, to watch. All this affords Murnau an excellent opportunity to render light and movement in terms of each other before actually presenting the Four Devils: for by now we have noticed that Fritz, hanging head down from his trapeze, is flying over the box of *la belle dame sans merci.*

The brilliantly-lit performance fades to the rehearsal in the cold light of the next morning. We see a general shot of the Four Devils flying on their trapeze, arms outstretched, twisting and turning in the air (they are doubled here by an actual circus act called The Four Codonas). The curious lighting gives the impression of four bodies flying unsupported through the air: neither the wires nor the trapezes are visible.

Then we see the ring, indistinctly at first through the vamp's binoculars. The roof of the tent seems to come close, the glasses follow the bodies, come to rest on Fritz and are adjusted. The image suddenly becomes clear, big, and bright. When the leap of death is announced we see again through the binoculars. The spectator seems to come even closer to the roof, and we rapidly see every detail: Louise and Adolphe high up, then Aimée standing in front of the trapeze that she will launch at the given moment towards her partner.

This time Fritz keeps the rose that the beautiful lady in the box throws to him in the ring. The first time he gave it, to the lady's annoyance, to Aimée. Mayer is not the man to miss a good symbol: Aimée, taking Fritz's hand to bow to the audience, pricks herself on a thorn.

The second encounter with the lady, when Fritz goes to see his injured horse in the stables during the interval, is fateful. Fritz's place at the acrobats' usual table in the little Parisian restaurant remains empty.

A voluptuous chiaroscuro in the lady's salon: beside the fire a tall lamp casts a subdued light. The walls are lost in darkness, the damask curtains are only lit up when the log on the hearth flares up for a second. A servant places the five-branched silver candlestick on a long low table, and lights the candles. The lady appears in a magic circle of light, while Fritz remains indistinct in the shadows. This seduction scene is intercut with a sequence in which the three other acrobats and the clown sit waiting for Fritz in the restaurant.

Then comes a scene that must have pleased the director of *Der Knabe in Blau*: the lady shows Fritz the portraits of her ancestors, and talks about the courage of one of them. The image becomes blurred and rippled until it is no more than a cloud from which emerges the story of a nineteenth-century officer. The tale of the hero's glory ends in the lovers' embrace.[4]

In the girls' room, Louise sleeps while Aimée, tired and disappointed, waits at the window. On a wall, the strange, elongated, enormous shadow of the five-branched candlestick. The shot is distorted. The candles are almost burned out. Fade to a similarly distorted and elongated image of the figures and hands of a clock. They are spectrally suspended in space, and the hands point to half-past two.

Then we see Aimée again, still at the window: at last she sees Fritz get out of a car and enter the house.

To convey that the liaison continues, Mayer has a series of roses falling one after the other into the ring, each accompanied by a passionate note from the lady. Adolphe tries to interfere, but Fritz gets angry and speaks sharply to him and to the old clown.

Fritz wakes one morning after a night of debauchery. This day he will fail his star trick – though at the last rehearsal, and the net is still fortunately there – and will realize that he must free himself from the temptress's toils. In a rapid series of superimposed flashbacks of varying form and brilliance, he remembers what has happened. First come violent embraces, kisses, and a sensual laugh, probably to be conveyed by a shot of the vamp's mouth. The couple drink avidly, and we see foaming glasses of champagne. Fritz smokes cigarette after cigarette until the whole screen is filled with smoke. The images succeed each other more and more rapidly and in ever greater confusion. Then through these fluid visions we see a large clear shot of Fritz's face: he believes he has the strength to overcome all these temptations.

There is another mental vision when Aimée, once again waiting for Fritz at the acrobats' modest hotel, makes a hole in the frost on the window and looks through it, at the wintry garden. The snow is falling slowly on the naked branches. Then everything blurs and the garden is transformed: it is spring, and Aimée sees herself walking there with Fritz, who is in love with her, under the same kind of flowering fruit-trees that Stroheim loved. Petals fall on the couple. Then everything changes: again the snow is falling thickly on the bare branches.

Aimée goes to see the vamp and implores her, in vain, to leave the young man alone – he does not belong to the same world as she does.

Fritz, wounded by the lady's sarcasm, blames her for having weakened him. He goes off in anger, thinking, as he assures Aimée, he has finally broken with the temptress. But Aimée unwittingly throws him back into the vamp's arms. She tells him to go to his dressing-room, where he will find a present.

---

[4] There are two different versions of this sequence in the script. In one, sequence 56, a girl takes refuge with her lover to avoid a forced marriage with another man, and the young officer risks death for her. In the other, sequence 57, the young officer, as in the tale of Gösta Berling, drives a sledge through the snow with a beautiful woman at his side. They are pursued by wolves, and he jumps from the sledge with drawn sword to save his lovely companion.

But when he goes there the first thing he sees is a bouquet of roses and a letter from the vamp. He ignores Aimée's humble gift. The vamp has won him back again.

As always, Mayer intersperses his images with symbols. Fritz, trying to forget the temptress, is drinking alone in a café. Some pieces of sugar fall on the table, he plays with them idly, and they form the word 'net'. Or he gets a little drunk, throws away an empty bottle, breaks a mirror, and again there is superimposed a net. But the image fades, the vamp's face appears close to his, smiling and triumphant, and in her arms he forgets everything.

Then comes the day of the gala performance, when Fritz has to do his turn without the net.

Mayer's plan for all this was as follows: Aimée, from her trapeze, sees the vamp enter her box. It seems to her as if the whole circus fills with mist. The ring seems to buckle, the sea of human faces to undulate and dissolve into patches of black and white. All that remains visible is the vamp's white neck with its string of pearls, and her white shoulders rising out of her furs. A new mist rises, through which appears the lady's face smiling upwards seductively: her teeth gleam as she puts a rose to her lips and kisses it.

Aimée forgets to send the trapeze to Fritz; Adolphe does so. Fritz catches it, but swings dangerously. Close-up of a spectator's face, distorted by fear, with other faces, out of focus, in the background. A pause, and the vamp seems to understand the danger; then she throws the rose into the ring.

Fritz lets go of the trapeze and flies towards the camera, his body twisting. Aimée's face is tense, her eyes desperate. She grips the trapeze as if she does not want to let it go, then closes her eyes as if to accept death and launches herself and the trapeze into the void. Fritz's hands seize not the trapeze but Aimée's body. They fly through the air, together, and Aimée sees below her the thousand upturned faces and, in superimposed close-up, the face of the vamp, her eyes fixed on the trapeze. With a tragic smile, Aimée deliberately lets go of the bar.

The camera falls with the two bodies, the roof grows small and distant, then we fade to the ring, with the bodies of Fritz and Aimée lying together broken beside the rose on the sand. A general shot of the horrified audience, and above it, in superimposed close-up, an empty trapeze.

This original script follows Hermann Bang in its tragic conclusion. But a happy ending was almost obligatory in the States, so the film had to finish on an optimistic note. The other couple, Louise and Adolphe, go off respectably on their honeymoon, hoisting the old clown on to the train with them at the last moment.

This looks rather like another example of that liking for popular farce,

The Four Devils: Mary Duncan and Charles Morton

The Four Devils: sketch by Herlth

which earlier made Mayer add the epilogue of the newly-rich porter to the properly tragic ending of *The Last Laugh*.

But this happy epilogue wasn't enough for William Fox, who wanted the hero and heroine to have a happy ending too. In a new, sound version (in which Aimée became Marion, Fritz Charles, and Adolphe Peter, and where the anonymous vamp significantly became 'la belle Hélène' – Helen) Aimée throws herself alone into the ring when she sees her triumphant rival. She is only slightly hurt, and Fritz throws himself at her feet to ask forgiveness.[5] Even this seems a more acceptable ending than the comic honeymoon for three.

Murnau must have given way to the demands of Hollywood. What is more, knowing that *Sunrise* had not recouped its cost, he took the American

[5] The text of the dialogue has been added to the English script. The sound version was shown in September 1929. It was largely only the last two reels that were affected. The dialogue begins with the quarrel between the two lovers after Aimée goes to see the vamp, and ends with the new happy ending, where Marion/Aimée says to the repentant Charles/Fritz: 'Don't cry, don't cry, darling! I love you, I love you.' Murnau must have liked this as little as he liked the modified version of *Our Daily Bread*, though in both cases the dialogue was limited at his suggestion to the climax of the story.

public's reactions into account for this, his next film.[6] He even agreed to sign
a questionnaire that the usherettes distributed to the audience at the première
of *The Four Devils* (see page 287).[7]

William Fox and Murnau must have gone through the fundamentally banal
answers conscientiously in preparation for the next production, *Our Daily
Bread*. Certain commercial aspects of this film are due essentially to the
results of the questionnaire. Contemporary critics in the international press
said that *The Four Devils* was already a long way away from the artistic
splendour of *Sunrise*, and that in spite of some very fine images due to
Murnau's mastery of visual effects, it was more popular, more suited to the
general public, and so assured of greater commercial success.

The cameraman on *The Four Devils* was Ernest Palmer, but I learnt
recently that Paul Ivano, then a young man, had also worked on the film,
though without credit. Ivano has given me some interesting details about the
shooting.

At first he found Murnau haughty and arrogant in manner, telling Ivano
(who even at that time had worked for Ford and some other major directors)
that it was an honour for him to be working with the great Murnau. After
introducing him, Herman Bing left by walking backwards, as if from royalty.
But relations improved when Murnau found that Ivano could produce what
Murnau wanted. For instance, he asked for the net to be seen over the ring
floor 'like a shadow, but with all its network meshes', an effect which recalls
the lacy network round the lovers' heads in the church in *Sunrise*. Murnau
was delighted with the result Ivano achieved with a newly developed arc-light
switch.

Similarly, when Aimée was to fall from her trapeze Murnau wanted to
repeat the effect of *From Nine to Nine*, in which as she falls she sees a
succession of images, possibly – as in that early script – images not only of

<hr />

[6] Murnau himself went to the Times Theatre in New York in January 1928 to observe the
audience reaction to *Sunrise*. It was not an easy public to please: according to *Motion Picture
Magazine*, the manager of a cinema in Albany, New York, had to take off Murnau's *Faust*
(which he had put on because of Jannings, the star) because it was too highbrow and the theatre
had been empty for three days. He had much better audiences when he substituted *Ankles
Preferred*.

[7] Let us take at random one of the twenty answers that Murnau kept. They were all written
on the back of copies of the questionnaire. This particular spectator congratulates Murnau in
the name of all the audience for having given them the chance to imagine the final scenes of the
'very human' film. 'And thank you for the realistic ending.' The writer also considers the
character of the circus manager very realistic, and thinks highly of the scene in which the boy
is made to ride the horse. But, forgetting about Hermann Bang, he objects to the title of the film
as misleading. He didn't understand certain psychological scenes between Miss Gaynor and
Charles in which the behaviour of the actors struck him as strange. Finally: 'It is a real
pleasure to congratulate you on having made such a splendid film.'

Our Daily Bread

the audience but of her whole life. For these shots Ivano built rails from high on the set and curving down to the ground, and on them in a triangular carriage he placed the camera, the movement of which was mechanically controlled.

Our Daily Bread (1929)

In *Our Daily Bread* Murnau again showed his preference for actors who were not too well established as stars. In the 1928 article in *Theater Magazine* he wrote:

I find it preferable to work with actors and actresses who have just enough experience to keep them from being great, but not enough to keep them from being pliable. Everything is subordinated to my picture, and just as I do not permit myself to be influenced away from what I think is the right thing to do and the right person to use, I will not do a picture that is based on a theme not to my liking or conviction.

Did he regret not having been firmer over *The Four Devils*? One has the feeling that difficulties are already looming ahead.

As early as 28 December 1927 Murnau had written to William Fox, following their correspondence about *The Four Devils*:

This summer I should like to make a picture, *Our Daily Bread*, a tale about wheat, about the sacredness of bread, about the estrangement of the modern city dwellers and their ignorance about Nature's sources of sustenance, a story adhering to the stage play *The Mud Turtle*.

Murnau also talks about a series of superimpositions to show a sort of 'Story of Wheat', from the field to the finished loaf, with all the intermediate stages. He also wanted to shoot in authentic Chicago locations, showing workers living and working in dark rooms surrounded by other buildings, where even the restaurants are underground. He wanted to make people realize how such surroundings oppress the inhabitants: they need not even be slums, just apartments where neither light nor air can penetrate because they are so closed in.

With that minute attention to authenticity which often makes people call him a 'realist', Murnau studied the production of bread, so that his series of images might be a sort of documentary that would complement the plot. Although as a Westphalian he was already familiar with wide open spaces, he now made a careful special study of the life of the farmers of Oregon.

He was glad of the opportunity of contrasting the oppressiveness of the city with the peace and quiet of the plains.

But *Our Daily Bread*, like so many great silent films, was mutilated and lost much of its vigour in the transition to talking pictures. William Fox, who had had 'every confidence in this German genius' for *Sunrise*, a very expensive film that enjoyed a poor box-office, realized that it was his interference in *The Four Devils* that had made it more commercial.

So there was reason for anxiety. This time Murnau didn't talk about making an inexpensive film, as he had in the case of *The Four Devils*. Delighted at being out in the open air again, he spent money like water, even going so far as to buy a farm in Oregon in order to be able to haul cameras on sledges through the oceans of ripe wheat.[8] He could be as mad as Stroheim. Fox wasn't at all easy in his mind. Although they had been able to take the script out of the hands of the weird Carl Mayer – who hadn't met the deadline – and so had escaped all his tortuous 'Central European' poetry and psychological digression, they were still stuck with a German author – Berthold Viertel. According to Huff, Fox, after seeing a working copy, objected that 'the film was too long and the peasants were not at all American', a criticism that would have been equally true of *Sunrise*.

Once more comic scenes had to be put in, and the gag-men were set to work. It didn't take them long to remove all trace of the great symphony of our daily bread, the Dürer wood-engraving Murnau had dreamed of.

Murnau terminated his five-year contract with Fox[9] and escaped to the South Seas; William Fox shortened the film and gave Murnau's former assistant, A. F. Erikson, an honest man of no imagination, the job of remaking some scenes and adding others. When the talkies came, dialogue was added, but the synchronization left much to be desired. The film was issued under the title *City Girl*.

Nothing throws a clearer light on Murnau's intentions than the 'suggestions for modifications of *Our Daily Bread*' which he sent to William Fox in a last attempt to save his film.

Suggestions of Changes for 'Our Daily Bread'

I would suggest the following changes which I would have made myself if I had worked longer on the picture:

1. I would suggest for the scene when the father meets the girl from the city, for the first time, and slaps her, to take that slap out of this sequence and put it in another place, which I will later suggest.

    I would take it out here because there is no sufficient reason for this girl, after she has received the slap, to stay on with the family instead of returning to the city.

---

[8] See Theodore Huff, *Index*, pp. 13–14.

[9] The contract with Fox was dated 8 July 1926 and covered a four-year period starting from July or August 1927. For the first year Murnau was paid $125,000; for the second, $150,000; for the third, $170,000, and for the fourth $200,000. He was expected to make one film per year; if he made more than four in all he was to get $125,000 more for each one.

Carl Mayer as author was to receive $20,000 to $25,000. Murnau was to make the films in New York or Hollywood and was under exclusive contract to Fox. He made only three out of the four films in the contract, and the third was finished by someone else.

2. To strengthen the danger that is in the person of Mac if possible, in all scenes where he appears with the girl, build up the danger, so that in the climax the final night, it already has its dangerous background.

3. On this final evening, the scene between Mac and the girl should be by far more sensuous, so that we, as an audience, really fear that the girl might surrender.

4. When the old man catches them both, in this scene, and tells her that he is glad that he has proof now, we should have the girl forget all her good feelings that might have grown through the love of the pure boy. She should become the hard-boiled waitress, who is only used to fighting men. She should yell at the old man all the truth this old tyrant could be told – of what he has done to her; what he has done to his son; what he has done to his whole family; and she should say it in the most bold, vigorous manner, so the audience would feel relieved that at last there is someone to tell him the truth.

   As an answer to this, which the old man considers an insult, outraged, he would slap her and call her a street-walker.

5. I think it might be good, after the scene where the girl breaks with her husband, to show how the girl escapes through the window of her room.

6. If talk should be added to the picture, I would suggest it start at the beginning of the final night sequence – that is to say, the scene where the girl sits alone at the table, in the living room, during the night, and all of a sudden Mac, with his wounded hand, steps into the room. But then the talk should go on to the finish. I suggest to start the talk there because the whole story has been built up to this night; all emotions have been shown and used and the whole situation is just right for an outburst, and there the opening would be given through the words. Just there would be the point where talk could be of big dramatic value.

7. In case no talking would be added, the titles, of course, ought to be changed entirely, as most of them at the end are impossible, not helping the story at all.

Murnau indicates the story clearly enough to allow us to limit ourselves to recapitulating the main outline of the narrative: Lem, a young peasant, virtuous and inexperienced, is sent by his father Tustine, a harsh, bullying old man, to sell their wheat in the city. There, in a low eating-house, he meets Kate, a waitress, who is treated like a drudge and persecuted by the lust of the men round her. She longs for purity, country simplicity, air and sun. She and Lem soon become friends and when he leaves she is in despair. At the station he turns back to go and ask her to marry him. He informs his father by telegram.

Tustine is furious and treats Kate as an intruder. He suspects her of having an affair with Mac, foreman of the harvesters, and she, seeing that her husband doesn't defend her against these accusations, decides to return to the city.

Meanwhile the harvesters, led by Mac, refuse to get the harvest in at night, although a hailstorm threatens. Lem wrestles with Mac on a wagon; the horses panic and bolt as the other men try to leap on it. Thinking the harvesters are leaving, Tustine fires, nearly wounding Lem. For the first time, Tustine is moved; he embraces his son and promises to accept Kate, who has gone away on her own, as his daughter-in-law. The harvesters bring in the crop before the storm, and Lem drives through the wheatfields to find Kate.

A peasant film, close to the soil. One German critic wrote that this was no longer the routine and conventional Murnau of *The Four Devils*: the style and direction recalled the mastery of *Sunrise* and the best early work of Sjöström. Murnau had, in fact, returned to the sort of *Kammerspielfilm*, harsh and heavy, which he had presented with all his visual genius in *Der Brennende Acker* and *Die Austreibung*. This quality is still visible even through the mutilations which turned *Our Daily Bread* into *City Girl*. It is marvellous, wrote another German critic, to see man become one with the landscape, with everything true and sincere and rooted in the earth, and to see the fever of the city and the bustle of the crowd thrown into contrasted relief.

In 1966, in Hollywood, I saw a print of *City Girl* which ran for only an hour. I was therefore rather surprised to read William K. Everson's programme note for a showing of the film at the Theodore Huff Memorial Society on 2 March 1970, in which he wrote that this was 'the full and untampered-with version as shot by Murnau'. Though he finds it curiously unadventurous for the man who had just made *Sunrise* and *The Four Devils* he calls it fascinating and rewarding, with some shots – the moonlit farmhouse, for example – quite breathtaking.

I thought I saw here a similar process to that rehabilitation [10] of *Hello, Sister*, the mutilation of which Stroheim spoke so bitterly. But in 1971 the Cinémathèque Française was able to show a new copy of *City Girl*. This copy runs for nearly an hour and a half, and I must acknowledge that there remain in it many traces of Murnau's unique visual style and lighting, mutilated as it is, with much of its nuance eliminated.

Some of the beauty of Murnau's soft modelling is preserved. The lamps and lights show the Murnau touch. The sequence in which Kate sees through the farmhouse window the lights of the harvesters going out to the wheatfields at night reminds one of the scene in *Sunrise* in which the city vamp sees the fishermen setting out for the rescue of the woman they fear may be drowned. The repetition of this sequence – when Kate sees the harvesters wanting to leave before bringing in the wheat – shows the degree of Murnau's involvement with this particular visual idea. Similarly, the enormous close-up of the hanging lantern on the back of the wagon in which Lem and Mac are struggling reminds one of the treatment of the ship's lantern during the storm in *Sunrise*.

[10] Elliott Stein, 'New York 1970: the Year of the Foof', and Richard Koszarski, 'Hello, Sister', both in *Sight and Sound*, Autumn 1970.

Likewise, the lamp on the farmhouse table, sometimes seen in close-up with its soft light gently moulding the darker zones around it, and the lamp held by Tustine in the barn, are shots which Murnau used, characteristically, to evoke an enveloping *Stimmung*. The subtle visual beauty of such moments remains, making one's awareness of the loss of rhythm – due to cuts and to final editing which Murnau was unable to supervise – the more acute. The emphasis on the sweetness of Charles Farrell's features against Mary Duncan's rather harsh prettiness is more than naturally increased by this false editing.

And elsewhere there are losses. The contrast, which Murnau wanted to emphasize, between the stifling closeness of the city and the endless, open wheatfields is hardly apparent. We see neither crowded street scenes, nor dark, narrow houses. And the wheatfields, which Murnau so loved to drive through with his camera, make little impression.

Here and there, there are echoes of *Sunrise*: passers-by seen through a restaurant window, for example. And here and there, also, there are jokes which might be Murnau's but which also might more justly be credited to Berthold Viertel's German taste as scriptwriter. For instance, in the train Lem has to empty all his pockets until at the last moment he finds his ticket in his waistcoat; then on the return journey with his bride he tucks the tickets in his hatband for the collector to find as they sleep. And in the restaurant, it is Lem's saying grace before his meal which first induces Kate to notice him.

There are undoubtedly signs of Murnau's genius visible in *City Girl*. Nevertheless I believe that many intimate digressions, matters of shading and psychological subtlety, have been lost in the final editing. The coming of sound brought a change of pace in film style. Murnau's slow rhythm had by this time become difficult to bear, and inevitably lent itself to savage cuts.

And nothing at all now remains of the superimpositions Murnau wished to use for his great symphony of *Our Daily Bread*.

13. The Culmination: Tabu

The melancholy strains of a South Sea island *Aloha Oe* can be heard through Murnau's last film. It is full of the painful nostalgia that always accompanies *la recherche du temps perdu*. This is not only because we are looking back with hindsight over a life doomed to end soon after. If Murnau himself died, the paradise he conjured up in his film had already been destroyed long since.

For Murnau himself failed to find the 'happy isles' of Van Zanten.[1] There is something tragic about the contrast he tries to make between his blessed isle, and the 'civilized' island of the pearl-fishers and Chinese merchants, a sad place steeped in alcohol and jazz. We know, alas, that all the islands have been like that for decades – tourist centres where the white man has transmitted to the beautiful, careless, childlike inhabitants his own civilization, including the Bible, brandy, syphilis, leprosy, and cheap cotton goods.

But Murnau tried to go back to nature. He found a dream landscape rising out of an emerald sea fringed with palms, with gentle flower-scented hills. He also found men who were as they had been before, and who when he stripped them of their ugly European clothes were as magnificent as on the first day of creation. They still knew how to move freely and proudly: when they threw their harpoons they were graceful, when they dived they were like bronzed young Greek gods.

Murnau offers us an apotheosis of the flesh: the feats and canoe races are

---

[1] *The Happy Isles of Van Zanten*, a novel by the Dutch author Laurids Bruun.

only pretexts for showing those godlike young bodies. He was intoxicated by them, just as Floyd Crosby's camera becomes intoxicated with light when a white sailing-ship appears among the sparkling waves, its bright colours inherent even in the black and white image. A sail unfurls like a sheet of shining silk, and suddenly the dark bodies of natives are seen among the rigging like ripe clusters on a grape-vine. Long, narrow canoes flash like fish through the transparent waters. In our appreciation of this complex entity we almost overlook the details, we almost forget – how could it be otherwise? – the love-story. The plot becomes a faint melody caught from time to time; finding its place like distant figures appearing in a landscape, like some desirable ornament.

The story Flaherty and Murnau tell is an old one which is always new, about love, renunciation, the curse of tabu, and the lover's death. They tell it without any elaboration, without too much Europeanization. Where it becomes too sentimental and out of keeping with the general tone, the fault is perhaps Murnau's. It remains a simple tale or song, as Murnau intended. He wanted to avoid turning it into something dramatic. He wanted to give himself up to a mood of adagio and explore and enjoy it to the utmost. The very things that might have been a break in style become successful, for we all, like Melville, have a sort of homesickness for the happy isles and for giving ourselves up to our dreams.

Tabu is no more a talkie than Flaherty's *White Shadows of the South Seas*.[2] It is a silent film in which here and there a song or the sudden mournful call of a conch is heard. Murnau and Flaherty deliberately adopt the methods of the silent films: instead of titles they use letters, the captain's log-book, a police report, the coconut leaf on which the lover writes his few words of farewell. The finale in its visual perfection is the apogee of the art of silent film: the young man, too tired to struggle any more, sinks silently beneath the waves, and the white sail disappears like a vision over the horizon. And the South Sea sings its eternal song.

When the film was finished, Réri, the heroine, a half-caste who used the name of her European father, became a dancer somewhere on Broadway. In the film Murnau managed to transform her and re-create her as a gentle native. It may be that for the girl herself it was only a sort of atavism, but this is rarely noticeable. She is not especially goodlooking, and as, like all the island girls, she has rather short legs, she doesn't compare very well with the magnificent young men. But she is charming, especially when she smiles.

Matahi, the hero, is closer to nature. He moves with a marvellous animal grace. Every movement of this young warrior with a body of bronze is unaffected and unique. He has the gift of corporeal expression as others have

---

[2] Co-directed with W. S. Van Dyke.

a gift for music. When he is distressed he recalls Michelangelo's young slave in the Louvre, abandoned to his grief.

The old argument about whether it is a documentary or a 'feature film' is pointless. Murnau did not make an expedition to observe native customs and record them in scientific detail. He was an artist who had set out with the endless European nostalgia for beauty and the sun. What he sought he found. And he transformed it, and gave us a glimpse of it.

I wrote the above as a young journalist, on 28 August 1931,[3] when the film first came out in Europe, only a few months after Murnau's death.

What can one add to this direct first impression? Everyone knows the film, and it has not aged. Today I would have talked about the marvellous skill of Murnau's cutting, his unparalleled sense of the rhythm of images, of camera angles, of the whole mastery of lighting that here attains its highest point; of the way he had all those slim canoes darting about in front of the ship, seen from many different aspects, shown interweaving swiftly in a rapid montage, and Matahi turning back on the pretext of collecting his little brother who is delayed; of the way Murnau delighted in orchestrating the coming and going of the narrow craft over the limpid waters. Or of the way he cut the shots of the girls bathing among the rocks, at the very beginning of the idyll, in a blaze of light and a swirl of harmonious movement. And of the way the search for the fugitives is handled, in the velvety darkness rent by zigzagging torches, and an atmosphere at once open and airy, and violent.

Murnau added occasional notes in English to the English script. But he always reverted to German in the case of anything especially important.

We see from these notes how one of the finest sequences in the film was created by Murnau alone.

	All with lighting from the side.
1. Medium:	Matahi's smiling face over the edge of the boat.
2. Medium:	He is disconcerted and his face grows more serious.
3. Nearer:	Matahi looks fixedly, as if not understanding, towards Hitu, then bows his head as if vanquished.
4. Close:	The garland of flowers – just that alone for some while – then we see Matahi's shadow fall on it, and a hand stretch out and slowly pick it up.

Matahi's dream, like all the vision sequences in Murnau, was entirely the creation of the director, and noted by him in German in the English script.

Dream: Matahi's head, very large, fills the screen; the eyes are open, thoughtful. The contours of the head remain distinct as the Chinaman appears inside, large, at first indistinct, then more clearly, holding in his hand a little bundle of bills. He shows

[3] In the *Film Kurier* of Berlin.

Tabu

205

the bills one by one, passing them from one hand to the other. As he does so we suddenly see the announcement of the departure of the 'Himano', first in Tahitian, then crossfaded to English or French, as if superimposed over the Chinaman.

While the lettering grows dim and the Chinaman is still showing the bills, the word 'tabu' suddenly appears in huge characters, then the Chinaman fades and the word 'tabu' has become the notice-board above the water. A lot of water in the foreground. Suddenly you can see into the limpid sea: oysters among fantastic corals. Suddenly you seem to see inside one of the oysters an enormous pearl, that grows larger and larger until it fills the whole picture.

And in the pearl the Chinaman reappears, this time holding a pair of scales, in one pan of which is a pearl of fabulous price.

The big pearl still fills the picture, and within it the Chinaman takes the other pearl out of the scale and tears up the bills. Then everything blurs, the outline of Matahi's head reappears, first with the pearl in the middle; then the pearl disappears and all that is left is Matahi's sleeping face.

Then Murnau adds, this time in English:

Start the dream with Matahi's head, his eyes still open (his face bent somewhat over his right shoulder), then overlap to dream, but for a while an outline of Matahi's face stays, so that it looks as if the dream takes place in his head. After the dream is finished overlap in same way to head again, but now head is against pole of hut bending over left shoulder. Matahi is sleeping.

After Friedrich Wilhelm Murnau's death his brother Robert went to Tahiti. Inspired by his brother's memory he filmed the place and wanted to continue his work. By chance I have been able to see, in Munich, two reels containing both rushes by Murnau and trials by Robert Plumpe.

The rushes are experimental location shots which Murnau must have taken with Flaherty. There is one marvellous fishing scene in which the young natives beat the water with branches to drive the fish into the net. Murnau must have left it out of the film because he already had enough colourful incidents.

Other scenes were shot by Robert Plumpe. Of course it is not surprising that these two reels show none of Murnau's skill in shooting and cutting.[4]

We are fortunate enough to be able to follow Murnau very closely on his

[4] There is a mystery here, on which I can throw some light. Robert Plumpe himself told me about these two reels containing rushes by Murnau and sequences of his own, which were stored at Graz, in Austria. After Plumpe's death they were sent to a Bavarian producer of documentaries.

On a visit to Bavaria I was able to verify that the thirty-five reels entitled *Insel der Glücklichen* (Isles of the Blest) are simply rushes of *Tabu*. Many of them were actually used in the film, and still have clappers reading 'Take Floyd Crosby' or 'Take Flaherty'; some are even marked 'Murnau', and one of these is dated 14 December 1930.

voyage to the southern isles. First, a telegram of 30 March 1929 to Kurt Korff, at Ullstein's of Berlin, the publishers of several illustrated reviews:

Leaving in about ten days on my yacht for South Seas, Marquesas, Society, Cook and Tanmota Islands, and perhaps Samoa. Are you interested? If so, what subject? Stop. How much dough will Ullstein give?

Murnau uses the German slang word 'Pinkus' in the last sentence. Throughout all that he wrote for Ullstein we find the curious mixture of journalese and poetry which Murnau often adopted out of a sort of shyness and desire not to reveal his innermost thoughts too clearly.

There is also a letter that he wrote in English to Korff, dated Papeete, Tahiti, 14 October 1929. Murnau had been in Tahiti for several months.

All in all, with the good luck and the bad, with the most wonderful days and the stormy, squally days, we had the most glorious trip imaginable, and a time which none of us will ever forget. It was the fulfilment of a happy dream, surpassing all expectations.

All our ports of call in the South Seas were French possessions, and in none of these places had the German flag been flown since the beginning of the war; and we had been told beforehand that the natives might act strangely, as the world war was still alive with them. But instead, wherever we appeared we were received in the most hospitable way – a hospitality that only one who has been to Polynesia can realize.

While the idea is to go on with the cruise as far west as possible through the Pacific, until west meets east, it looks to me as though I might stay for some time longer around these waters, because together with Robert Flaherty, whom you know as the director of those marvellous pictures *Nanook of the North* and *Moana of the South Seas*, I am going to make a picture that will be called

TABU

A story of the South Seas

As it is based on the still paradise-like conditions and life of some of the islands here, to keep the real spirit of the thing I am staying away from white actors, and all professionals. All people appearing before the camera, whether whites, half-castes or natives, are people who have never been in front of a camera before. You know and you understand that for a dramatic story this will be quite an experiment – but I shall enjoy doing it, as I hope to catch some of the true unspoiled Polynesian spirit, which, if we succeed, ought to be well worth the harder work.

We have gathered our cast from some of the remotest corners of the islands, first having combed all the islands looking over and testing hundreds of people. We believe now that we have the very best, and we are going to start shooting soon.

The reels containing the 'Fishdrive' which I had seen in a more or less clandestine showing in Munich must have been abstracted from those in Graz. A Milan distributor now hires them out to Italian film societies as a 15 minute 16 mm. film, 'Battuta nel Mare del Sud'. Robert Plumpe entitled his material *Insel der Glücklichen*; he added some other material from documentaries on the South Seas with the intention of thus making up a new film, but died before carrying out his plans.

I am sending you herewith some photographs of our main characters, who, we think, while they have all the qualities of the pure native appearance, still will appeal to a white audience. Personally I think these people, with their childlike charm and grace, would be a sensation if they entered European or American studios.

Besides these photos of the cast, I am sending you quite a number of pictures of the trip. On the back of each picture I am giving you a short indication of what it is, or where it was taken. If you want to publish any of them in *Illustrierte Zeitung* or *Dame* or *Querschnitt* ... they are at your disposal.... All pictures must carry the note 'Murnau–Flaherty Production' and also 'Murnau Photo' or 'Flaherty Photo' – whichever will be marked on the back of the print....

Before I left the States I promised to send you also reports of the trip and its outcome, for publication; but I find now that it is a difficult undertaking to fulfil that promise, as to do it well would require more time than I could take away from the work of the picture, or would like to take away from my lazy lying around in the sun and enjoying the beauty of this paradise. At the same time the whole atmosphere – nearly every stone and every reef and every house – is full of stories, true or legendary, just inviting one to write them down if one could only find the time....

Murnau also enclosed a letter that he had written to Salka Viertel, wife of Berthold Viertel, a German dramatist and director living in Hollywood, in which he talks about the beginning of his voyage. If he wanted to, Korff could publish this under the title of 'Letter to Salka', and Murnau would send more material later.

The letter to Salka is written in German, and recounts in somewhat comic vein the misfortunes of Eddy the cook, 'who says he has been at sea for twenty years and is still seasick all the time except when it's calm'.

Murnau writes that the Southern Cross had always been for him the symbol of tropical exuberance, a dazzling fairy story, the emblem of all stories of adventure, exploration, and South Sea pirates, the sign of Melville, Stevenson, and Conrad. He expected to see it near the Equator, and was surprised when it appeared only eight hundred miles from Los Angeles. The gramophone was playing some popular tune when a small, dull, slightly misty, unromantic star came into view. Murnau felt this disillusionment like a physical pain.

Now [the letter ends] when we are nearer the Southern Cross, it has become luminous, and for us it is a sort of symbol. Soon, when we have crossed the Equator, it will shine down on our books and our dreams, for it is towards our books and our dreams that we are voyaging.

Murnau's brother also gave me an article by Murnau running to thirty-four typewritten pages: it is called 'Meine Fahrt zu den Glücklichen Inseln' (My Voyage to the Happy Isles), and places for photographs are indicated in the margin.

Tabu: in the picture top left Murnau is in the bow of the boat and Matisse in the stern

As the Ullstein archives were partly destroyed I do not know whether this account was ever published in one or other of their reviews.

Again we encounter the mixture of slanginess and poetry. Murnau is proud of his yacht *Bali*, which has a red heart painted on the stern and for which the former air-pilot had taken a captain's ticket. He gives a loving description: it is long and slim, 65 ft by 16 ft, drawing $8\frac{1}{2}$ ft of water. It belongs to the Gloucester Fishermen class, with two sails and a 50 h.p. diesel engine.

He tells how he took with him a whole collection of books about the South Seas: Conrad, Stevenson, Pierre Loti, Melville, Frederick O'Brien (author of *White Shadows of the South Seas*), Hal and Nordhoff – all of a kind to strengthen his nostalgia for the islands. He recounts little anecdotes about the helmsman, who has one leg in plaster and walks with crutches, reminding Murnau of Long John Silver, with his stories of the seven seas. He also tells about the little cook Ole [5] and his seasickness.

The first port of call was Mazatlan on the west coast of Mexico. There was a cinema there which to Murnau's great amusement was showing an 'apocryphal' film called *Sister Angelica*, 'directed by F. Murnau', but which Murnau had never heard of.

The first place they called at in the South Seas was Tai-o-Hai on the rocky island of Nukuhiva in the Marquesas, known to Stevenson and O'Brien and famous as the setting of Melville's *Typee*. A hundred years before there had been a population of 160,000; now, thanks to the coming of the white man, there were barely a thousand people. Murnau could still see the white sand, the tall slim coconut palms, the shrubs with their fantastic red flowers, the frangipanis, white as alabaster, which perfumed all the island, and in contrast the jagged dark mountains rising against the clouds like angry gods. But the natives were no longer gay and singing as in Melville's day: they stared at Murnau and his team without a smile. Great yellow flowers fell heavily from the 'burao' trees in the midday sun, and Murnau suddenly realized the time, patience, love, hard work, and research that would be needed to capture, bit by bit, the shattered image and the destroyed and fugitive splendour of this former paradise. He would have to search everywhere for men who still had the pride, the beauty, and the intelligence of their ancestors.

A French trader told Murnau that all these people wanted to do was die. What had they to live for? The missionaries had taken away their faith and replaced it by a religion they didn't understand; they had forbidden them to go about half-naked, to dance their gay pagan dances, to carve their idols. They had been given cheap cotton clothes and rum; they were riddled with tuberculosis, influenza, and syphilis; the old clothes the missionaries collected

---

[5] Presumably the cook also called Eddy, mentioned above.

for them had infected them with leprosy. They had no resistance to all these new diseases, and so they died.

In Tai-o-Hai Murnau was told by a painter that the sort of natives he was looking for were only to be found on the island of Ua-Pu. The land was rocky and infertile, so they were forced to depend largely on fishing. This was what saved them from just lolling about waiting for death like the inhabitants of Tai-o-Hai. Ua-Pu was off the usual shipping routes; as it was unproductive its people were left in peace.

Murnau went there. He found it one of the most beautiful of all the islands, with a population that was 'witty and pure'. The young men, handsome in face and figure, upright, energetic, vivacious, and polite, invited him to go fishing with them. They dived down to the limpid submarine caves to harpoon fish; they overflowed with joy, everything they did was a game. Although the missionaries had forbidden them, too, to dance, for Murnau and his companions they performed the ancient ritual dances and sang the Tahitian 'Himini'. They were 'like pictures by Gauguin come to life'.

Between the dances Murnau played them some gramophone records. They listened politely – they were too polite to criticize. But only one record really aroused their enthusiasm. This was a disc of Paul Robeson singing a spiritual: their faces lit up and they swayed to its rhythm. When Murnau went away the islanders rowed out in their canoes with coconuts, breadfruit, bananas and other fruit, and fish. They wouldn't take the money he tried to give them – these were presents for a friend.

Murnau visited the valley of Typee, an idyllic spot where Melville had been a prisoner. He also went to see Paul Gauguin's grave at Atuona, and thought of the painter's words: 'All that your civilization gives rise to produces only disease.' Like him, Murnau had fled from the horrors of a baneful civilization.

Then, at Hanavave, the 'bay of the virgins', on the island of Fatuhiva, he discovered a dream landscape: a green valley watered by a little gently meandering silver river, with huts thatched with palm leaves. Here Murnau found Mehao. 'His smile was like a ray of bright sunshine; you only had to clap your hands for his whole body to sway in a dance of delight.'

Again, away from the priests, under the breadfruit trees, they danced the 'tapraita'.

It was a dance for the arms and body more than for the feet [wrote Murnau]. The hips are rolled sideways and forwards, faster and faster, more and more voluptuously, perfectly freely. Mehao had more grace, a finer figure, greater passion than any of the rest.

Would he not be perfect for the film? Murnau took a photograph of him. Underneath he wrote:

He was an orphan from early childhood and grew up freely and independently, like an animal in the jungle. A pure-bred Polynesian, of extraordinary physical beauty, slim and strong, with simple, natural movements. The marvellous harmony of his figure makes him look like a Greek god, a model for the Olympic games, a delight of nature.

But in the end it was Matahi that Murnau chose.

Then Murnau set sail for flower-scented Takapotu, one of the Thunder Islands. Unlike the Marquesas, they boasted a large bustling population, dressed, alas, in American cotton. It was an ugly industrial centre for the copra trade, and Murnau looked with horror at the hovels of corrugated iron intermingled with gaudy Chinese shops. The natives who came on board threw themselves hungrily on the fruit from the Marquesas. Their island did not produce any, and they ate the lot before the sailors could stop them.

Some Mormon missionaries told Murnau about the work of the pearl-fishers: of the sharks, and Pahua the giant crawfish that seized its victims in its claws and held them down to drown on the bottom of the sea; of the conger that lived in the coral caves and whose bite was as dangerous as a shark's. They told him about the tricks of the Chinese merchants to get hold of the pearls won with such hardship, and how they themselves tried to protect the childlike natives against them.

Murnau witnessed a very civilized Christian dance: all those taking part were got up in their European Sunday best, and boys and girls went meekly and correctly through the prescribed motions, waving long sticks in all directions. 'Naturally religion and business were mixed, and this meagre entertainment had to be paid for.'

He discovered Takaroa lagoon, a 'marvel of colour' in which the green of the ocean shaded to the blue of the sky and the downy white of the clouds, in contrast to the red of the natives' loin-cloths. Nowhere was colour so alive and vibrant as here on the atolls of the Paumotis. It was there that Murnau met Matisse, who said 'the colour here is a revelation'.[6]

Then Murnau watched the pearl-fishers, men and women, at work, as he was to show them in *Tabu*.

In the evening he would walk in the moonlight.

Never have I seen such moonlight. You could read a newspaper by it. The sky was never dark nor nocturnal, but luminous and a brilliant blue. The light of the moon nearly blinded us!

Murnau entered a tent where couples were dancing American fashion to a band of guitars, and gambling: 'it all had the bitter taste of civilization'. He recreated this dance in *Tabu* for the 'civilized' island.

Then the Mormon missionaries left and the natives danced a genuine ancient dance for him, accompanied by drumming on a petrol tin.

[6] Murnau took a photograph of Matisse, which as George Pratt of George Eastman House, Rochester, has informed me, appeared in Alfred H. Barr's book, *Matisse*, with the acknowledgement, 'Photo by F. Murnau.'

Then they had to go on to Tahiti, which Captain Cook, Wallis, and Bougainville had all described as a paradise. Murnau pondered over all the tales about this marvellous island, and about the mutiny on the *Bounty*.

It was evening. Papeete was bathed in a sea of light and rose up out of a thousand beams. The ship *Tahiti*, all its cabins lit, lay alongside the quay.

With the arrival at Tahiti Murnau's account ends.

In a letter to his mother, whom he loved very much, Murnau described the careless life in which 'there is no work and no worries, where the shining days go by in games and dancing, bathing and fishing, and the night innocently brings all lovers together.'[7]

He delights in the 'immaterial beauty of the tropics', in 'the mild air, the scent of flowers, the nobility of the people of these happy isles'.

And in another letter he says:

Tahiti was our headquarters. We had built a laboratory there where we developed our own negatives, and had trained some of the natives to help us. Our preparations for the film were carried through without haste, like everything here. It took several months to build up a team. I used to go from island to island to find the people we needed.

In a third letter Murnau wrote:

When I think I shall have to leave all this I already suffer all the agony of going. I am bewitched by this place. I have been here a year and I don't want to be anywhere else. The thought of cities and all those people is repulsive to me. I want to be alone, or with a few rare people. When I sit outside my bungalow in the evening and look at the sea, towards Moreo, and see the waves break one by one and thunder on the reef, then I feel terribly small, and sometimes I wish I were at home. But I am never 'at home' anywhere – I feel this more and more the older I get – not in any country nor in any house nor with anybody.

And then sometimes he was seized with a more precise homesickness:

First of all I must go to Europe. It's four years since I saw my mother.

Then I'd like to study the development and technique of talking pictures in Germany, France, England, and the United States. I was far away from civilization when the talkies came in, and I must inform myself about the situation and the direction in which they are developing.

It is ridiculous to say that talking pictures will disappear again. No invention that shows itself to be of value will ever be rejected. The talking picture represents a great step forward in the cinema. Unfortunately it has come too soon: we had just begun to

[7] For these letters see the quotations in an article 'Aus Briefen F. W. Murnau' [Der Mensch und der Künstler] by Ernst Hofmann for the *8 Uhr Abenblatt*, Berlin, 27 April 1931.

find our way with the silent film and were beginning to exploit all the possibilities of the camera. And now here are the talkies and the camera is forgotten while people rack their brains about how to use the microphone....

David Flaherty, Robert Flaherty's brother, says that Murnau deliberately made *Tabu* as a silent film, not for financial but for purely aesthetic reasons.

The fact was that Murnau, with his great devotion to the camera, knew that he could not sacrifice, for the sake of sound, the enormous visual possibilities that the subject offered him.

It seems astonishing that Murnau, who wrote so enthusiastically about the songs of the Polynesians, never thought of recording them. Emile Savitry, the Surrealist painter who died recently, told me not long before that Murnau's idea of music for the film was not Hugo Riesenfeld's insipid score. Savitry himself had been on a trip to the South Seas as a young man, travelling on a sailing ship in search of adventure. He took a great many photographs which he showed Murnau when they met by chance: Murnau was particularly struck by one of a wreck – a sort of ghost ship with a curious aura, dim and half shrouded in mist. He later asked Savitry to work with him, and to choose interesting locations for him among the other islands. Murnau himself was just leaving for Tuamotu, said Savitry, to make recordings of Polynesian music. This suggests that Murnau wished to use a native score for his film.

One is surprised to find almost no mention in Murnau's accounts of his journey of his collaboration with Robert Flaherty. An article by David Flaherty fortunately fills this gap.[8]

Robert Flaherty was unhappy about the film on Indians which he was making in Mexico for Fox. To soothe his feelings William Fox suggested that he go on to make another film afterwards in Tahiti. It was David Flaherty who was supposed to assess the possibilities of Tahiti, but before he could set out he had to hang about Hollywood waiting for the company's decisions. He felt very lonely there, and was very glad to meet Murnau, who took him on the set of *Our Daily Bread*. Murnau was as tired of commercial considerations and methods as Bob Flaherty: he was kind and charming, and kept telling David that Bob's films were the best. This was almost praise from Olympus to David, for Murnau was already a 'big shot' in Hollywood. There was also something godlike about him personally – tall, slim, and straight, with his clearcut features, keen eyes, and beautiful golden hair.

Then David left for Tahiti. When he got back to Hollywood Murnau sent him an urgent invitation, and was almost annoyed to hear that David was not free that very evening.

[8] See also the article by Mrs Frances Flaherty, first published in *Canadian Newsreel* in May 1954, and subsequently in *Film Culture*, 20, 1959.

He came the next day. At that time Murnau was living in a big house right up in the hills of Hollywood, alone except for his domestic staff.[9] David, the only guest, was installed at a long table from which one had a bird's eye view of the lights of Hollywood and even Los Angeles below.

Murnau's face lit up when he told David of the beautiful yacht he had bought, of the Gloucester Fishermen class, the *Pasqualito*. Murnau was to re-name it the *Bali*, an island he wanted to visit. Hollywood was wearing him out, he hated the artificial atmosphere and the pressure the studio exercised over him. David poured out his enthusiasm about Tahiti, and Murnau listened, fascinated.

Suddenly he said, 'Would you like to come with me to Tahiti?' David couldn't believe his ears. But unfortunately he was obliged to go back to his brother in Mexico.

It was at this point that David learned from Murnau that Bob's film in Mexico was on the point of being suspended: Bob and the company had differences of opinion about the plot, and there had been a fire at the camp near Tucson. Why shouldn't Bob and he join forces to make a film after their own hearts in Tahiti?

The very next day he and David set out to see Bob in Tucson. Bob told him the story of a pearl-fisher, which he had been thinking about ever since his unfortunate experiences working on *White Shadows of the South Seas*. Murnau listened with passionate eagerness.

Finally they signed a contract with a new company called Colorart, which left them much freer than a more established organization like Fox. On 18 April 1929 Flaherty cabled Murnau that the film would cost less than 150,000 dollars.

At the end of April 1929 David sailed with Murnau from San Pedro on the *Bali*. Bob left a month later on a steam ship. He arrived first, for Murnau and David were two months on the way, with stops in the Marquesas and the Paumotu islands. When they got there Bob told them Colorart hadn't sent the money that had been agreed in the contract; he and his assistant had been living on credit. After sending cable after cable, they finally learned that Colorart were in financial difficulties and on the verge of bankruptcy.

Murnau then offered to finance the film himself, with what remained, after he had bought the *Bali*, of the money he had earned in Hollywood. The crew had to be paid off; the only people he kept on were the cameramen. For the yacht he recruited a crew locally.

[9] Murnau seems to have moved house often in Hollywood. Sometimes, Salka Viertel told me, he lived in a luxury hotel; another time in a small old hotel near the sea, in a 'little room full of sun, where you could smell the apples and the sea'. He also lived for some time at 903 Wilcrox Avenue, Hollywood.

Since Murnau was economical by nature and Flaherty, according to David, was not, there were bound to be difficulties. Murnau wanted to direct the film himself, and Floyd Crosby was to be behind the camera; what fell to Flaherty, therefore, was simply the plot. Flaherty wanted to make a sort of documentary after the style of *Nanook* and *Moana*; Murnau wanted to make a feature film. It was there that the difficulties began.

The two directors, so different from one another in their way of living and looking at things, were very discreet about any misunderstanding between them. Each greatly admired the other's achievements so far. If they quarrelled it was not because Murnau was tight-fisted, as David Flaherty suggests. On the contrary, he was generous by nature. But he knew that all the money he had earned in Hollywood would be used up, and that if the film took too long to make, he, as the sole producer, would get badly in debt. Nor was the trouble that, while Murnau didn't drink (his kidney trouble made him a total abstainer), Bob Flaherty was overflowing with energy and liked more than one drink. Hollywood gossip, which trailed them step by step, even went so far as to allege that Flaherty, who knew how fond Murnau was of the yacht, purposely wore heavy-soled shoes which would scratch the polished deck.

But all these pinpricks have nothing to do with the fundamental differences between these two extraordinary directors. Richard Griffith, who treats this divergence discreetly in *Film Culture*, says that Flaherty, disappointed by the conventional romanticism of *White Shadows of the South Seas*, had said before they set out for Tahiti: 'We're going to make the sort of film they wouldn't let me make out of *White Shadows*!' Flaherty told Griffith that what he didn't like about *Tabu* was that Murnau had not only romanticized but also 'Europeanized' the traditions and customs of the Polynesians as far as psychology and motive were concerned; he also found the lighting and photography of the film more European than 'Pacific'.[10]

The same issue of *Film Culture*, 20, also gives us the opportunity of comparing two original plots, both presented as by Flaherty and Murnau. *Turia* is clearly more up Flaherty's street than *Tabu*: Flaherty, a born maker of documentaries, was only interested in the social conditions of the natives, and here the subject is the exploitation of the pearl-divers by the Chinese traders. The story takes place first on the little atoll of 'Avura', 'less touched by civilization', then on the completely industrialized island of Tahiti, and is basically the second part of *Tabu* with a few fragments added from the first

---

[10] See *Film Culture*, 20: 'Flaherty and Tabu' by Richard Griffith. Griffith's article relies on one by Maurice Scherer (Eric Rohmer), 'La Revanche de l'Occident', in *Cahiers du Cinéma*, 21, March 1953, though this only speaks of 'the white blood under their brown skins' and the Greek bas-relief of the Sleeping Hunter. Seymour Stern has sent me a note refuting the insinuations that *Tabu* was shot by Flaherty, not Murnau.

part. There is no 'tabu' either on the dangerous fishing-place or on the young half-caste girl Turia, whose father was a white man.

In the end Tino, a young diver, seeing that all their resources, and even the pearls entrusted to him by his friends, have been swallowed up by the easy life of Tahiti, goes back with Turia, his sweetheart, to Avura, where he once was innocent and happy. He dives again in the dangerous spot where, at his first meeting with Turia, he found an unusually large and perfect pearl. But this time he does not return from the mysterious depths. Only bubbles rise one by one to the surface. Then all is still, and the only thing left on the water is the flower which Tino, in a last impulse of love, took from the hair of the sleeping and unsuspecting Turia.

This story, less ornate than that of *Tabu*, must have been rejected, according to the letter written by Murnau, before 14 October 1929. But *Turia* itself is so romantic that it may be regarded as proof that even before *Tabu* Flaherty had given way to Murnau.

As for the 'Europeanization' in *Tabu*, it is not as simple as Richard Griffith thinks, with his allusions to the 'Germanization' of the plot, 'Teutonic' Priestesses, and the resemblance between Matahi and the 'Dying Gaul' (*sic!*). Murnau had set out for the islands dreaming of all the tales of the Pacific he had read. But neither Jack London, nor Stevenson, nor O'Brien, nor Melville, nor even Conrad, were German authors.

David Flaherty wrote to me in February 1960:

Turia was written some time before *Tabu* which did not evolve until some months after we had arrived in Tahiti.

. . . When Murnau decided to break with Colorart, we had many conferences with regard to writing a new story upon which Colorart could have no legal claim. *Tabu* evolved only after we had been many weeks in Tahiti, left stranded there by Colorart's failure to send production funds as stipulated in the contract.

After Murnau's death, Colorart filed suit against the Murnau Estate and Robert Flaherty for the money (some 50,000 dollars if I remember correctly) they had actually put into the picture, which had been budgeted at 150,000 dollars. When the suit was finally heard in Los Angeles, it was quickly thrown out, since Colorart obviously had no legal grounds.

In another letter David Flaherty writes:

I do not recall the exact date of the break with Colorart, though it must have been toward the end of 1929, any time I would say, from October to December. Nor do I recall the date of the termination of the Murnau–Flaherty partnership, which was about a year after the break with Colorart. At a guess I would say it occurred between October and December, 1930, not long before we all left Tahiti by mail steamer for San Francisco and Hollywood.

One more observation on the *Turia* and *Tabu* stories. The *Turia* story was first told to Mr Murnau verbally by my brother. We all worked together setting it down on paper, Murnau contributing to its dramatic construction. (You will note the joint authorship credit: F. W. Murnau and Robert Flaherty.) As for *Tabu*, its basic idea, the sacredness of the *taupou*, or village virgin, was contributed by Bob out of his experiences in Samoa. At our story conferences in Tahiti I was always greatly impressed by Murnau's skill in translating the ideas we discussed into detailed dramatic scenes, shot for shot. Many weeks were spent in working out the *Tabu* script, and we had more than one version – one of them containing more than 600 scenes.

As for the 'Murnau touch': I also had heard that much was due to Carl Mayer. From my experience of working with him, I can confirm that Murnau worked out every detail, of script, direction and camera angles, most thoroughly. It is my opinion that he dominated completely any film he ever made, including the editing.

These letters of David Flaherty are interesting, as they show that the theme of the virgin proclaimed as *tabu* was not – as so many critics have charged – Murnau's invention, but comes from Flaherty's experiences in Samoa. On the other hand, David Flaherty confirms Murnau's independent way of working.

If Murnau had agreed to film *Turia* all the legends about his accidental death would have lost their foundation. For a great deal of invention was afterwards brought to bear on his life on the islands and the difficulties he encountered during the making of the film.[11]

Murnau was said to have brought misfortune upon himself by shooting his film in certain sacred places. According to this legend, Faarere, the local chief, is supposed to have warned Murnau; and, curiously enough, Murnau – who liked consulting fortune-tellers and was extremely superstitious, with a strong taste for the supernatural – disregarded his warning. Misfortune then followed misfortune: as he approached a reef that was 'tabu', in order to set up the camera there, an enormous wave arose, the canoes were flung against the rocks, two cameras sank to the bottom, and many feet of exposed film were spoiled. Some of the extras fell inexplicably ill, and even the principals, Matahi and Reri, injured themselves on the coral reefs and suffered from slight blood-poisoning. The Chinese cook was drowned in mysterious circumstances.

It had rained a good deal before the scenes of the lovers' flight by night were shot, and the palm-branch torches didn't give enough light in the humid

[11] See Wilmon B. Meard's articles, which have also been published in German papers. Moreover the 'curse' continued to operate: Douglas Fairbanks went to Murnau's bungalow at Tainuu Point, 11 kilometres from Papeete, to shoot *Robinson Crusoe*. Apparently he was pursued by bad luck, and there were all sorts of strange incidents. At all events it is certain that Fairbanks hastily left the island.

atmosphere. So Murnau sent for magnesium flares. After several satisfactory tests had been made, one of the flares suddenly exploded and a young white man was burned in the face and hands. He later recovered.[12]

Moreover, Murnau had built his big bungalow on a former native burial-ground, and set up his cameras on reefs where sacrificial victims used to be exposed. All this was of course 'tabu'! It was said that an old man called Tuga had cursed Murnau for all these acts of sacrilege. Murnau became more and more nervous, harassed by the work and the obstacles he encountered on all sides. The sense of anxiety became more and more intolerable. Then one day the old priest Tuga appeared again, and there was a great exorcism scene: 'Deliver him, O Gods, from darkness. Return to the darkness, your home, and return no more to trouble this man.' But in spite of all the magic formulas the natives still murmured, and it was only because of Murnau's great kindness that they didn't desert.[13]

On 23 August 1930, after Murnau had already left his island, a native of Punaavia composed a song in Tahitian:

> *Greetings, Mr Murnau,*
> *To you and your friends,*
> *On this pleasant night,*
> *Greetings, greetings!*
> *I think your place*
> *Was like a branch of jasmin.*
> *That is why I came on the 'One arara'*
> *To play a tune on the guitar.*
>
> *I heard a crowd*
> *Lamenting at the 'taipari',*
> *And why are you weeping,*
> *Marara, the flying fish?*
> *I beg you, Mr Murnau,*
> *Let me come back to you,*
> *Not in your room,*
> *Only there where you are,*
> *So that I can return*
> *There where you are.*

[12] I was able to discover a bill from Dr F. Cassian, of Papeete, dated 27 July 1929, for 2 dollars for an anti-tetanus injection given to a patient called Harry Cruse, presumably a young German.

[13] Murnau had installed himself in great comfort, and even had his huge library sent from Berlin. I have found here and there some figures that give some idea, but an incomplete one, of the enormous production expenses: for a fortnight's shooting Matahi was paid 90,000 francs; for the village constructed specially at Moto Tapu Murnau paid 8,495 dollars.

Murnau used up his entire resources during the eighteen months' shooting of *Tabu*. He was in debt, and his creditors were impatient. I discovered a letter among his brother's papers, dated 29 April 1930, from the Pacific Entomological Survey of Papeete in which they say they have heard that he wants to sell his yacht. But Murnau refused their offer: he wanted to make other journeys and other films among the happy isles. Later the yacht was stolen.

At last Paramount came to the rescue. Flaherty cabled Jesse L. Lasky, Famous Players Lasky Paramount Building, New York City, that he and Murnau would sign an agreement with the company on a fifty-fifty basis after deduction of production costs from the gross amount. A ten-year contract was waiting for Murnau at Paramount: they liked *Tabu*. (Though at the first private showing, without sound, everyone had got up and gone out at the end without a word of encouragement to the director.) So he would be able to make more films among the islands! Murnau was overflowing with ideas: Melville's *Typee* was one of them.

But fate struck. The New York première of *Tabu* was fixed for 18 March 1931. Murnau died on 11 March.

14. Murnau's Death

Murnau's accidental death is also surrounded with legends.

He had wanted to go and visit his mother in Germany, and as was his habit, he consulted a fortune-teller. He was told that he would arrive at his mother's on 5 April, but in a different manner from what he expected. In fact his coffin arrived in Hamburg on a ship of Norddeutsche Lloyd's on the exact day the fortune-teller had predicted.

He had enjoyed talking to Salka Viertel about this forthcoming journey. He always liked doing things elegantly and in the grand manner, and had hired a Rolls Royce to take with him on the boat. Salka Viertel had found a chauffeur for him to take with him. 'But how ugly he is!', said Murnau. It was of no matter, as he had already found himself a handsome young Filipino to drive him in Germany.[1] Salka was partly reassured because in Hollywood, at least, the Rolls Royce was hired with the chauffeur as well.

Murnau was to visit the well-known author, William Morris, at Carmel del Monte, before the première of *Tabu* and his trip to Germany. He was to talk to Morris about the film so that he could write a book about it, and he wanted to discuss his new projects for the cinema.

It was said later that Rose Kearin, Murnau's secretary, had a presentiment and persuaded Murnau to go by car instead of flying; but it is not clear

---

[1] Murnau had once had a very handsome Malay servant when he lived in the Douglasstrasse, Berlin-Grunewald, who had run amok and killed a chambermaid while his employer was absent. The police had to break down part of the house to get at him.

whether it was the journey to Carmel del Monte, or the one to Germany, that she had in mind.

Salka Viertel has told me that Murnau, who was a close friend of the family and always welcome there, came to her house on the morning of 11 March to get some sandwiches for the journey. She was out. The same evening she received a telephone call from a clinic in Santa Barbara: Murnau had had a serious accident. She and her husband Berthold Viertel, and Murnau's secretary Rose Kearin, hurried to Murnau's bedside.

Just after they had filled up with petrol before reaching Santa Barbara, it appeared that the young Filipino had wanted to show Murnau what a good driver he was. The chauffeur of the hired Rolls Royce, who was responsible for the car, at first refused to let him. Murnau said he would take the responsibility.

The young Filipino drove at top speed, a lorry came in the opposite direction, he lost control, a collision was inevitable, and the car hurtled down the bank. The other occupants of the car – the chauffeur, Stevenson the Filipino, Ned Marin, manager of the company that did the synchronization for *Tabu*, even Pal, the German sheepdog – were almost unhurt. But Murnau, who had fallen against a post, had suffered a serious fracture of the skull. . . .

He was still alive when Salka Viertel arrived. His face was drained of colour, and there was dried blood at the corner of his mouth. His eyes still recognized her as she bent over him gently whispering, 'Mur'.

And then she closed the eyes that had so loved to 'see'.

The ancient Greeks represented death as a handsome young man, with the sombre and enigmatic beauty which the young Filipino who drove Murnau to his death no doubt possessed.

Everyone's private life is sacred, and if we here touch in passing on the homosexual tendencies in Murnau which his brother Robert always tried to refute, it is merely because they may explain certain elements latent in his style, and for example certain vagaries of sensibility in *Faust*. Murnau's natural predispositions were as decisive a factor in the subtlety of his art as in his premature death.

Venomous tongues did not fail to set to work in the great Babel of Hollywood.[2] Not many people had the courage to come and bid the great director a last farewell in the funeral parlour on 19 March: the two Viertels, Greta Garbo, George O'Brien, William K. Howard, Thomas Mirande, Edgar Ulmer, Herman Bing, and three others – eleven people in all.

For a long time Greta Garbo kept the death-mask of this man who had been as solitary as she.

[2] See the insinuations mentioned by Kenneth Anger in *Cahiers du Cinéma* and in his book, *Hollywood Babylon*.

Rochus Gliese wrote and told me that by chance he had met in Munich one of Murnau's colleagues who claimed to have witnessed the accident. He and another friend and assistant, Herman Bing, had been following in another car.[3] His tale was rather curious.

Murnau had invited the two colleagues, who had helped him finish *Tabu*, to come to New York with him for the première. But suddenly he told them he'd given up the idea of going right across America by car and would go by sea via Panama. When they expressed surprise at this strange idea, he finally admitted that an astrologer had predicted that some catastrophe would happen on the journey.[4]

According to this account they were driving from Los Angeles to San Francisco to join the boat, when Murnau, who was driving, and for once going more slowly than he usually did, turned the wheel too sharply to avoid a lorry that was approaching in the other direction, and the car went off the road on to the bank. His Filipino driver, who was sitting next to him, was unhurt. But Murnau had been terribly injured, and died in Bing's car on the way to the hospital.

Salka Viertel's account seems more likely to be authentic.

And here are the facts according to the report of the case brought against the Tanner Motors Livery Inc., the car-hire firm from which Murnau had hired, for two days, on 10 March 1931, a Packard (not a Rolls Royce as Salka Viertel thought) to go from Los Angeles to Monterey.

Murnau's mother prosecuted the company on the grounds that the chauffeur of a hired car was not allowed to let anyone else drive, and that in doing so in this case he rendered Tanner Motors responsible for her son's death. The chauffeur, John Freeland, having seen that Murnau's valet, Garcia Stevenson, was a very inexperienced driver (he had had to be told several times not to go so fast), was also culpable, according to the plaintiff, for having done no more about it, but just gone to sleep beside Stevenson.

It emerges from this report that 12 miles outside Santa Barbara, Freeland had bought some petrol and had the tyres tested at the Rio Grande Oil Station at Elwood. When he came back to the car he saw Garcia Stevenson sitting at the wheel. He asked him if he was going to drive. 'The old man told me to,' he answered casually. (It was an irony of fate that for this handsome young man, Murnau, who was only forty-two, and a great artist at the height of his career, was 'the old man' who paid.)

[3] Bing committed suicide a few years later in Hollywood.

[4] The astrologer had said he would lose his life on a car journey, and according to Edgar G. Ulmer, Murnau ordered tickets on a boat via Panama. But in order to get to the port, San Diego, he had to take the fatal car. He is supposed to have said to Ulmer, when the latter wanted him to send the boat tickets back, 'I must cheat fate by going by boat.'

Murnau with Berthold Viertel in Hollywood

Murnau, sitting in the back with his dog, apparently didn't hear this off-hand remark. He just nodded as a sign of agreement.

During the five miles that Garcia was driving, Freeland told him several times 'You'd better slow down', for as he said later, 'He couldn't keep his foot off the throttle.' But Freeland got drowsy and was unable to do anything when he felt the car first skid, then fall down the bank on the left side of the road.

Everyone was thrown out of the car. Murnau was lying 20 feet from the Packard, groaning. The accident happened at five in the afternoon. Murnau, the only person seriously hurt, died during the night.

According to Edgar G. Ulmer the money could not at first be found to have the body embalmed and sent to Germany. Bing went round asking everyone to help. Jannings gave 3,000 dollars, in spite of the fact that he and Murnau had not been on friendly terms for the past few years.

When the coffin had been put on the boat the sailors at first refused to sail with it on board. It was twice taken off the ship before they would agree.

On its arrival at last in Berlin from Hamburg – after all sorts of forms had been filled in and rules and regulations dealt with – a crowd of directors gathered round. The coffin contained a strange sort of image of Murnau, rosy and made-up, like a waxwork from Madame Tussaud's. Carl Mayer, Herlth, Röhrig, Emil Jannings, Erich Pommer, Carl Hoffmann, Fritz Arno Wagner, Rochus Gliese, Fritz Lang, Ludwig Berger, and the film writer Hans Rameau were there. So was Flaherty, who was passing through Berlin. Fox had sent Winfield Sheehan.

Robert Herlth has written an account of the funeral:

One morning in 1931 Carl Hoffmann telephoned to tell me of Murnau's sudden death. I immediately got in touch with Rochus Gliese, who told me there were difficulties over transportation of the coffin because of some questions of inheritance in the United States.

When the coffin at last arrived in Berlin, we assembled in the chapel of the cemetery at Babelsberg. A choir sang, and a minister tried to convince us of the religious devotion of a man he had presumably never met.

I was already stunned by the loss of such a unique person, and all this made me profoundly desperate and depressed. I was trying not to listen to the conventional banalities, when Carl Mayer went up to the coffin to place some roses and say his last farewell.

I was drawing breath and plucking up courage for my own turn to speak, when Fritz Lang stepped forward.

As he said himself, he was Murnau's old adversary, but he now spoke in sincere praise. He described Murnau striding into the studio, always good-tempered, smiling affably, able by his mere presence to kindle enthusiasm. He seemed like some great aristocrat interesting himself in the cinema partly out of curiosity and partly by way of amusement — which was in fact what a lot of people believed. In reality he was a tireless and thorough worker: behind his gaiety was an indefatigable energy that was none the less there because he liked to hide it.

'It is clear,' said Lang, 'that the gods, so often jealous, wished it to be thus. They favoured him more than other men and caused him to rise astonishingly quickly, which was all the more surprising because he never aimed at success nor popularity nor wealth.

'Many centuries hence, everyone would know that a pioneer had left us in the midst of his career, a man to whom the cinema owes its fundamental character, artistically as well as technically. Murnau understood that the cinema, more than the theatre, was called to present life as a symbol: all his works were like animated "ballads", and one day this idea would be triumphant.' And Lang ended with an exhortation: 'Let all sincere creators take the dead man as their example.' 'Aloha oe Murnau', was Lang's last farewell.

I have remembered this speech so clearly because it expressed what I myself felt, and because he who uttered it had an entirely different conception of the art of the cinema.

We stepped forward in silence for a last farewell towards the solid bronze coffin, which seemed so long because Murnau had been so tall.

His face could still be seen through a sheet of glass. The marks of the accident were no longer there: it was an expressionless wax mask, without even that slightly haughty smile behind which he had liked to hide.

The coffin was carried out, a crowd of friends following, led by Erich Pommer, Emil Jannings, Fritz Lang, and Ludwig Berger. It was put down in front of the unfinished chapel.

And so ended the life that after a meteoric rise met with so sudden an end.

Jannings had said nothing: he was rarely so moved. He just stepped forward and gently passed his hand over the glass that covered Murnau's face.

Later he spoke of Murnau, for once without histrionics:

Of all the great personalities of the cinema, Murnau was the most German. He was a Westphalian, reserved, severe on himself, severe on others, severe for the cause. He could show himself outwardly grim, but inside he was like a boy, profoundly kind. Of all the great directors, he was the one who had the strongest character, rejecting any form of compromise, incorruptible. He was a pioneer, an explorer, he fertilized everything he touched, and was always years in advance. Never envious, always modest. And always alone.

His successes and failures both arose from the same source. Each of his works was complete, authentic, direct, logical. If one ever seemed to be cold, it was still fundamentally lit by the fire of his artistic will, which always remained incorruptible. It was harsh and absolute, like Gothic art.

The newspapers said that for lack of money Murnau's coffin remained in a cellar instead of being laid to rest in the Waldfriedhof, the cemetery in the forest of Stahnsdorf. And in the damp atmosphere the corpse, hastily and inefficiently embalmed, was decomposing. . . .

An announcement in *Film Kurier* denied all this. They were waiting for the funeral chapel to be finished, the plot of land had been paid for. Today Murnau lies at rest in the Stahnsdorf cemetery in the Russian zone. It is not easy for his near relatives to visit the grave. According to recent information the sumptuous tomb of the man who was always alone stands deserted on a hump of neglected land. Apparently this too is only legend: for his brother Robert Plumpe was buried in the same place, in the Plumpe family vault.

All that remains is his work. That is still young. Eternal.

Nosferatu
Murnau's own copy of the Script

Murnau's own copy of Henrik Galeen's script for *Nosferatu* was entrusted to me by Robert Plumpe Murnau and has been translated here by Gertrud Mander.

The prime interest of Galeen's script lies in what it has to tell us about script-writing in the Expressionist period. For this reason, in translating it into English an attempt has been made to follow the original syntax, punctuation, and line division as closely as possible. Much of the original, with its oddly-broken lines, looks like blank verse; and we have tried to reproduce this effect. We have followed the original in its prolific use of exclamation marks, words in capitals, and letter-spaced lower-case matter. Most noticeably, we have tried to keep the staccato rhythm of the original, with its incomplete sentences, clauses, phrases, and idiosyncratic punctuation; and we have avoided the temptations of grammatical tidiness or narrative smoothness. In one respect, the liberal use of series of full points (...), we have standardized to three points, and not attempted to follow the apparently arbitrary use, in Galeen's typescript, of any number of points from two to six. We have also italicized speech and quoted passages in the titles.

Murnau scribbled alterations and notes on the typescript in his own hand, and all these amendments appear in the translation in bold type. Where he deleted a word or passage in the original we enclose the deleted portion in square brackets [/]. We have used round brackets (/) where they appear in the original, and also for a few necessary editorial comments, and for Murnau's deletions of his own notes.

There are two features of the script which we have not attempted to reproduce. The first is the repeated use of a roughly drawn grid, rather like a noughts-and-crosses frame, which Murnau used as a working tool for listing the characters, their clothes, and the time of day. The second is the presence throughout the script of Murnau's rough sketches for the sets and camera set-ups. Examples are shown on page 235.

The script begins with a complete list of titles. The main text follows. In the notes at the end I comment upon some points of difference between the script and the film as it survives in the copies known to me.

L.H.E.

List of Titles (*Nosferatu*) **Murnau**

1. *Nosferatu*, a symphony of horror
2. based on the novel *Dracula* by Bram Stoker and freely adapted by Henrik Galeen
3. Direction: F. W. Murnau
4. Costumes and sets: Albin Grau
5. Photography: F. A. Wagner
6. Music: Hans Erdmann
7. Characters:

Count Orlok	Max Schreck
Hutter	Gustav von Wangenheim
Ellen, his wife	Greta Schroeder
Harding, a shipbuilder	G. H. Schnell
Ruth, his sister	Ruth Landshoff
Professor Sievers, municipal doctor	Gustav Botz
Knock, a house agent	Alexander Granach
Professor Bulwer, a Paracelsian	John Gottowt
Captain	Max Nemetz
1st Sailor	Wolfgang Heinz
2nd Sailor	Albert Venohr

8. Act I
9. (Diary) A chronicle of the Great Death in Wisborg in the year 1843 A.D. (Three real crosses are painted under the title.)
10. **Diary.** page 1: Nosferatu. Doesn't this name sound like the midnight call of the death bird? Beware of uttering it, or the pictures of life will turn to pale shadows, nightmares will rise up from the heart and feed on your blood. For a long time I have been meditating on the rise and fall of the Great Death in my home town of Wisborg. Here is the story of it: In Wisborg there lived a man called Hutter with his young wife Ellen.
11. 'Why have you destroyed them . . . the beautiful flowers?'
12. 'Don't be so hasty, my young friend! No one escapes his destiny.'
13. (Diary) There was also a house agent called Knock, the centre of much gossip. Only one thing about him was certain: he paid his people well.
14. 'Count Orlok – His Grace . . . from Transylvania . . . wants to buy . . . a beautiful house . . . in our little town . . .'
15. 'You could make a nice bit of money.'
16. 'It will take some effort, however . . . a few drops of sweat and . . . perhaps . . . of blood.'
17. 'He wants a handsome deserted house . . .'
18. 'That house . . . just opposite yours. Offer him that!'
19. 'Have a quick journey, have a good journey into the country of ghosts.'
20. 'I shall travel far away to the country of ghosts and robbers.'
21. (Diary) Thus Hutter gave the grief-stricken woman into his friends', the rich shipbuilder Harding's and his sister's care.
22. 'Be without fear.'
23. (Diary) page 7: and young Hutter travelled on many a dusty road until finally the peaks of the Carpathian mountains loomed up ahead. The horses were pulling the coach with difficulty.

24. 'Quickly ... my meal – I must go on to Count Orlok's castle!'
25.
26. (Vampire Book) Pentagram
27. (Vampire Book) Of vampires, monstrous ghosts, feats of magic and the seven deadly sins.
28. (Vampire Book) From the seed of Belial came the vampire Nosferatu which liveth and feedeth on the blood of mankind and, unredeemed, taketh his abode in horrible caves, graves and sarcophagi filled with cursed earth from the graveyards of the black death.
28a. (Vampire Book) Pentagram
29. 'Drive on! The sun is setting!'
30. 'Pay whatever you like! We are not going any further!'
31. 'We are not going any further. The other side of the pass is haunted.'
32. (Diary) Hutter had barely crossed the bridge when he was seized by the sinister visions he often described to me later.
33. 'You have let me wait – wait too long. It is almost midnight now. The servants are asleep.'
34. End of Act I.
35. Nosferatu, Act II.
36. 'You have hurt yourself ... Your precious blood!'
37. 'Shall we stay up together for a while, dear sir? It's a long time to go till sunrise and during the day I sleep, my friend, I truly sleep the deepest sleep.'
38. (Diary) As soon as the sun started to rise the shadows of night left Hutter too.
38. (Hutter's letter) Darling! Dearest!
     Do not grieve because your beloved is far away ...
40. (Hutter's letter) ... the mosquitoes are a real pest. I have been stung at the neck by two at once, very close together, one on each side ...
41. (Hutter's letter) One's dreams are heavy in this deserted castle, but do not fear ...
42. (Diary) The ghostly evening light made the shadows cast by the castle appear as if they were alive again.
43. 'Your wife has a beautiful neck ...'
44. 'I shall take the house ... the handsome deserted house opposite yours ...'
45. (Vampire Book) From the seed of Belial came the vampire Nosferatu which liveth and feedeth on the blood of mankind and, unredeemed, taketh his abode in horrible caves, graves and sarcophagi filled with cursed earth from the grave-yards of the black death.
46. (Vampire Book) At night the said Nosferatu sinketh his fangs into his victim and feeds on the blood that constitutes his hellish elixir of life.
46a. Beware lest his shadow turn into a nightmare with horrible dreams.
47. (Diary) At the same hour.
48. 'Ellen!'
49. 'Fetch a doctor ... a doctor!'
50. 'Hutter!'
51. 'Harmless blood congestions!'
52. (Diary) The doctor described to me Ellen's anxiety as if it had been an unknown illness. But I know that in that night her soul had heard the call of the death bird. Already, Nosferatu was raising his wings – yet at dawn Hutter set out to fathom the horrors of his nights.
53. 'Ellen! Ellen!'

54. (Diary) The raftsmen knew nothing about the sinister load they were taking down the valley.
55. End of Act II.
56. Nosferatu. Act III.
57. 'The peasants brought him into the hospital yesterday. They said he had fallen from a mountain. He is still feverish . . .'
58. 'C o f f i n s—'
59. (Diary) page 17 Nosferatu was on the way, danger was afoot for Wisborg. The Paracelsian Professor Bulwer, who was attempting at that time to discover the secrets of nature and its basic principles, told me that the two-masted schooner 'Empusa' had taken on a consignment of coffins filled with earth.
60. 'The schooner is supposed to set out this very night.'
61. (Diary) I must report that during those days Professor Bulwer, the Paracelsian, explained to his students the horrible habits of carnivorous plants. They caught a terrifying glimpse of the deep mysteries of nature.
63. 'Isn't it – just like a vampire!'
64. (Diary) Already, Nosferatu's approach seemed to affect Knock, the house agent.
65. 'The patient who was brought in yesterday has a fit of raving madness.'
66. 'Blood is life! Blood is life!!!!'
67. 'And this one . . .'
68. '. . . a polyp with tentacles . . .'
69. 'transparent . . . almost incorporeal . . .'
70. 'No more than a phantom . . .'
71. 'S p i d e r s ———'
72. (Diary) Ellen was often seen in the lonely dunes on the beach. She longed for her beloved. Her eyes were searching the waves and the distant horizon.
73. (Hutter's letter)
74. (Hutter's letter)
75. 'No, I have to get away . . . reach home by the shortest possible way!'
76. (Newspaper clipping) Plague:
77. 'A sailor has fallen ill below deck. He is talking in a fever.'
78. (Diary) Like an epidemic it spread over the whole ship. The first sailor who had shown the symptoms was followed by the entire crew into the dark grave of the waters. In the light of the setting sun the captain and his first mate said farewell to the last of their companions.
79. 'I shall go down! If I haven't come up again within ten minutes . . .'
80. (Diary) The ship of death had a new captain.
81. End of Act III.
82. Nosferatu. Act IV.
83. (Diary) It is not easy to describe how young Hutter, his energies sadly decimated, managed to surmount the difficulties of his homeward bound journey while Nosferatu's deathly breath swelled the sails of the ship and made it speed towards its destination in ghostly haste.
84. 'I must go to him. He is approaching!!!'
85. 'The master is near . . . The master is near . . .!'
86. (Diary) I have given a lot of thought to the notion that Nosferatu had travelled with coffins filled with earth. Then I read somewhere that vampires draw their shadowy power from the cursed ground in which they are buried.
87. 'I have examined everything – there is no living soul on board!'

88. (Log-book) Varna – July 12. Crew, apart from myself, the captain – one helmsman, one mate, and five sailors. Departing for the Dardanelles.
89. (Log-book) 2nd day: July 13. One sailor has contracted a fever.
    Course: SSW. Direction of wind:
    Third day: July 14. Mate has begun to hallucinate, says a strange passenger is below deck. Course: SE. Direction of wind: NE. Volume of wind: 3.6.
90. (Log-book) 10th day: 22 July. Discovered rats in ship's hold. Danger of plague . . .
91. 'There is a danger of plague! Go home! Shut all your windows and doors!'
92. (Proclamation) All citizens are notified that the honourable magistrate of this town prohibits the moving of plague-suspects into hospitals to prevent the plague from spreading through the streets.
93. End of Act IV.
94. Nosferatu. Act V.
95. (Diary) Hutter had made Ellen promise not to touch the book which had given him such terrifying hallucinations. Yet she was unable to withstand its strange fascination.
96. (Vampire Book)
97. 'This is how I see it – every evening . . .!!!'
98. Panic seized the population. Who was still well? Who already ill?
99. 'I shall run over there quickly . . . I shall get Sievers . . .'
100. (Vampire Book) Wherefore there is no salvation therefrom except that a woman without sin were to make the vampire forget the first crowing of the cock. Of her own free will she would have to give him her blood.

101. The panic-stricken town was looking for a scape-goat. It chose Knock.
102. 'He was seen – he ran away from the house – he strangled the attendant.'
103. 'He strangled him ... the vampire!'
104. 'Bulwer! Fetch Bulwer!'
105. 'Knock has been captured!'
106. 'The master ... the master!'
107. 'The master ... is ... dead.'
108. 'Hutter!'
109. (Diary) page 113   and the miracle shall be told in truth: at that very hour the Great Death ceased and the shadow of the death bird vanished as if it had been overcome by the victorious rays of the living sun.
110. The end.

Characters:

Count Orlok, the Nosferatu	**Schreck**
Thomas Hutter	**Wangenheim**
Ellen, his wife	**Schroeder**
(Lord) Harding, **a shipbuilder**	**Schnell**
Anny, his sister (Ellen's friend)	**Ruth Landshoff**
Professor Sievers, municipal physician	**Botz**
Knock, a house agent (Hutter's employer)	**Granach**
Professor Bulwer, a Paracelsian	**Gronau**
The Carpathian innkeeper	**Herzfeld**
An old servant	
1 Captain	**Nemetz**
3 Mate	**Witte**
2 Helmsman	**?**
4 Sailors	**Venohr**
Doctor	**Hardy von François**
Nurse	
(An old woman)	

(Citizens, sailors, Huzules, Transylvanian Jews and others ...)
(Time – the 1840s.   Place: a small harbour town
Transylvania
and the open sea ...)

I
Act I

Fade-in.	**8 metres location shot: Wismar** Townscape. View over the roofs of a small old-fashioned town built in the style of the 1840s. The sun shines peacefully on pointed gables and leafy squares.
Fade-out.	[**Two shots, one from the church tower onto the town**] **the other from the harbour over towards the town.** **1st: view of Lübeck** **Dissolve to harbour of Wismar.**
Scene (2) **3** Fade-in. Outside a window.	**4 metres 2x** There are flowers in green window-boxes. On the window sill a kitten is playing in the morning sun. With graceful movements she tries to catch a ball that dangles from a thread. Now the ball is being pulled in through the window. The cat jumps in after it.
Scene [3] **4** [Small neat kitchen]	**Ellen's sitting room 7 metres 2x** The morning sun casts the shadow of a window frame onto the floor. Ellen, by the window, is pulling in the thread with the ball, the cat follows it with a leap. Then she puts the little animal on her arm. **Playing with it she sits down on the window sill bathed in sunshine and looks out dreamily.** She squats on the floor opposite the animal and plays with it. Her dressing gown moves in the breeze, her big childlike eyes are laughing.
Scene [4] **3a** A small sitting room (attic)	**20 metres Hutter white jabot blue waist coat** [Poor-looking and tidy. A bed], a chair in period style. Hutter is standing in front of the mirror. He is about to put his jacket on. He pauses to listen, takes a look through the side window. Smiling happily he finishes dressing and goes out.
4a A small flower garden [**in front of Hutter's house**].	**Shot from above. Hutter appears, gardening knife in hand, looks up beaming with joy. He finds a clump of carnations, cuts the flowers with a quick gesture and makes a bouquet.**
Scene 5 (The small kitchen)	**Ellen's room 18 metres 2x** Ellen, still playing with the kitten, hears Hutter coming and jumps up.
[Shot of cooker.	Ellen comes over and begins to busy herself with the saucepans, with a childlike earnestness towards her housewifely duties.]
Shot of door:	Hutter is standing in the door-way and laughs and laughs; **hiding the bouquet behind his back, he laughs and laughs.**
Shot of cooker:	[Ellen turns round, catches sight of her husband and seems a little ashamed that she hasn't yet made breakfast. Now Hutter moves closer to her, looks into the sauce-pan, holds it upside down indicating that it is empty, and looks at her reproachfully.
Title:	*Ellen!*

She is sulking now and trying to placate him. But he pulls out his watch; it is late already; he has to go. He kisses her good-bye, but she calls him back again to confess that she hasn't got any money left to do the shopping. He pulls out his purse with a sad look and holds it up: there is nothing in it! They both sigh. He leaves with a heavy heart. The moment she is alone she takes a small basket of potatoes, which is all she can find, the last resort of the poor housewife, and starts peeling them. A potato drops on the floor, the kitten comes up and plays with it.]

Fade-out.

Long shot: **They are rushing towards each other, Ellen throws herself into Hutter's arms.**
He produces the bouquet,
hands it to her beaming all over his face.
She is touched then, saddening, she takes the flowers
looking at the stems and stroking them. His voice
asks for the reasons of her behaviour.
She says:

Title: *Why have you killed them . . .*
. . . the beautiful flowers?
Hutter is taken aback for a moment.
He apologises and kisses her. Then she forgives
him, they stand in an embrace.

Fade-out. **2x**

Scene 5a   **10 metres   Lauenburg.**
Fade-in.
Street with front gardens.
Title: *Professor Bulwer.*
Professor Bulwer is walking vigorously, yet slowly along the road, enjoying the morning and the sunshine. His stick strikes the ground energetically.
Suddenly he stops and turns round. Who is following him in such haste? Isn't it Hutter? He grasps the passing man by his sleeve; he holds on to it. Hutter greets him, looking pleased. Bulwer laughs and, looking deep into his eyes, says:

Title: *Why so hasty, my young friend? One reaches one's goal soon enough.*
Hutter, of course, doesn't understand him. He has to get to the office quickly. He greets him again and again. Until he manages at last to break free with a laugh and rushes off.
Bulwer stands there for a moment, then he resumes the regular rhythm of his walk.

Scene 6   **6 metres   Caption: Knock – a house agent**
Fade-in.
Dusty cramped office.
Pale light is falling through tiny blind window-panes into the strange room which is eccentrically decorated with bits of old-fashioned furniture. Knock is standing at a high desk. People call him a house agent.

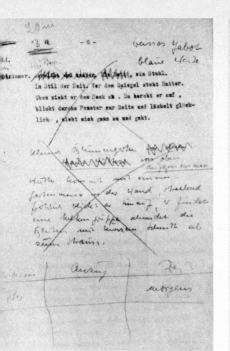
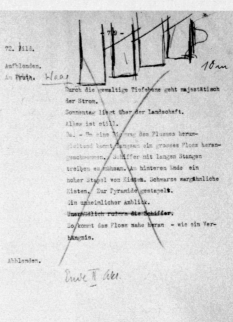
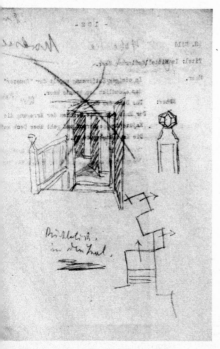
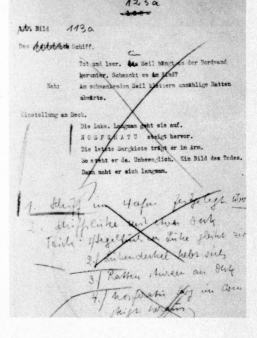

Nosferatu: four pages from the script

Close-up:	Knock's spindly hunch-backed figure. Grey hair, weather-beaten face full of wrinkles. Around his mouth throbs the ugly tic of the epileptic. In his eyes burns a sombre fire. He is reading a letter.
Close-up:	The letter. On a sheet of paper decorated on the margin with grotesque vignettes a medley of intricate and quite illegible signs.
Medium close-up:	Knock seems to be able to make sense of the strange letter, for his ugly mouth sets into an understanding smile. Then he turns and opens a door.
Scene 7	**5 metres**
Small room adjoining the office.	Very narrow and dark, totally without sun. Hutter, buried in files. Knock looks through the door and calls him in. **Another clerk is present.**
Scene 8	**30 metres**
The dusty and cramped office.	Knock and Hutter enter; Knock points to the letter with mysterious gestures and tells Hutter:
Title:	*Count Orlok – His Grace ... From Transylvania ... wants to buy ... a beautiful house ... in our little town.*
Close-up:	Knock's demonic face with wide-open eyes.
Title:	*You could make a nice bit of money ... It will take some effort, however ... a few drops of sweat and [blood] ... **perhaps a little blood.***
Close-up:	In Hutter's face expressions of mounting joy and strange apprehension are fighting each other. Yet joy wins in the end.
Long shot:	Knock digs up an old atlas from the depths of the cabinet and opens it. His finger runs over a page:
Close-up:	The route from England to Transylvania on the map.
Long shot:	Transylvania? asks Hutter, his eyes suddenly shining at the thought of a journey. Yet Knock has turned back to the letter, now reading the back page.
Close-up:	The back page of the letter, covered with the same illegible squiggles.
Long shot:	Knock seems to be able to make sense of this page too, he turns back to Hutter who is already day-dreaming about his journey.
Title:	*He wants a handsome deserted house.*
	For a moment Knock is lost in thought, then he has an idea. He limps over to the window.
Scene 9	**4 metres Window frame, take in Knock**
Section of a window.	View down the street.
Dissolve.	The deserted house. A dilapidated façade. Black and hollow windows. Not a sign of life. Shadows on it.
	Daytime – Sun
Scene 10	**15 metres**
The dusty and cramped office.	Knock walks back from the window and says to Hutter:
Title:	*That house ...*
	just opposite yours. Offer
	him that!

Hutter seems to be a little taken aback, but he rallies round quickly. Knock urges him to set out on the journey at once, hands him some money and documents and pushes him to the door.

Fade-out.
Scene 11
(A room in Hutter's house)
Ellen's room.

18 metres 2x As in scene 8
Ellen is sitting by the window. Now she can see him coming. She waves to him. Her face lights up with joy. She hurries over to the door. Presently Hutter enters. Moved and happy, he puts his arms round her and tells her his great news:

Title:

I shall go on a journey far far away ...
to the country of [blood-red] mountains where
there are bandits and ghosts still.
Ellen is startled. A shadow passes over her forehead. She wants to hold him back. But he is not listening. He has got to pack; already he is leaving her.

Fade-out.
Scene 12
The attic room.
Fade-in.

15 metres Frau Schroeder without shawl saddle bags

Hutter is packing his little travelling bag. Ellen appears in the door behind him. Suddenly she starts to beg him tearfully, entreatingly: Do not go! I am worried about you! But he rejects her remonstrations. Now he has finished packing. He gets up. Ellen, realising that he has made up his mind steps back, resigning herself. But there is fear in her eyes. Seeing her like this he hesitates for a moment. But then he embraces her again with determination, takes up his bag and leaves the room with her.

Fade-out.
Scene 13
(Lord) Harding's park.

15 metres
Hutter, all ready for the journey, takes his leave from Harding and his sister Anny. Ellen, weeping, is supported by Anny.

Close-up:

The two men. Hutter, taking both of Harding's hands and looking deep into his eyes:

Title:

I entrust Ellen to your care.
Harding promises his friend to look after Ellen, she can live here, she will never be alone.

Long-shot of all the characters.

Hutter gives his hand to Anny and then to Ellen. One last farewell kiss. [At this moment her grief is over. As if she had a premonition she says:

Title:

Farewell! There is no escape left.
At first they are all startled by these words.] Then Hutter breaks away. Another farewell, another wave of the hand and Hutter vanishes into the park. Ellen is staring vacantly into the distance.

Scene 14
Square with fountain.

10 metres saddle bags
A number of healthy-looking people are walking about in the sunshine. Tied to the fountain a lonely, saddled horse. Hutter

appears, mounts the horse, gives one last backward look and gallops off.

Fade-out.
Scene 15
Title:

8 metres   Schlesische Hütte
The Carpathian Mountains.
Wild and rocky mountains. Contre jour.

Fade-out.
Scene 16
Outside the Carpathian inn.
Long shot:

Evening
10 metres

The big mail coach drawn by four horses drives up and comes to a halt.

Shot of door of inn:
Shot of coach:
Long shot:

The inn-keeper, a small old Jew, comes out and sees the coach.
Hutter jumps out first. He looks around.
The house. One part brick-walled living area, the other coach house and open stables.

Shot of coach:

In the meantime the other passengers have got out. Long-haired, black Huzules. All identically dressed and of identical appearance like ghosts. They go into the house.

?

The **inn-keeper** has gone up to Hutter and greets him with an inviting gesture.

Shot of coach:

The horses are now unharnessed, the coach is being pushed into the coach-house. Night is falling.

Scene 17
Inside the inn.

8 metres   servant: Frau Kurz
A large smoky room with an enormous tiled stove. A central hanging lamp throws out dazzling light. At tables in the background the passengers. Hutter, who came in last, is standing in the foreground, he looks around and sits down right in front. At once the old servant approaches with a glass and puts it down in front of him. He overcomes a strange anxiety that was brought on by the evening mood in a strange country and puts on a sudden show of liveliness. He knocks on the table and says:

Title:

Quickly, my meal – [and then]
I must be off to Count Orlok's castle.
The servant recoils in horror. The strangely identical-looking passengers, sitting in the background, rise up abruptly to stare at him.

Shot of bar:
Long shot:

The old hunch-backed Jew pricks up his ears.
Hutter looks around in embarrassment, then takes up his glass resolutely and downs it at one gulp.

Scene 18
A grassy slope behind the inn.

4 metres   Walddorfsenke
The ground falls away towards the back. Night mists are creeping up from the valley. The horses are put out here to graze. Suddenly, they raise their heads, as if frightened and, scattering, gallop away.

Scene 19
Inside the inn.
Shot of window:

8 metres

The passengers, seen from behind, are standing by the window, looking out apprehensively. The old servant has not got the

	courage to go up to where they stand and makes the sign of the cross. Hutter stands alone, looking around. He is perplexed and wants to ask what is happening. The old servant comes up to him and whispers into his ear.
Title:	*You mustn't go* *there now, there are wolves about.* *Spend the night here.* Hutter understands and decides to stay.
Fade-out.	
19a	**Hyena**
19b	**Horses, panicking**
Scene 20	**6 metres**
A room at the inn.	A tiny white-washed room with sharp angles: a flickering light from the old servant's candle. Now Hutter enters. She puts the candle down, goes out without a word. Her eyes expressing concern for him. Hutter alone. He goes over to the window, throws it open and looks into the starless night.

(Scene 21 is missing from the script)

Scene 22	**5 metres**
Inside the inn.	The pale passengers, now without Hutter in the enormous room, look frightened. They, too, are listening to the horrible howling. They look at each other and are crossing themselves in terror!
Scene 23	**20 metres**
The tiny white-washed room.	In the light of the candle Hutter, shivering, closes the window. He is no longer sleepy. He walks up and down the room restlessly, stopping in front of a little bookcase.
Medium close-up.	Looking for something to distract him Hutter pulls out a book at random.
Long shot.	He moves back to the candle, sits down on his bed and opens the book. He gets interested in it.
Close-up:	The book's title page: V A M P I R E The page is being turned over. T H E N O S F E R A T U. *From the bloody sins of mankind a creature will be born which will seek revenge for the sin committed by the parents and visited on their children and children's children. Whosoever lusts after blood without reason is under his spell, the spell of the vampire* N O S F E R A T U.
Shot of bed. **Close-up:**	**Hutter, shaking his head, continues reading.** **Book: ...** *grown up on his native soil – from which alone he draws his powers.* Hutter shuts the book, having lost interest. It seems confused to him. He yawns and puts out the candle.
Fade-out.	
Scene 24	**12 metres**
Fade-in.	

The small white room at the inn.	Morning sun is flooding in from the window. Hutter wakes up. Yawning like someone who has slept deeply but not well. He sits up rubbing his eyes. They fall on the book on the bedside table. He reads the title:
Close-up: Normal shot:	V A M P I R E spits on the floor in contempt of the confused rubbish and throws the book playfully into a corner. Then he pauses to listen, goes over to the window to open it. He takes a deep breath of the morning air.
Scene 25	**6 metres Walddorf** The grassy slope in the morning light. Coachmen and grooms are rounding up the horses with long whips and lots of shouting.
Scene 26 The small room.	**5 metres** Hutter steps back from the window. His eyes are laughing, as he turns round. He stretches himself happily; then he takes off his shirt, goes over to the washstand, pours water over his body. He has a proper wash.
Scene 27 In the yard.	**Dolny Kubin** The old servant, mother to all animals, throws corn to her chickens. There are sparrows, too. Everything is bathed in sunlight.
Scene 28 Outside the inn.	**10 metres** The bustle of departure. The horses are in harness. The passengers have got into the coach. Now, in the morning light, one can see their differences. They are much less uniform than they had seemed the previous nightfall. They are chattering noisily to the people who are staying behind and with the peasants and nosy children who are gathered around the coach.
Close-up:	The coachman is about to climb onto his seat, but the small Jewish inn-keeper holds him back: one passenger is missing. They look up to the windows; angry about the delay the coachman cracks his whip a few times.
Shot of inn:	Hutter appears in an upstairs window, still only half-dressed; he gives a wave: I am coming. And disappears again.
Shot of door: Shot of coach:	Hutter comes rushing out with his travelling bag. He climbs to his seat on the coach-box, the horses start moving.
Scene 29 Outside the inn.	The Huzules take off their hats. The children are waving. The old servant has joined them. God bless the travellers. May he guard them against evil spirits. They stretch out their hands as if warding them off.
Medium close-up: Fade-out.	Hutter breaks into loud laughter.
Scene 30 A Mountain range. Long-range shot:	**12 metres Westerheim** In the distance a steep path cutting through the wild scenery, on it the mail coach creeping slowly upwards.

Scene 31	**10 metres road to the Schlesische Hütte**
The mail coach.	
Medium close-up:	The mail coach is moving into the setting sun.
Medium close-up:	A coach window. [An old woman] **Hutter** leans out, giving the coachman a push with an umbrella.
Title:	*Drive on!*
The sun is setting.	Next to her another old woman, identical looking. She is staring into the abyss. Now the first one turns to look in the same direction: two identical faces.
Scene 32	**4 metres View from Schlesische Hütte**
A rocky gorge.	Wisps of mist are rising and falling in the last rays of the setting sun. Patches of sun and shade.
Fade-out.	
Scene 33	**10 metres Close to Arler Hütte**
Title:	At the crossroad.

[A carved madonna casts a long shadow across the road. Behind it an old woman on her knees, deep in prayer. She lifts her head and looks down the road.] The mail coach approaches, the horses are pulling with difficulty, breathing hard. She seems to ask herself: do they want to drive to the haunted castle? and gets into the middle of the road to warn them off. The mail coach stops. Hutter gets off the coach box. Now he stands at the crossroad. The passengers are anxious to move on, gesturing violently to him not to take the left fork. But Hutter disregards their shouting. He waves farewell with his hat and walks briskly off.

33a	**Hutter walking past the carved madonna.**
Scene 34	**8 metres Vratna Pass**
Distant mountains.	View through the cut made into the rock by the road into the far distance. In the background the fantastic castle of Count Orlok in the evening light. One can see a steep road leading straight up into the sky. Something comes racing down. A coach? A phantom? It moves with unearthly speed and disappears behind a ground-swell.

1) Castle Orlok, dissolve with	
2) Steep road between	
boulders	
Scene 35	**4 metres Near Schlesische Hütte**
At the crossroad.	
Angle as in Scene 33:	Mortally frightened, the coachman beats his horses. [The old woman has disappeared as if swallowed up by the ground.] Astonished, Hutter follows the vanishing coach with his eyes. He is all alone now, standing like this for a while. Then he pulls himself together and walks resolutely along the road on the left.

Fade-out.	
Scene 36	**Vratna Pass**
Fade-in.	
Carpathian virgin	The trees are casting long shadows on the forest path.
forest.	Hutter appears.

He halts: what's that? Something comes racing up, turns round as if moved by a hidden force and moving jerkily. Stops dead. Hutter likewise. A black carriage. No wheels? Two black horses – griffins? Their legs are invisible, covered by a black funeral cloth. Their eyes like pointed stars. Puffs of steam from their open mouths, revealing white teeth. The coachman is wrapped up in black cloth. His face pale as death. His eyes are staring at Hutter. Raising his whip he makes an inviting, almost commanding gesture. He waits. Hutter cannot rally enough strength to follow the invitation. Yet those eyes assert their power. Step by step, as if pulled by invisible threads, Hutter approaches the uncanny creature. He gets into the carriage. It reverses quick as lightning, dashes off and disappears.

Scene 37
A fairy-tale forest.

5 metres   At the Vratna Pass, behind Tyer Hora

Empty. By the roadside a wise, man-sized raven. Its shoulders hunched up. It turns its head listening. Then takes two hops forward and looks down the road. Who's coming? The familiar vehicle sweeps up and past. A young man, holding on desperately, sits inside, looking terrified. [It] **The raven** follows him with mocking eyes behind glasses. **Coach drives at top speed through a *white forest*!**

Scene 38
Long shot of a snakelike bend.

5 metres

[Valley] Deserted lane. Only a lonely twisted willow-tree with a straggly top can be seen. Again, the carriage races past. Like an ancient man who has been disturbed in his rest the tree looks after the vehicle with blank eyes. Isn't there a grin on its mouth?

Drive over stone bridge across deep gorge.

15 metres   Poczamok

Scene 39
Count Orlok's castle.
39a

The arch of a gate in the shade. The silhouette of the carriage drives underneath it at a sharp angle and disappears in the moonlit spacious castle yard.

Shot of castle yard:
Medium close-up:

The porch. The carriage stops in front of it. Almost in a faint, Hutter slides down. As if in a whirlpool, the carriage circles round him and disappears. Hutter turns round and follows it with his eyes. He stands in front of the closed gate, holding his bag.

39b

Then, very very slowly the two wings of the gate open up. Somewhere far back in the dark corridor a man can be seen standing motionless. He is holding a candle which lights up his chalkwhite face. He is waiting. Who is that? Hutter bounds up the two steps and stands in the doorway. He would still like to go back. Yet it is too late now. Hesitantly he walks towards the stranger. Behind him the gates close.

Fade-out.

End of Act I

Act II

Scene 40 **Hall.** Medium close-up:	In the centre Orlok, the candle in his hand. The walls of the hall are plunged in darkness from which Hutter's back emerges. He faces the motionless figure. Is this pale, ghostly creature with hollow eyes and thin mouth the lord of the castle himself?
Close-up:	The face twists into a polite grimace. Sharp ratlike teeth appear over the lower lip.
Medium close-up:	They are now face to face. It must be the count for this is no servant's gesture with which he now takes hold of his visitor's bag.
Title:	*The servants are asleep.* *It is **almost** [after] midnight.* Hutter's clenched fingers let go. Bag in hand, Orlok turns round. He holds up the candle and walks ahead. Hutter follows.
Scene 41 **Gallery of ancestors' portraits.** Medium close-up:	One of the castle owner's ancestors, frontal view. [For centuries he has been asleep like this with his eyes closed. Now something approaches. His eyes begin to move.] Two figures are passing: Orlok and his visitor.
Long-shot panorama:	He follows them with his eyes. They walk close to the wall where portrait follows portrait. **Omitted.**
Scene 42 **Dining room.**	**25 metres** Gigantic dimensions. In the centre a massive Renaissance table. Somewhere in the distance a fire place. Flanked by two armoured figures. Black and motionless. In olden times, this must have been used by knights for their drinking bouts. Are these things their armour? Is that long line that runs across the wall a crack in the old structure? Or a lance left hanging there? Suddenly, Hutter notices that the count is waiting. Quickly he hands him the plans of the deserted house and Knock's letters. With a smile Orlok takes them and begs him to take a seat. The meal is waiting. Hutter sits down. Orlok lifts up the papers and studies them.
Close-up:	Orlok reading. The back page of the letter shows a confusion of numbers, legible and illegible letters. The holy number seven is repeated several times. In between, cabbalistic signs. The spindly fingers holding the letter cover up the rest like claws.
Close-up:	Hutter is spell-bound, his eyes wide-open.
Close-up:	Over the top margin of the letter Orlok's eyes appear. He is looking over to Hutter like a snake about to hypnotize its victim.
Close-up:	Hutter eating. He puts a morsel into his mouth. He lifts up his eyes. His look turns into a stare. He is unable to swallow.

Long shot:	The hall with the halo of light in the centre; the figures are looming above the table.
Close-up:	An antique clock with a pendulum. A hammer strikes the hour. The big hand points to 12 o'clock.
Medium close-up:	Hutter staring into space as if transfixed. After the twelfth stroke he drops his knife and fork. The knife grazes his hand, it is bleeding.
Medium close-up:	Quick as lightning the count rushes up to him offering his help. He prevents Hutter from wiping off the blood. The knife might have been poisoned. [The sticky blood should be removed from the cut.] His lips are sucking at the hand [hastily]. Frightened, Hutter pulls away his hand from his grip. He moves backwards **towards the fireplace.**
Medium close-up:	By the fireplace. The count is polite; he has lost his ghostlike appearance. He is asking for something in a friendly, almost sad manner.
Title:	*Shall we stay up together* *for a little while? It's a* *long time to go till sunrise . . .* *And during the day I am always out and about.* The count sits down. And Hutter cannot resist his chivalrous manner. He sinks back into the massive chair.
Scene 43 Fade-in. The same hall.	**18 metres**
	Hutter wakes up in the large armchair near the fireplace. He can hardly remember the events of the night. The armchair opposite seems to be empty. But there is light on it. Hutter's gaze wanders across the hall over to the window.
Shot of window:	It is very high and divided up into small panes. Morning light is streaming in.
Shot as before:	An old-fashioned window. An ancient hall, very dusty. Nothing strange about it. Hutter yawns. His eyes fall on the cut in his hand and he remembers a few more things. What has he got on his neck? He touches his throat. Must have been mosquitoes. A mirror! His bag is nearby on the floor. He takes out his mirror and looks at his neck.
Close-up: Normal close-up:	The mirror shows two red spots on his neck, very close together. Why should he worry about a few little spots? he thinks and puts the mirror away. He yawns once more. But suddenly he stops. What's this? He looks at the table, astonished.
Close-up:	A still-life of food: fruit, a joint, all kinds of gastronomic delicacies.
Normal:	He is overjoyed. He rushes over to the table and begins to eat as if he were starved.
Scene 44 The dilapidated terrace. ?	**22 metres Poczamok** Still eating, Hutter steps out into the sunlight. He looks around, seeming relaxed. He holds a sheet of paper and a **pencil** in his hands. Then he casts about for a suitable place and, leaning against the stone wall, he begins to write a letter.

Close-up:	The beginning of the letter: *My dearest, my only one* . . .
Normal:	Hutter stands upright, looking at the clouds. Why does that stupid mosquito buzzing round his nose stop him from concentrating? He catches it quickly. And now he knows how to continue. He puts pencil to paper again:
Close-up:	Part of the letter: *. . . the mosquitoes are a real pest. I have been stung at the neck by two at once, very close together, one on each side* . . .
Long shot:	Hutter continues writing.
Scene 45	**14 metres Poczamok**
Forest near the castle.	A man on horseback is approaching. He stops occasionally and peers over to the castle as if he were scared of it.
Outside the porch.	Hutter stands there, waving with the letter. The rider comes up cautiously and takes the letter without dismounting. Then he dashes off at a gallop showing signs of great fear.
Scene 46	**15 metres**
Fade-in.	
Dining room.	Orlok is sitting by the fireplace bent over some plans. Hutter is standing behind him. Orlok shows more interest in the young man than in the papers lying in front of him. Looking over his shoulder he asks for some more information. Hutter rummages among the papers in his bag. A little picture falls on the table. He wants to hide it quickly, yet Orlok was quicker. He has picked it up and is looking at it.
Close-up:	A miniature portrait of Ellen.
Medium close-up:	Orlok asks about the person in the picture. And Hutter is forced to answer him.
Close-up:	Orlok's eyes open wide. His lips look even thinner than before. Contemplating the picture he whispers:
Title:	*What a beautiful throat your wife has* . . .
Medium close-up:	Hutter is breathing hard. The fear which grips him in the count's presence is replaced by a sudden fear for his wife. He forgets himself and reaches for the miniature. For the first time he touches Orlok's body. The count jumps up. He raises himself to his full height with triumphant determination and a glazed look in his eyes, and says, anticipating the horrors to come with pleasure:
Title:	*I shall buy the house* . . .
	The handsome deserted house opposite yours . . .
	Quickly, he takes up the contract and signs it. He hands it back to Hutter. Hutter bows uneasily and retires. Orlok watches him go, a satanic look has come into his eyes. His hands have turned into claws.
	Hutter takes his bag with him
Fade-out.	
Scene 47	**15 metres**
Fade-in.	**A candle is burning**
A small room in the castle.	Hutter is standing in the middle of the room, quite dazed. He shakes off his misgivings. He decides to leave to-morrow. He

245

	kisses the picture and starts to undress, when to his amazement he discovers a book in his pocket. The old book from the inn. Did the inn-keeper's wife put it there? Mechanically, he opens it.
Close-up:	The book.
	Chapter II.
	Night is the vampire's element.
	He can see in the dark
	which is a wonderful ability to have in this world,
	half of which is night.
	We humans, however, are helpless and blind at night . . .
Normal:	Hutter shuts the book. A horrible thought has occurred to him. He is feverish. Is it this book, these ancient walls which make him believe in the existence of ghosts? Did not the count seem to have vampire-like claws and rat's teeth? He jumps up, first running, then sneaking to the door.
Scene 48	**4 metres**
Dining hall.	
View from door deep into the dining hall.	By the fireplace Count Orlok, no, not Orlok but a gigantic vampire, a motionless, sombre watcher in the night.
Medium close-up:	He looks at Hutter with a fixed gaze.
Scene 49	**6 metres**
The small room.	
Shot of door:	Hutter. He supports himself against the doorpost. A terrible realisation has dawned on him. Shut the door, shut it quickly! There is no bolt. No lock. He looks around, puts the heavy oak-chair against the door. Is it possible to escape?
Medium close-up:	Window. Hutter rushes up and flings it open.
Scene 50	**3 metres Tegeler Forest**
	Night. Undergrowth. A pack of wolves, raising their heads, howling.
Scene 51	**8 metres**
The small room.	
Long shot:	Hutter falls on his knees by the side of the bed. Hands clutching the bedclothes, he stares at the door behind which the horror is waiting.
	What is this?
Medium close-up:	Moved by an invisible hand the door opens to half its width in one single jerk.
Long shot:	Hutter. Terrified, he covers his eyes with his arms, pulls at the bedclothes and shields his eyes. He mustn't see it. He mustn't look!
Fade-out.	
Scene 52	**6 metres**
Title:	The same night.
Ellen's bedroom at the Hardings'.	Ellen wakes up suddenly. She has been dreaming. As if she had seen a vision . . . She has a premonition of danger . . . Now she gets up. Moves over to the window and steps out on to the balcony.

Scene 53 Harding's study.	**6 metres** Night. Harding is sitting at his desk. He hears a noise. Rushes out. **Picture of ?ung** **12 metres**
Scene 54 Ellen's bedroom. Medium close-up of door leading to the balcony. Title:	Ellen is perching on the edge of the balcony. Harding rushes into the room. Discovers that the bed is empty. He shouts: 'Ellen!' *Ellen!* He catches sight of the sleepwalker at the moment when, woken up by his shouts, she loses her balance and falls over. He runs up to her and gathers her in his arms. He carries her over to the bed. A servant, alerted by the noise, appears in the door. A doctor! shouts Harding. The servant disappears.
Scene 55 Fade-in. The small castle room. Long shot:	**6 metres** Hutter in bed, tense and doubled up. Slowly, Nosferatu creeps up on him. Irresistible, he bends over the terrified and helpless man and buries his fangs in his throat.
Fade-out. Scene 56 Fade-in. Ellen's bedroom. Long shot: Title: Long shot:	**7 metres** Ellen shouts: *Hutter!!!* Ellen in bed ... in delirium. Anny is kneeling by her side. A doctor, Professor Sievers, is taking her pulse. Harding. Ellen trembles like a wounded bird. She doubles up, throws herself about and retreats into a corner of the bed.
Scene 57 The small castle room. Medium close-up: Long shot:	**8 metres** Night. NOSFERATU turns his head. He is listening intently as if he could feel – hear the **terrified** shouting in the distance. NOSFERATU moves away from Hutter's bed. He [dissolves into the air] **leaves the room.**
Scene 58 Ellen's bedroom. Medium close-up: Title: Fade-out.	**8 metres** Ellen is calming down slowly. Her terror turns into apathy. Breathing weakly. She settles back listlessly into her pillows. Sievers can tell the improvement from the pulse-rate and says to Harding *Normal congestions of the blood ... caused by an awkward position during sleep ...* He has assumed an academic air. His beard trembles in his eagerness.

Scene 59

3 metres   Poczamok
Behind a pointed gable of the castle the sun is rising slowly.

Fade-out.
Scene 60   **7 metres**
Fade-in.
The small castle room.   The light of dawn is falling through the window as through a sky-light and moving along the wall until it reaches Hutter's face, looking half-fainting, half asleep.
Suddenly he wakes up.
He starts up and clutches his throat. He jumps out of bed, clenching his fists, runs over. To the door. Carefully ... he looks out.

Scene 61   **6 metres**
Dining hall.   Daytime.
The room is empty ... Hutter, pale and hollow-eyed, staggers in. He looks around ... nothing. Shaking his head, fists clenched with wild determination, he drags himself forward.

Scene 62   **6 metres**
Portrait gallery with flight of   Hutter is dragging himself along with difficulty. He goes down
stairs.   a few stairs. At the end of the corridor he finds a door. He opens it.

62a. A curving gallery, ex-   Hutter opens one door after the other.
terior.
Scene 63   **15 metres**
A vault.   Empty and dark.
In the centre of the darkness a black coffin. Hutter has pushed the door open and enters. He starts back. He stares without understanding. Fear grips him. But he must make certain. Trembling heavily, he lifts up the coffin lid. He recoils in horror. Dropping the lid, he retreats into the darkest corner. For inside the coffin he has seen, black and long, the lifeless body of NOSFERATU. Horror-stricken, Hutter almost collapses. Then he rushes out.

Fade-out.
Scene 64   **3 metres   Poczamok   Vratna Pass   Tatra**
Fade-in.
Sunset.   Between a line of bizarre tree-trunks evening approaches like a ghost . . .

Fade-out.
Scene 65   **6 metres**
Fade-in.
(A niche inside the castle)   **The small castle room.**
Hutter is crouched on the floor. His body is twisted with fear. His hair is standing on end ... his eyes are staring. Suddenly, he starts up and listens. Can he hear a noise in this desolate place? Could it mean his salvation? With difficulty, he drags his weakened body over to the window.
Window frame for out-door shot.
Scene 66   **3 metres   Poczamok**

The walls of the castle seen from outside.	Hutter stares from a window. He refuses to believe what he sees.

The crossbar of a window

[12] 6 metres   Poczamok

Scene 67
Castle yard

One can see a low-wheeled cart with the two fantastic horses harnessed to it. And now:
is it a shadow? A ghost? Nosferatu. He is moving to and fro, to and fro. From the cart to the castle. And back again. Carrying boxes. Black coffinlike boxes. From the back door of the castle to the carriage. He piles them up. Box on box. Into a gigantic pyramid. All this happens at an uncanny speed.

Scene 68
Part of the castle wall.

3 metres   Poczamok
Hutter, staring at the phantom with glazed eyes.

Scene 69
Castle yard.

6 metres   Poczamok
The carriage is now loaded. Suddenly the phantom jumps on to the topmost box and disappears inside it. Instantly the horses dash off with the cart at lightning speed. The big gate closes behind them with a bang.

Scene 70
The small castle room.
Title:

8 metres
Hutter jumps back from the window.
Ellen!

NOSFERATU is on his way, Ellen is in danger. He has to hurry. Save Ellen. Ellen! Ellen! Suddenly, he starts tearing [down the wallhangings] **up the bedclothes**. He tears them, making long pieces and knotting them into a rope.

Fade-out.
Scene 71
An abyss.

coat

10 metres   Poczamok
Hutter, dangling from a window in the castle walls on a rope. But the rope is too short.
Beneath him, the abyss still opens up.
And yet he risks the drop – dead or alive.

Medium close-up:

So he hurls himself down. Hutter is lying at the bottom of the abyss, between trees and boulders. Tossing and turning in fever and pain. So he tries to lift himself up. But pain seizes him again. Then he faints.

Hutter coat

Scene 72
Fade-in.
By the river [Pruth]
Waag.

10 metres

The river flows majestically through the immense plain.
The scenery is bathed in sunshine.
All is peaceful.
Then a large raft appears round a bend in the river and floats slowly into view. Boatmen with long poles are pushing it with considerable effort. At the stern a high pile of boxes. Black, coffinlike boxes. Stacked into a pyramid. An uncanny sight. [Indefatigably, the boatmen go on punting.] The raft is coming closer and closer – like doom.

Fade-out.

End of Act II

Act III

Scene 73 Title: Hospital ward.	**12 metres** A Budapest hospital. A long line of white beds. In a bed in the foreground, Hutter. In bandages . . . his eyes closed. The doctor comes to him now. He examines him. Questions the nurse. She tells him about the case:
Title:	*He was brought in yesterday by Huzules who said he had fallen down a mountain. He is still feverish . . .* As the doctor continues his examination Hutter wakes up, opens his eyes. There is fear in his feverish look still. The nurse hurries up to him to hold him. Yet he crawls away to the end of the bed. Spreads out his hands to defend himself. Suddenly his eyes go dead. He collapses. His lips are murmuring something . . . The doctor bends over to hear what he is saying.
Close-up: Title: Medium close-up: Fade-out. Scene 74 Fade-in. The port of Varna.	Hutter, muttering to himself *Coffins———* Doctor and nurse look at each other without understanding. **18 metres** At the quayside, ready for loading, and next to other cargo, the pile of black coffins. Customs officials are examining the letter- ing and papers. They are approaching the boxes.
Close-up:	The customs inspector questions the official who accompanies him about the boxes. The man searches among the papers and hands over the freight letters to his boss.
Close-up:	Freight letter. *Mixed cargo, from Varna to Whitby.* *Content: garden soil for experimental purposes.*
Normal shot:	The inspector smiles incredulously. He orders a search!! Barefooted dock-workers drag up one of the apparently very heavy boxes, heaving and swearing. The inspector gives an order. They open the lid with difficulty. There is **earth** [sand] inside! The inspector gives another order: turn it out! The workers obey. [Sand is falling out] . . . nothing but [sand] **earth**. Satisfied, the inspector turns to another pile of cargo. Yet in the sand . . . something moves violently . . . something is alive . . . jumps out . . . horrible animals . . . rats!! One of the dock-workers, who bends over to scoop the scat- tered sand back, hits out violently. Did not one of the animals . . . reeling from the blow . . . bite his foot?

Long shot:	The big **hand pulley** [steam crane] hauls up one of the boxes and drops it into the belly of the sailing-boat that is anchored at the quay. At the ship's stern one can discern a name, underneath the baroque figure head: DEMETER.
Scene 75	**12 metres**
Title:	*Professor Bulwer, a Paracelsian, explains the nature of carnivorous plants to his students.*
The institute.	
Medium close-up:	Professor Bulwer, surrounded by a few students, quiet and simple people. They are listening to his lecture. Now he points emphatically to a plant with a very strange shape.
Close-up:	A flower. Its petals reaching out like tentacles. Motionless. Now. An insect. Hovering, attracted by the scent . . . settles on the colourful calyx. There in a flash the tentacles have gripped it. The insect is caught. Its struggling is in vain. With irresistible force the flower has drawn it into the recesses of the calyx . . .
Medium close-up:	Bulwer pointing at the flower. Slowly his lips are moving:
Title:	*Isn't it like a vampire??*
Scene 76	**6 metres**
Title:	**Dr Sievers.**
Medical laboratory.	Professor Sievers turns away from his bench. Because the attendant has entered and seems alarmed.
Title:	*The patient who came in yesterday has had an attack.*
	At once, Sievers follows the attendant who leads the way.
Scene 77	**12 metres**
Lunatic's cell.	Sievers and the attendant stop short at the doorway. Straining their eyes to see into the semi-darkness. There, in the corner. Something moves slowly. It is a man. Now his face is in the light. Like a panther preparing to leap, his ferocity restrained, he raises himself up slowly. His crazed burning eyes staring at Sievers. And now we recognise him at last . . . it is Knock!!! Suddenly, in one leap, he is at the window. Sievers is startled, says something to the attendant. Who prepares the straitjacket he brought along. Yet the expected attack does not come. Knock remains at the window, arms jerking, he begins . . . to catch flies which he puts into his mouth. Horrible food. The madman's face twists into a grin that resembles distant lightning. His swollen lips are murmuring something:
Title:	*Blood is life! Blood is life!!!!*
	Suddenly, the madman starts up and throws himself with all his might on the unsuspecting Sievers. Who can barely ward him off. But the attendant comes to his help quickly and throws the straitjacket over the raging man's head.
Scene 78	**8 metres**
The Institute.	Bulwer, in a quiet, scholarly manner with his students. He points to an aquarium.
Close-up:	On a piece of rock in the water hangs a small polyp. Now it

stretches out its tentacles, grabs a small fish and pulls it up to its mouth. It is almost transparent, colourless and of a jelly-like consistency.

Close-up: Bulwer's face. He is talking.

Title: *And this one . . . a polyp with tentacles . . .*
transparent . . . almost incorporeal . . .
almost a phantom. **3 titles**

Scene 79   **8 metres**

Lunatic's cell.   On the floor, in his straitjacket, whining pitifully, mad Knock.

Close-up: His face. Turning his sad eyes upwards. He notices something there. His lips form a word:

Title: *Spiders . . . !*

Close-up: A spider-web with a live spider which clutches, vampire-like, an insect and is sucking its blood.

Normal: Knock in exultation.
Sievers stands motionless . . . does not understand.
Brusquely, he gives an order and leaves.

Fade-out.

Scene 80   **4 metres**

Fade-in.

The graveyard of Whitby.   View from the pier-head towards the shore. In the foreground the surging sea. Further back, where the shore rises steeply, the graveyard of Whitby.

Closer: The graveyard. Afternoon light. In front of the graveyard [a long row of benches. People are strolling up and down looking out on to the sea . . . sitting on the benches and enjoying the view.]

Medium close-up: A bench, somewhat apart from the others. Ellen is sitting there. Dreamily, her eyes searching a distant country beyond the sea. She seems to be wrapt in an anxious day-dream about her distant lover. Now she shuts her eyes, because tears are welling up.

Scene 81   **4 metres**   **Croquet?**

In Harding's park.   Harding, youthful and athletic, is batting. The shuttlecock(**??**) flies high up into the air. Anny, in a light dress, shouts with joy . . . catches it . . . throws it back. The shuttlecock flies backwards and forwards. It is a picture of health and light.

Scene 82   **6 metres**

At the park gates.   The postman, a small old man, rummages in his leather bag and produces a letter which he hands with an air of importance to Harding's servant who is as old and wizened as he. Before he leaves, the postman points to the stamp which seems to be of special value, lifting his eyebrows: This letter has travelled far . . . it comes from a very remote country. The two old men bend over the rare letter.
Then the old servant takes it in.

Scene 83   **6 metres**

In the park.   As the servant approaches, Harding and Anny stop playing. Anny takes the letter, reads the address and runs to her brother. It is for Ellen, she says, pointing into the distance.

Shall we take it to her straight away? Harding agrees, they hand their rackets over to the servant and walk off.

3 metres

Scene 84
At the graveyard.
Medium close-up:

Ellen is still sitting there, looking over the vast waters, lost in her sad longing thoughts.

Scene 85
The sea.

3 metres   Heligoland
Distant view over the sea. A sand bank skirted by rocks, jutting out into the surf waters.

Scene 86
At the graveyard.

12 metres
Harding and Anny are approaching. They are joining the lonely Ellen, shaking hands and trying to cheer her up. Guess what we have brought you! They show her the letter. Ellen trembles. She takes the letter quickly and tries to open it. But her hands are too weak. Does she foresee disaster? Looking pained, she gives the letter to her friend. Open it! I cannot do it. Gladly and quickly, Anny takes over. You'll see, he is safe and sound and sends you good news. She starts to read it, gives a joyful laugh, she was right. All is well. The worries were unfounded. Happily she gives Ellen the letter.

But barely has she read the letter when Ellen's face assumes an expression of hurt certainty. Does she derive evil premonitions from these lines?

Close-up:

The letter.
. . . the mosquitoes are a real pest. I have been stung on the neck by two at once, very close together, one on each side . . .

Normal:

Ellen's face is distorted as if she were suffering physical pain. Harding and Anny are perplexed.

Scene 87
Title:
The port of Galaz at night.

GALAZ
The 'Demeter' is anchored off the jetty. Nobody is about on the quay. A stormy night, strange uncertain light. Suddenly – a gentle movement from the ship down the gangway to the shore . . . rats . . .

Fade-out.

The coffins are reloaded
Omitted

Scene 88
The hospital at Budapest.

10 metres
Hutter, dressed, stands in front of his bed. He looks pale and weak still, yet full of resolution. The nurse notices his unsteady stance. She fusses around him. You ought to stay a few more days! Have some more rest! But he wards her off. His gestures are restless and fluttering, a strange force has taken possession of him.

Title:

I have to get home by the shortest possible way!!
So he says goodbye, disregarding the nurse's advice, thanks her for her care and goes out quickly.

Scene 89
Title:
The port.

Constantinople.
Night. Wild dogs are barking from the debris in the street up to the distant firmament, writhing in the mud like snakes.

253

Nosferatu

Focus on quay:	The 'Demeter' at anchor. What's scuttling over there? ... A shadow from the ship to the land ... rats ... one ... four ... ten ... an endless stream ... they carry terror with them. **Omitted.**
Scene 90	**8 metres Polnischer Kamm Non-stop rain** **Entry to the Vratna Gorge**
Title:	In the Hungarian plain.
Coach station in the Pussta.	The mail coach is arriving at top speed. The coachman whips his exhausted horses into a last effort. The coach has barely stopped when Hutter jumps off. He calls for more speed. Now fresh horses are being brought along. Hutter joins the grooms and tells them to hurry on! To hurry on! The tired horses have been taken out of harness and are being led to the stable. Bring fresh horses! Hutter gives a helping hand. Now the straps are done up. The coachman blows his horn. Some late-comers appear. They get into the coach, Hutter is the last. And the heavy coach rumbles off, the horses galloping, sparks flying from the hooves, dust rising, into the pathless country.
Fade-out.	**Hutter leads a limping horse through heroic** (illegible)
Scene 91	
Fade-in.	
The port of Constantinople.	
Long shot.	In a fresh breeze, the 'Demeter' emerges from the confusion of mast-heads and gains the open sea. **Omitted** **15 metres**
Scene 92	
Lunatic's cell.	In a stupor, Knock is perching on his bunk. The attendant, holding a broom, is about to leave the cell. At this moment Knock lifts his eyes. With a look of artful cunning and with rigid concentration he follows the attendant's movements. Now, he seems to have discovered an opportunity; softly, he sneaks up on the unsuspecting man and takes away the newspaper that sticks out of his pocket. The attendant does not notice and shuts the door behind him. The moment Knock is alone he unfolds the paper [trembling with expectancy] and starts reading [searching for something] with wide-open eyes. [Now he has found what he was looking for. He is riveted to this passage:]
Close-up:	The Newspaper. PLAGUE *In Transylvania and in the Black Sea ports of Varna and Galaz a plague epidemic has started. Young women in particular fall victim to it in large numbers. All the victims show the same peculiar wound marks on the neck whose origin is still an enigma to the doctors.* *The Dardanelles have been closed to all ships suspected of carrying the epidemic. [It is out of the question that the epidemic will reach Western Europe.]*

Medium close-up:	Knock's mocking, triumphant face assumes an expression of demonic grandeur. He straightens himself up, lifts up his head, raises his arms as if greeting the evil.
Scene 93	**8 metres North Sea**
Title:	[The Mediterranean] **Open sea.**
Sea.	In the distance, the 'Demeter' sailing through the waters gleaming in the evening light.
Dissolve. Medium Close-up:	The ship's deck.
	The ship's mate is running up the companion-way in great agitation and crosses the deck on his way to the captain's cabin.
Scene 94.	**8 metres**
In the captain's cabin.	The captain of the 'Demeter' bent over maps, making entries in the log-book. The mate enters and reports excitedly:
Title:	*Below deck a sailor has fallen ill.*
	He is talking in a fever.
	The captain looks up, shocked. He leaves his work and follows the mate.
Scene 95	**12 metres**
Below deck.	In the background the ship's hold. Among other cargo in the deep darkness the coffins. To be seen through an open door. In the foreground the crew's cabin with hammocks. In one of them the delirious sailor.
Medium close-up:	Captain and mate go up to the patient who stares at them as if they were ghosts. He seems to listen intently. Every noise makes him start.
Shot of hold:	Brooding, intense darkness. The lid of one of the coffins seems to open a little . . .
Medium close-up:	The captain, more angry than concerned, advises the patient in his uncouth sailor's way to have a strong drink.
	Promptly, the mate produces his bottle and gives it to the patient. The smell seems to wake him up from his lethargy and he takes a long sip. The captain tells him to have a good rest and goes out again with the mate.
	The sailor alone. His eyes are wandering . . .
	Suddenly, they remain fixed, as if spellbound, on the door leading to the hold.
	In horror he sits up and remains in a crouching position as if turned to stone.
Pan to the door leading into the hold.	There, horrible and awe-inspiring, stands NOSFERATU.
Fade-out.	And . . . he . . . approaches.
Scene 96	**10 metres Hornunger Moor Lüneburger Heide**
Wild and desolate scenery.	In the distance a galloping horseman on the plain. He comes closer and closer . . . moving at tremendous speed. It is Hutter.
Dissolve.	
Medium close-up:	Hutter, standing near his horse and examining its injured hoof. With a desperate gesture, he lets go of it. Yet he has made his decision. He must go on. He takes the horse by the reins and walks on, dragging the limping animal after him.

255

Scene 97	**12 metres**
Title:	[The gulf of Biscay] **Open Sea** **North Sea**
On deck, the 'Demeter'	Evening. In the last light of the sun captain and mate are about to push the shrouded corpse of the last sailor over the railing. They have covered their mouths and noses with cloths for protection.
Shot of ship's side:	The corpse is slid down into the water by ropes.
On deck.	For a moment the two last survivors pause in quiet contemplation of the horror of death. Suddenly, the mate's body stiffens, he has made a resolution. For a short moment, he shuts his eyes and tries to master the horror that is rising up inside him. Then he pulls himself together, tears the cloth off his face, takes up an axe and, brandishing it in the air, calls out:
Title:	*I'm going down!!!*
	If I haven't come back
	in ten minutes ...
	With the courage of a desperate man he hurries over to the companion-way.
Scene 98	**12 metres**
Below deck.	There are the black boxes. They are the mate's target. He lifts his axe at the first one and shatters its lid. There it is: he is tempted to retreat.
	Rats! All round his ankles he feels the crawling of horrible creatures. Yet he pulls himself together for a second time.
	Another box, smashed by a second blow. And the same thing happens again: rats! only rats! He is wading through wriggling bodies which surround him from all sides. Yet he withstands the horror. There, a third box.
Close-up:	The mate. In despair, foaming at the lips, he prepares for the third blow.
Long shot:	The axe falls from his hand. His hair is standing on end. Quick as lightning NOSFERATU rears up from the box.
	Now the mate is finally overcome by horror. ... Covering his eyes with his hands he runs upstairs, crazy with fear.
	[Slowly and steadily, NOSFERATU is approaching.]
Scene 99	**8 metres**
Fade-in.	
On deck.	The captain is guarding the helm. Then, from the hatch, the mate emerges ... his hair has turned grey ... his face looks crazed, ... he is foaming at the mouth.... Trying to escape ... he sways ... turns deliriously in a circle ... loses his sense of direction ... does not see the railing ... and overshoots it, falling head first.
	The captain watches in horror. Now he is left all alone. But his face remains determined. He picks up a rope and ties himself to the helm, not to be tempted to leave it. Thus he awaits the horror....
Fade-out.	

End of Act III

Act IV

Scene 100 Fade-in. A cliff by the coast.	**5 metres Heligoland** Night, roaring surf. The storm is howling. A gigantic wave moves up, breaks, the water splashes high up. **Moving coach**
Scene 101 Anny's room.	**5 metres** Night. Anny is asleep. The storm is pushing against the windows, opening them. The curtain is billowing and fluttering in the wind. Anny wakes up. [Confused] **Terrified,** she jumps up. She tries to shut the window, yet **cannot bring herself to do it**. [The storm is pushing her back . . . she recoils.] **She runs out of the room.** **Waves** **Ellen** [**Anny wakes up**] **Carriage** **Ellen walking forward** [**Waves**] [**Carriage Hutter**] **Anny wakes up** **Waves** **Ellen Anny** **Boat**
Scene 102 Ellen's room at the Hardings'.	**3 metres** The storm is sweeping through the open window. The bed is empty. . . . Anny enters. **She knows at once what has happened, – rushes out.**
Scene 103 The roof of Harding's mansion.	**4 metres** Ellen, her clothes fluttering in the wind, her hair like a flag, is sleepwalking in the storm. She stretches out her arms defensively. A white figure against the black night sky. **Contre jour! Clouds!**
Scene 104 is missing Scene 105 Sea.	**6 metres Contre jour North Sea** **High Sea.** The storm is raging, enormous tidal waves . . . In the distance a sailing ship, the 'Demeter', at full sail, racing to its perdition. **Trick**
(Scenes 106 and 107 are missing) Scene 108 [View across the town at night.	**6 metres** The storm is tossing the trees.] **Sailing boat moving towards its objective.**
(Scene 109 is missing) Scene 110 Sea.	**12 metres Wismar.** The storm rages violently. The sand bank threatens. 'Demeter', the fatal ship, has come closer, still moving at full speed.

View from the sea towards the harbour.
Sailing ships are coming in at full sail.
Contre jour (Wismar).   Trick.
Ellen runs out [room]
Broken axle
Ellen runs through garden
Ship moves towards objective
Knock I
Ship coming into the harbour
Hutter, running through street. Knock
Ship in harbour. Nosferatu appears
Hutter running through street
Nosferatu through gate with coffin
Door   Hutter
Knock escape
Nosferatu square or street
Room

Scene 111
[Roof] **Balcony** of Harding's mansion.

4 metres
Ellen in Anny's arm. Her hair is fluttering in the wind. Ellen, stretching her hands towards the sea, as if trying to defend herself.

[Title:]
Scene 112
At the graveyard.
View over the sea.

[*I must go home. He is coming.*]
6 metres

Medium close-up.

In the foreground the crosses. In the back sandbank and cliffs. In the far distance people, hurrying to rescue the ship-wrecked. The sand bank. The ship crashes into it ... turns over on its side. **View through archway: the sailing boat is moving past. (Wismar)**

Scene [116] **113**
Lunatic's cell.
Long shot:

4 metres
Knock alone. He drags up a chair ... to the window. He climbs up on it.

Medium close-up:

Knock pulls himself up by the bars, trying to look out. The wind, blowing in, makes his hair stand on end uncannily.

Scene **113a** [120]
The [stranded] ship.

10 metres
Dead and forsaken. [The] a rope is dangling from the deck. Is it swaying in the wind?

Medium close-up:
Shot of deck.

An endless number of rats climbing down the swaying rope.
The hatch. It opens slowly. N O S F E R A T U climbs out. He carries the last coffin. Remains standing. Motionless. The image of death. Then he approaches slowly.
1) Ship anchored in the harbour. Dissolve.
2) Ship's hatch with a piece of deck.
Trick: 1) Canvas glides away from hatch.
       2) Hatch lid is lifted.
       3) Rats are rushing on deck.
       4) Nosferatu coffin in arm climbs out.

Scene [113] **114**
8 metres   Lauenburg or Travemünde

Town centre. Medium close-up:	Trees, shaken by storm. A carriage races up, stops abruptly. Hutter jumps from the carriage. An axle is broken. The coachman seems at a loss. Hutter cannot wait. He leaves the carriage and runs off.
Scene 115 **Archway with view of the** **harbour:** Scene [119] **116** [The roof of Harding's mansion] Title:	**5 metres Wismar** **Nosferatu enters the town.** **6 metres** **Ellen's room at the Hardings'.** Ellen and Anny. Ellen suddenly breaks away. Overjoyed and as if she had a happy vision she throws her arms up and shouts: *I must go to him. He is coming!!* She moves off and vanishes. Anny wrings her hands in despair.
Scene (120) **117** Park of Harding's mansion.	**4 metres** Storm-tossed trees. A white figure comes out of the house. It is Ellen. She is running through the park.
118 **118a** Scene [122] **119** Lunatic's cell. Long shot: Medium close-up: Title: Long shot.	**4 metres perhaps Lüneburg** **Street. Shuttered windows. Nosferatu striding.** **Hutter, running along a street.** **8 metres** Knock, moving away from the window wall. The madman is listening for outside noises, as if he had received a signal from the other world . . . triumphantly . . . he whispers to himself: *The master is near . . . the master is near . . .!* Suddenly, he listens attentively. He creeps over to the door. There he waits expectantly. . . . The door opens. The attendant appears. He looks around the room. Not noticing that Knock is behind him. Knock creeps carefully behind his back. Suddenly frightened, the attendant turns round. Knock makes for his throat like a vampire. The atten- dant falls over. The madman is at his throat, **for a moment** **only, then he lets go and sneaks out.**
Scene [124] **120** In front of Hutter's house.	**5 metres** Hutter comes running up. He looks up: no light. He is just about to enter when – somebody is calling. He turns round. Ellen!!!!! They fall into each other's arms.
Scene 121	**Square with fountain. 5 metres** **Nosferatu, coffin under his arm, is standing in the middle of the** **square. Looking around to orientate himself. Then he strides on.**
Scene [126] **122** [Hutter's parlour.]	**4 metres 2x** **Ellen's sitting room.** A lamp is shining. Hutter and Ellen. They are sitting on the chaise longue. The happiness of being reunited was too much. Overpowered by emotion, he sinks down on her arm.
Scene 123	**4 metres.**

In front of Hutter's house.
Scene **124**
Fade-in.
[Hutter's parlour]

Title:

Scene (129) **130**
Street in front of Hutter's house.

[Shot of Hutter's house]
The deserted house.
Medium close-up:

Fade-out.
Scene [113] **126**
On the [stranded] ship.

Close-up:

Close-up:

[**Close-up:**]

Scene **127** [114]
[Sandbank] **Harbour.**
Long shot:
Close-up:
Medium close-up:

Title:

Scene [115] **128**
On board ship.
Long shot:

Captain's cabin:

Nosferatu, staring up.
6 metres   2x

Ellen's room.
Hutter and Ellen, on the chaise longue. He sits up, looking deep into her eyes.
Thank God ... you are well ... now everything has come all right.
She does not understand him. But the joy of being together again is stronger than anything else. And the room is bright.
10 metres
There is nobody about. But in the middle of the street stands NOSFERATU, hidden by the night, carrying the coffin. Slowly, he turns his head and looks over to Hutter's house.
[There is a friendly light in the window]
Empty! Carrying the coffin – Nosferatu appears in the picture.
NOSFERATU. Once more he turns his head. He looks over to the other side. [The deserted house is over there]. He makes for that now, walking slowly. **Then he goes into the house.**

12 metres
The captain, collapsed in death, is tied to the helm. In the foreground, some men, Harding among them, are climbing up on deck. They are aghast at the terrible sight.
The dead captain. Tied to the helm in discharge of his duty! One hand is still on the helm. The other [holding a crucifix] clutches his chest in mortal agony.
His head sunk back, face distorted. There are two red marks on his neck. . . .
Harding. He cannot comprehend the horror. . . .
(The ship has anchored.)
[**The ship's deck. A hatch opens. Nosferatu, coffin under his arm, climbs out, steps on the quay.**]
6 metres
The [stranded] ship is in sight. [It is night-time.]
In the blowing wind [nocturnal figures] ... Townspeople.
Down the tilted hulk a man is climbing along a rope.
[By the light of a torch] the captain of the harbour with a number of old people. . . . Looking like fishermen. The climber approaches and reports.
Everything has been examined. . . . No living soul on board.
The captain receives the report ... jots down some notes.
10 metres   [is inserted below]
Night.
Back-board with helm.
Some men are lifting up the dead captain, and carry off the corpse.
Harding alone ... he finds a book next to a masthead that is affixed to the helm. [In the light of a dim lantern he reads]:

Nosferatu: scene 98

Close-up:	A page of the book.
	Varna – July 12.
	Crew – apart from myself the captain – one helmsman, mate and five sailors.
	Departing – for the Dardanelles.
Normal shot:	Harding shakes his head.
	He is puzzled.
	On deck. Harding emerges from the cabin with the book in his hand.
Fade-out.	
Scene [121] **129**	**15 metres**
Fade-in:	
Port Authority building.	[Night] **Daytime.**
	A large hall. On the walls a number of figure heads.
	Models of ships are suspended from the ceiling.
	The dead captain is [carried in] lying in state.
Medium close-up:	Dr Sievers is examining him. He notices the marks on his neck.
Close-up:	
Medium close-up:	Dr Sievers turns to Harding. He, too, cannot make sense of this case. Nevertheless he talks incessantly. Harding **comes closer**, shows him the log-book. Both of them are reading:

Close-up:	The log-book. A page: *Second day: July 13.* *A sailor has fallen ill with a fever.* *Course: SSW. Direction of wind:* *Third day: July 14.* *Mate is talking strangely. He says there is an unknown pas-* *senger below deck.* *Course: SE. Direction of wind: NE.* *Volume of wind: 3.6.*
Normal shot:	Sievers and Harding are looking at each other. Sievers' white beard is trembling. They continue reading. *Tenth day: July 22.* *Rats in the ship's hold.* *Danger of plague.*
Normal shot:	Harding has been reading this aloud. Now Sievers understands at last. He points to the book with his finger. Danger of plague! That's what it is. Danger of plague, he calls out.
Title:	*Danger of plague!* *Go home!* *Shut all your windows and doors!*
Long shot:	Deeply frightened, the bystanders move away. The women put the ends of their head-scarves into their mouths. Panic-stricken, the crowd leaves the room.
Fade-out.	
	(perhaps end of act)
Scene 130	**15 metres**
Fade-in.	
A deserted square.	Nobody is about. Except in the centre of the square, the town-drummer with his large drum.
Medium close-up:	The drummer. He beats a mighty roll.
Medium close-up:	A closed window. The hatch opens and a woman's head appears: totally emaciated, sunken cheeks, long dishevelled hair. The disease has gripped her too. On her neck the ominous little marks.
Medium close-up:	The drummer has produced a piece of paper and reads it aloud:
Title:	*All citizens are notified that the honourable magistrate of this* *town prohibits any movement of plague-suspects into hospitals* *to prevent the plague from spreading through the streets.* The drummer has finished reading and goes off.
Fade-out.	

End of Act IV

Act V

Scene 131 Fade-in. A bend in a street.	**15 metres** A man emerges from a front-door. He shuts the door behind him. Quickly and with circumspection he chalks a [black] **white** cross on the door. Then he goes on.
Panning shot:	The adjoining house. The man knocks hard on the door. From a window above a head looks out. There are still people living here. The man moves on.
Panning shot:	The next house he knocks at remains quiet. He grabs the door handle, it is locked. Again he draws a cross on a deserted house. Then he goes on.
Panning shot:	The first house in the side-street. A coffin is being carried out. The men carrying it have white bandages over their mouths. The man comes along and draws a [black] cross on this house, too. Then he walks on, following his horrible business. . . .
Fade-out. Scene 132 Ellen's bedroom Close-up:	**15 metres 2x shaded candle on table near armchair** **Book-cover. Inscription.** **(Vampire). See Chapter I of book.**
Dissolve to	**Ellen by the window, the book on her knees, continues reading, overcoming her aversion.** **Chapter II appears.**
Medium close-up:	**Ellen is pondering on what she has read.** **Hutter comes into the picture, with agitation, almost hostility he grabs the book.** **Ellen, standing now, looks straight into his eyes, turns and points over to the deserted house.** **compare the following** **black dress and shawl.** **Hutter, black waist-coat and jacket.**
Scene [135] Ellen's room. Long shot: Medium close-up:	**2x** [Ellen by the window. Hutter approaches her from the door.] [Suddenly, she grabs his arm, stares out of the window,] pointing out, she shouts: There!!! **Her body is tensed up like a bow, trembling with excitement.**
Scene [136] **133** [The deserted house] Almost at once dissolve to Window. Medium close-up:	**3 metres** [Seen through Ellen's window-frame] A window, divided into four rectangular panes. Light from behind. Stuck to the window, almost completely covering it, something looking like a black four-legged spider. It takes a moment before one can make out Nosferatu's fingers which are clawing the window frame. In the centre of the body, grinning lasciviously, the waxen face with the ratlike teeth.

Scene **134** [137]
Ellen's bedroom.

Title:

8 metres   2x
Ellen holds frantically on to Hutter's hand. [Shaken] **Breathing heavily,** she turns her head towards him, saying:
This is how I see it – every evening . . .!!!!
She bends her head back. She knows all she has to know.
And there is peace in the knowledge.
Hutter has not come to that yet. He finds her calmness disturbing. He follows the retreating figure with his eyes.

Medium close-up:
Medium close-up:
Fade-out.
Scene [134] **135.**
In front of Hutter's house.

Ellen is swaying.
Hutter, despairingly, presses his fists against his face.

6 metres
It is now evening. The lamp-lighter comes down the darkening street and lights up the street-lamps. Then he walks on.
!remains!

Scene [138] **136**
Fade-in.
Anny's **bedroom** (boudoir).
Long shot:

10 metres

Anny crouching on a chaise longue. Bent over her Harding, who is holding her hands and trying to calm down the struggling woman who is shaking fitfully. She collapses with exhaustion. Then he pulls himself together and decides:

Title:

I will run over quickly . . .
I shall get Sievers.
And he is gone.

Medium close-up:

Anny, having almost fainted with fear, comes to again. She opens her eyes. She lifts up her head. Nobody around?? Is she all alone?? Isn't there something moving about in the corner? Something fluttering at the window?

Medium close-up:

The window, covered by the curtain. Behind it, the shadow of a giant bat.
It grows and grows. Soon it isn't a bat any longer.
A vampire?! NOSFERATU?!

Medium close-up:

Anny's body hits the wall. She jumps up and pulls the bell.
[Then, half crazed with fear, she runs into the background.]

Scene [139] **137**
Anny's bedroom.
Long shot:

Night. Servants running to and fro in the direction of the boudoir.

137a
137b

The bell is ringing.
Servants' room. A servant asleep, doesn't hear, turns over in his sleep.

Scene [140] **138**
Anny's [boudoir] **bedroom.**

3 metres
Anny pressed close to the wall. Servants are rushing in.
There!
she shouts, pointing to the window. Like a flock of chickens the women are huddling together. Anny rushes over to them, but they are already so gripped by fear that they imagine her fingers, which they are trying to push back, to be the vampire's

claws. Shrieking, they run off in all directions. The door is slammed shut.] Anny beats against it **the door**. She is waiting for the horror, but she doesn't want to see it, much rather die first. She grabs a tablecloth and covers her head and neck. Then she collapses.

Fade-out.
Scene [141] **139**
Fade-in.
Ellen's **bed**room.

3 metres

Daytime. Ellen by the window ... looking out. She stands motionless. Paralysed by misery she witnesses the daily scene of wretchedness.

Scene [142] **140**
Street in front of Hutter's house.

8 metres
Ascending. In the distance, a strange procession is wandering across the street. One coffin after another carried by survivors. Past Hutter's house, towards the procession, a man is dragging himself along, tired to death. He supports himself by a stick. He catches sight of the distant procession and lifts up his hands to heaven in misery.
with window-frame. Ellen.

Scene [143] **141**
Ellen's room.

10 metres
Ellen, on the point of fainting, turns away from the window. She cannot bear the sight of this wretchedness any longer. She sinks into a chair, resting her head in her hands.

Close-up:
Close-up:

The book, open. She has been reading it for days.
A page of the book:
ONLY IF A CHASTE WOMAN
CAN FEARLESSLY MAKE
HIM
MISS THE FIRST CROWING
OF THE COCK WILL HE DISINTEGRATE
IN THE LIGHT OF
DAWN.

Close-up:

Ellen lifts up her head, staring into space like a visionary. She knows. She shuts her eyes.

Fade-out.
Scene [144] **142**
Fade-in.
In front of Harding's mansion.
Medium close-up:

The porch. Harding – haggard – a broken man, comes out. He closes the door and supports himself against the door-post. His hand reaches up, paints a black cross on the door ... and falls down. His hollow eyes refrain from looking at his work again ... they cannot bear to see the symbol. [He moves forward with a glazed look in his eyes.]
Harding: black cape, dark trousers.
Omitted

Fade-out.

Scene [145] **143**
Fade-in.

7 metres

(In front of deserted house)	**Street.** A group of emaciated men with a fanatical look about them are standing around. An unkempt-looking woman is haranguing them. [They are raising their fists.]
Title:	*He has been seen!* *He ran out of the house!* *He strangled the attendant!*
Scene [146] **144** Well in the market-place.	**8 metres** Two ancient women are sitting by the well. Death has no terrors for them. Since every new day is a present to them.
Close-up: Title:	They are whispering to each other; their heads are trembling. [*In the deserted house . . . that's where it is hiding.*] *He strangled him. The vampire.*
Medium close-up:	**Further back agitated people are running across the square, shouting excitedly to one another. The two women turn round gesturing fiercely.** They clench their bony fists threateningly. Harding can be seen behind the well. He has heard everything.
Close-up: Long shot. **Scene 144a** **Street (shot from above).**	He utters a bitter and mocking laugh. Harding walks on. **10 metres** **Crossing. Crowd gathering from all sides, then moving in one direction.**
Close-up:	**A street-corner with a man** **who points at something above. People rush up to him;** **they all turn to face the same way,** **look up, make threatening gestures.** **Somebody throws stones.**
145 **Gable of a house.** **Medium close-up:**	A figure is crouching on a roof-top. **It is Knock. He is looking down with a sneer on his face** **and pokes out his tongue.** **A stone whizzes past him. He suddenly gets up and clambers off.**
Scene [149] **147** Ellen's **bed**room.	**8 metres** Ellen in an old armchair, busy embroidering a cushion in the cross-stitch manner of the 1840s. An inscription reading: <div align="center">I LOVE YOU.</div>She puts down her work, resting her head.
Close-up: Medium close-up: Scene [154] **148** Back of deserted house.	Tired, she falls to day-dreaming. **Then she lights a lamp.** Ellen takes up her work again, determined to finish it. **Evening 4 metres** The street is empty. Knock jumps down a wall and runs off. In the distance some men appear, chasing him. They catch sight of him and rush after him.
Scene [156] **149** Meadows outside the town.	**8 metres** Shot against a wide expanse of sky. In the distance running figures, no more than silhouettes. (Turn slowly) Knock in front. His pursuers following a long way behind.

Scene [162] **150** Fields.	**3 metres** Evening mists. Cornfields waving in the wind. Suddenly, right in front between the ears of corn a head. Dishevelled hair. Then a bony back. The head turns round slowly. It is Knock.
Scene [163] **151** A lane between fields.	**3 metres** The landscape has grown dim in the evening light. The men chasing Knock are approaching. They stop. They seem to have lost the trail. Suddenly, one of them sees something. He opens his eyes wide, shouting: there!!! They all look one way. They all dash off in that direction.
Scene [164] **152** Cornfield. Long shot.	**10 metres** In the distance one can still see the back and dishevelled head. Is it Knock? He seems not to hear or see his pursuers. The men are coming near, rushing towards him across the field. They lift up their sticks and fists.
Medium close-up:	A scare-crow. A black coat is dangling on a stick. Bits of straw and tattered rags. The men fall on it in their disappointment. Suddenly they stop. There! What can that be!!!
Long shot.	A hundred feet away a head has appeared. Then the figure of a man. It is moving away quickly. The chase starts up again.
Fade-out. **Scene 153** **Title:** **Deserted house. Medium close-up:**	**3 metres** **Night.** **Nosferatu at the window.**
Dissolve **Scene 154** **Ellen's bedroom.** Medium close-up:	**8 metres 2x** **Ellen wakes up. She sits up in bed, listening as if she had heard somebody calling her.** **She gets up, walking as if pulled by invisible threads.**
Long shot:	**She goes over to the window. In the foreground Hutter asleep in an armchair, looking worn out.**
Medium close-up: **Scene 155.** **Deserted house.**	**Ellen is clinging to the window. She sees.** **3 metres** **Nosferatu at the window.** **He raises his arms slowly.**
Scene 156 **Ellen's room.** Medium close-up:	**8 metres 2x** **Ellen is about to collapse by the window.** **Shaking with fear she struggles violently with herself. The last battle.** **Twice her hand comes up to open the window and drops down again weakly; then, with sudden determination, she pulls herself up dead straight and deliberately throws the window wide open.**

Scene 157 Deserted house. Medium close-up:	4 metres
	Window. Nosferatu moves away from the window, turns round and disappears.
Scene 158 Ellen's room. Close-up:	4 metres Ellen trembling with fear and apprehension.
Scene 159 Deserted house. Medium close-up:	6 metres
	Locked-up gates. Suddenly the gates swing open; Nosferatu appears.
Scene 160 Ellen's room. Medium close-up:	12 metres 2x
	Ellen is covering her face with her hands, seized with mortal fear.
Long shot; (window moves out of picture)	Ellen at the window. She wants to call for help. She staggers forward. She stops in front of Hutter. One last moment of indecision. Then she wakes him up. Hutter jumps to his feet. He catches the trembling figure in his arms and carries her over to the sofa. She begs him, hands raised as if in prayer:
Title:	*Bulwer . . . Fetch Bulwer!* She entreats him to go. Hutter takes her hands, she quickly kisses his head, then he rushes out.
Scene 161 In front of Hutter's house.	3 metres A path bordered by flowers. Hutter rushes out. Trousers, pleated shirt, collar without tie. No hat, no waistcoat.
Scene 162 Ellen's room. Long shot.	5 metres Ellen is still looking in the direction she saw Hutter leave, then she gets up and walks towards the window.
Scene 163 Deserted house. Long shot:	5 metres Nosferatu is walking forward and moves out of the picture. The house looks more deserted than ever!
Scene 164 In front of Hutter's house.	6 metres Nobody is about. Nosferatu is approaching. He comes to a halt. (He is preparing to jump, looks up.) He enters the house.
Scene 165 Ellen's room.	6 metres Ellen turns round suddenly. She is shaking with fear, anticipating the horror about to happen. And it is coming – slowly, tensed like a predatory animal. She recoils, moves backwards step by step, and step by step it follows her. !Heart – Hand!

Scene 166
Bulwer's laboratory (cum living room).

6 metres
In addition to the already familiar fish tanks there is a large telescope by a window. A profusion of antiquated scientific gadgets, globes etc. A lamp is burning. Bulwer asleep in dressing-gown and night-cap in the armchair. Cages with birds and all kinds of animals. Hutter rushes in. He wakes Bulwer, begs him to come with him. Bulwer starts to get dressed.

Scene 167
A municipal building of the period (town hall).

A large crowd is gathering in front of the town hall. Knock has been captured. More people keep pouring in from all sides.
Omitted.

Scene 168
(An office type room inside the town hall.)

5 metres
Dr Sievers' laboratory.
Sievers rushes in excitedly from the adjoining room, accompanied by a man who has brought him the news. From the other side Knock is being brought in. The lunatic is trembling with fear.
exit

Scene 169
Ellen's room.

4 metres
Night. Ellen in bed, the strangler is at her throat, his fingers clawing her arms. Her eyes, widened in mortal fear, have a glazed look. Then she seems to have heard something.

Scene 170

A cock jumps on to a still-life of farm implements. He flaps his wings, puffs up his throat and heralds the morning.

Scene 171
Sievers' lunatic's cell.
[Inside the town hall]

6 metres
Knock.
Knock at the window, held by two men. Trying to ward them off, he shouts anxiously:

Title:

The master . . . the master . . .!
He tries to break free. At Sievers' order he is put down brutally.

Scene 172
Ellen's room.

Nosferatu raises his head. He looks drunk with pleasure. Ellen's eyes are full of terrible fear. She must not allow Nosferatu just to go. She puts her arms round him; he cannot resist and bends his head over her again.
Omitted

Scene 173

3 metres
The sun is rising over the small town.

Scene 174
Ellen's room.

Ellen's last moment of apprehension. There, isn't that a flicker of sunlight on the wall over the bed? Her eyes light up hopefully and remain fixed on this first sign of the new day. She stretches out her hand for it. And look: it is moving; it is moving downwards.
Omitted

Scene 175
Street with front gardens.

5 metres
The long shadows of sunrise. Nobody is about. Then the

Scene **176**
Ellen's room.

shoulders of Hutter and Bulwer appear. They are hurrying on and turning into a side street.
8 metres
The bed is bathed in sunlight. Ellen's eyes are full of anticipation. Has she sacrificed herself in vain? Suddenly the horrible figure jerks himself up. He looks about in amazement. He clutches his heart. The bestial tenseness of his bearing relaxes. For a moment he stands, legs apart, as if trying to regain his balance. He clutches his heart again and falls on his knees, his face turned to the sun, distorted by pain.

Scene **177**
Sievers' lunatic's cell.
[Town hall]
Medium close-up:

Knock.   5 metres

Knock, in a straitjacket, alone in the sunlight which is falling through a barred window. He is mumbling disconnected words:

Title:

The master ... the master ... is dead.
His head sinks on to his chest.

Scene **178**
Ellen's room.

8 metres
Nosferatu on his knees, supporting himself with one hand on the ground. He raises the other in the direction of the sun to shield himself from the light that brings him death. But he cannot hold out against the sun. His fingers, his hand, his arm are dissolving in the light. The sun seems about to strike his heart. Now his body is disintegrating in the light. Ellen throws up her hands, [triumphantly] calling:

Title:
Scene 179
In front of Hutter's house.

Hutter!
4 metres
Shot looking out from the doorway into the distance. Bulwer and Hutter are running, not just walking into the house.

Scene **180**

8 metres
Ellen in bed. In anticipation, her hand reaches out for Hutter. Hutter comes rushing in, falls on his knees by the bed. He takes hold of her hand.

Close-up:

Her hand grasps his, then it lets go weakly and drops away. Ellen's head falls over – – – –
Bulwer is standing at the window, hands behind his back, looking out.

Variations from the Script in the Final Screen Version

Scenes 1–4:	These scenes are less detailed. The business with the kitten and Ellen's forgetting to prepare breakfast is omitted. Murnau instead emphasizes the bouquet scene and the happiness of their marriage.
Scene 8:	Instead of the old atlas there is a large map hanging in the office.
Scenes 14, 16, 28:	The people walking in the square are omitted (Murnau and the rather small firm had to be careful with money and extras). Similarly with the coach. On the journey to the Carpathians we see no other passengers. The people in the inn are not fellow passengers but belong to the village.
Scene 27:	The old servant feeding the chickens is omitted. (Murnau was to make use of this scene later, in *Sunrise*.)
Scene 29:	The children waving goodbye: omitted,
Scenes 30–33:	The two old women are omitted. Likewise the old woman praying who tries to warn them. Titles 30, 31, and 32 are omitted.
Scenes 37, 38:	The man-size raven and the grinning tree are omitted. Murnau has no need of such devices to create terror.
Scenes 41, 62:	The gallery containing family portraits is omitted. Murnau used a real castle for the exteriors and only two studio-built sets: the dining hall and the small room.
Scenes 62, 62a:	We only see a flight of stairs.
Scene 80:	Instead of a real graveyard the film simply presents some crosses on a sand-dune, the graves of those lost at sea.
Scenes 81–83:	The game and the postman are omitted.
Scene 110:	There is no sandbank threat to the *Demeter*.
Scene 112:	No rush of people, and the ship simply glides into harbour.
Scene 113a [120]:	Nosferatu emerges without his coffin. He is, however, carrying the coffin when he enters Wismar.
Scene 127 [114]:	Simplified to a few workers, owners etc.; no bystanders.
Scene 130:	Instead of a deserted square the film shows us the narrow (and real) street along which the coffins will later be carried. When the drummer reads the proclamation several people, including a child, all apparently healthy, open their windows and look out.
Scene [138] 136:	The superfluous bat is omitted; the curtains merely flutter.
Scene [140] 138:	No servants rush in. There is one only, who sleeps through the ringing of the bell.
Scene [142] 140:	The man dragging himself along is omitted.
Scenes [144] 142, [146] 144:	The film shows us no more of Harding, and we are left to suppose that Anny died of the plague.

Scene 164:	Murnau bases his interpretation of this scene on a picture by Moritz von Schwind.
Scene 165:	Murnau's sequences of Nosferatu's shadow gliding up the stairs and standing at the entrance door do not appear in the script.
Scene 180:	Murnau's ending includes a scene in a landscape and a (different) castle ruin, not provided for in the script. See pages 115–16, for mention of the use of more of this material in the German copy of the film preserved at the Cinémathèque Française.

Filmography

(Compiled with the assistance of Frau Erika Ulbrich and Herr Werner Zurbuch, Munich.)

1919   *Der Knabe in Blau* (*Der Todessmaragd*) [The Blue Boy]
5 acts, finished on 28 June 1919.
Production: Ernst Hofmann Film Gesellschaft.
Script: Hedda Hofmann and Edda Ottershausen.
Sets: Willy A. Hermann.
Camera: Carl Hoffmann.
Cast: Ernst Hofmann (Thomas v. Weerth); Blandine Ebinger (a beautiful gypsy); Karl Plathen (the old servant); Margit Barnay (a young actress); Georg John (the gypsy chief); and Leonhardt Haskel, Rudolf Klix, and Schmidt-Verden.

1919   *Satanas*
First shown about 30 January 1920 in the Richard Oswald-Lichtspiele, Berlin.
Production: Victoria Film Co. (Ernst Hofmann).
Script and artistic direction: Robert Wiene.
Sets: Ernst Stern.
Camera: Karl Freund.
Cast:
1st episode: Fritz Kortner (the Pharaoh Amenhotep); Sadiah Gezza (Nouri, a harp-player), Ernst Hofmann (Jorab); Margit Barnay (Phahi, Pharaoh's wife); Conrad Veidt (the Hermit from Elu, and Lucifer).
2nd episode: Conrad Veidt (Gubetta, a Spaniard, and Lucifer); Kurst Erhle (Gennaro); Elsa Berna (Lucrezia Borgia); Ernst Stahl-Nachbauer (Alfonso d'Este).

3rd episode: Conrad Veidt (Ivan Grodski according to the synopsis, Wladimir G. according to the programme, and Lucifer); Martin Wolfgang (Hans, a young student, later 'Führer' of the Revolution); Marija Leiko (Irene); Max Kronert (Father Conrad); Elsa Wagner (Mother Conrad).

1920   *Sehnsucht (Bajazzo)*
The picture of a life in 5 acts (1,700 metres) or:
'The Tragedy of a Dancer', licensed on 18 October 1920 – 1,765 metres.
Production: Mosch Film 1920, or:
Production: Lipow Film, according to an advertisement and to a writer, Frau Lindau-Schultz.
Script: Carl Heinz Jarosy.
Sets: Robert Neppach.
Camera: Carl Hoffmann.
Costumes: Charles Drecoll (a *haute couture* company).
Cast: Conrad Veidt, Gussy Holl (Russian grand duchess); Margarete Schlegel, Eugen Klöpfer, Paul Graetz, and Helene Cray, Danny Gürtler, Albert Bennefeld, Ellen Bolan, Marcella Gremo.

1920   *Der Bucklige und die Tänzerin* [The Hunchback and the Dancer]
5 acts. First shown 8 July 1920 at the Marmorhaus.
Production: Helios Film Gesellschaft.
Script: Carl Mayer.
Camera: Karl Freund.
Sets: Robert Neppach.
Cast: Sacha Gura (Gina, a dancer); John Gottowt (Wilton, a hunchback); Paul Biensfeld (Smith, a rich bachelor); Anna von Pahlen (Mrs Smith, his mother); Henri Peters-Arnolds (Baron Percy); Bella Polini (a dancer).

1920   *Der Januskopf (Schrecken)* [Janus Head]
6 acts – 2,300 metres. First shown 26 August 1920 at the Marmorhaus.
Production: Decla Bioscop Sensations Klasse (according to the censor's certificate: Lipow Film).
Script: Hans Janowitz.
Sets: Heinrich Richter.
Camera: Karl Freund, Carl Hoffmann.
Cast: Conrad Veidt (Dr Warren and Mr O'Connor), in the script still Dr Jeskyll (sic) and Mr Hyde; Margarete Schlegel (Grace – Jane in the script); Willy Kayser-Heyl, Margarete Kupfer, Gustav Botz, Jaro Fürth, Magnus Stifter, Marga Reuter, Lansa Rudolph, Danny Gürtler.

1920   *Abend . . . Nacht . . . Morgen* [Evening . . . Night . . . Morning]
5 acts – 1,700 metres.
First shown beginning of October 1920 at the Decla Lichtspiele Unter den Linden.
Production: Ein Decla Detectiv Film der Decla-Bioscop (one of the group of Decla Detectiv Films 1920–21).
Script: Rudolf Schneider-München.
Sets: Robert Neppach.

Camera: Eugen Hamm.
Cast: Bruno Ziemer (Chester, a rich gentleman); Gertrud Welker (Maud, a demi-mondaine); Conrad Veidt (Brilburn, her brother); Carl von Balla (Prince, a gambler); Otto Gebühr (Ward, a detective).

1920   *Der Gang in die Nacht* [Journey into the Night]
A tragedy in 5 acts – 2,000 metres.
Trade showing 13 December 1920. Première: January 1921.
Production: Goron Films.
Script: Carl Mayer, based on the Danish script 'The Conqueror' by Harriet Bloch.
Sets: Heinrich Richter.
Camera: Max Lutze.
Cast: Olaf Fønss (Professor Dr Eigil Boerne); Erna Morena (Hélène); Gudrun Bruun Steffensen (Lily); Conrad Veidt (the painter); and Clementine Plessner.

1920–21   *Marizza, genannt die Schmuggler-Madonna* [Marizza, called the Smuggler's Madonna]
First title: *Ein Schönes Tier, Das Schöne Tier.*
Tragedy in 5 acts – 1,800 metres.
First showing 20 January 1922 at the Johann Georg Lichtspiele am Kurfürstendamm.
Production: Helios Film.
Script: based on the script 'Green Eyes' by Wolfram Geiger, adapted by Hans Janowitz.
Sets: Heinrich Richter.
Camera: Karl Freund.
Cast: Adele Sandrock (Mme Avricolos); Harry Frank (Christo Avricolos, her elder son); H. H. von Twardowski (Antonino, her second son); Leonhard Haskel (Pietro Scarzella); Greta Schroeder (Sadja, his daughter); Maria Forescu (Yelina); Tzwetta Tzatscheva (Marizza); Albrect von Blum (Mirko Vasics, a smuggler); Max Nemetz (Grischuk, a smuggler); Toni Zimmerer (Haslinger, a customs man).

1921   *Schloss Vogelöd*
First shown beginning of April 1921 at the Marmorhaus.
Production: Decla Bioscop.
Script: Carl Mayer, adapted from the novel by Rudolf Stratz.
Sets: Hermann Warm.
Camera: Fritz Arno Wagner, Laszlo Scheffer.
Artistic adviser: Graf Montgelas.
Cast: Arnold Korff (the Master of Vogelschrey auf Vogelöd); Lulu Keyser-Korff (Centa von Vogelschrey, his wife); Lothar Mehnert (Graf Johann Oetsch); Paul Bildt (Baron Safferstädt); Olga Tschechova (the Baroness, his wife); Paul Hartmann (Graf Peter Paul Oetsch, the Baroness's first husband); Hermann Valentin (retired judge); Julius Falkenstein (the frightened gentleman); Rudolf Leffler (the butler); Walter Kurth Kuhle (a valet); Victor Blütner (Father Faramund); and Leoni Nest, the little girl.

1921–22   *Nosferatu (Eine Symphonie des Grauens)* [Nosferatu, a Symphony of Horror]
5 acts. First showing 5 March 1922.
Production: Prana Film G.m.b.H.
Script: Henrik Galeen, based on *Dracula* by Bram Stoker.
Sets and costumes: Albin Grau.
Camera: Fritz Arno Wagner.
Original Music: Hans Erdmann.
Cast: Max Schreck (Graf Orlok, Nosferatu the Vampire); Alexander Granach (Knock, an estate agent); Gustav von Wangenheim (Hutter, his assistant); Greta Schroeder (Ellen, Hutter's wife); G. H. Schnell (Harding, a shipbuilder); Ruth Landshoff (Annie, his wife); John Gottowt (Professor Bulwer, a Paracelsian); Gustav Botz (Professor Sievers, town medical officer); Max Nemetz (captain of the ship); Wolfgang Heinz (first sailor); Albert Venohr (second sailor); Herzfeld (the innkeeper); Hardy von François (hospital doctor); Heinrich Witte.

Readapted for sound:
1930   *Die Zwoelfte Stunde – Eine Nacht des Grauens* [The Twelfth Hour – a Night of Horror]
Length: 1,893 metres.
Applicant for censor's certificate: Deutsch-Film Produktion.
Artistic adaptation: Dr Waldemar Roger.
Sound: Organon GmbH im Polyphon Grammophon Konzern.
Cast: In addition to the original cast of *Nosferatu* under new names (see pp. 115–17), a new character, the priest, is played by Hans Behal.

1922   *Der Brennende Acker* [The Burning Earth]
6 acts. First shown 16 March 1922.
Production: Goron-Deulig Exklusiv Film.
Script: Willy Haas, Thea von Harbou, Arthur Rosen.
Sets and costumes: Rochus Gliese.
Camera: Karl Freund, Fritz Arno Wagner.
Cast: Werner Krauss (Rog, the old peasant); Eugen Klöpfer (Peter his son; in the script Piotr); Wladimir Gaidarow (Johannes, the second son; in the script, Bosko); Eduard von Winterstein (count Rudenberg; in the script, Rodomir); Stella Arbenina (Helga, the Count's second wife; in the script, Marina); Lya de Putti (Gerda, his daughter by his first marriage; in the script, Helena); Greta Dierks (Maria, a young peasant; in the script, Grischka); Emilie Unda (an old servant; in the script, Marfa); Alfred Abel (Baron Ludwig von Lellevell; in the script, Ludwik); and Olga Engl, Elsa Wagner, Unda Faliansky, Eugen Rex, Leonhard Haskel, Gustav Botz, Adolf Klein, Albert Patry.

1922   *Phantom*
6 acts – 2,905 metres.
Presented on 29 October 1922 on Gerhart Hauptmann's sixtieth birthday at the Ufa Palast am Zoo.
Production: Uco Film of Decla Bioscop.
Script: Thea von Harbou and H. H. von Twardowski, based on a novel of the same name by Gerhart Hauptmann published in the *Berliner Illustrierte*.

Sets: Hermann Warm and Erich Czerwonski.
Camera: Axel Graatkjär and Theophan Ouchakoff.
Costumes: Vally Reinecke.
Original music: Leo Spiess.
Assistant: Herman Bing.
Cast: Alfred Abel (Lorenz Lubota); Frieda Richard (his mother); Aud Egede Nissen (Melanie, his sister); H. H. von Twardowski (Hugo, his brother); Karl Ettlinger (Starke, the bookbinder); Lil Dagover (Marie, his daughter); Grete Berger (Frau Schwabe, moneylender); Anton Edthofer (Wigottschinski); Ilka Grüning (the Baroness); Lya de Putti (Melitta, her daughter, and Veronika Harlan); Adolf Klein (Harlan, a rich steel merchant); Olga Engl (his wife); Heinrich Witte (a clerk at the town hall).

1923   *Die Austreibung* [The Expulsion]
4 acts – 1,557 metres.
First shown 23 October 1923 at the UT Kurfürstendamm.
Production: Decla Bioscop A.G.
Script: Thea von Harbou, based on the play by Carl Hauptmann.
Sets: Rochus Gliese and Erich Czerwonski.
Camera: Karl Freund.
Music: Joseph Viet.
Cast: Carl Götz (Steyer, the old peasant); Eugen Klöpfer (his son); Ilka Grüning (his mother); Lucie Mannheim (Aenne, daughter by an earlier marriage); Aud Egede Nissen (Ludmilla, young Steyer's wife); Wilhelm Dieterle (Lauer, a hunter); Robert Leffler (the minister); Jacob Tiedtke (a notary).

1923   *Die Finanzen des Grossherzogs* [The Finances of the Grand Duke]
6 acts – 2,250 metres.
First shown 7 January 1924 at the Ufa Palast am Zoo.
Production: Union Film.
Script: Thea von Harbou, based on a novel of the same name by Frank Heller.
Sets: Rochus Gliese and Erich Czerwonski.
Camera: Karl Freund and Franz Planer.
Cast: Harry Liedtke (Don Ramon XX, Grand Duke of Albacco); Mady Christians (Olga, Russian Grand Duchess); Guido Herzfeld (Markowitz, a moneylender); Hermann Valentin (Monsieur Binzer); Alfred Abel (Philip Collins, alias Professor Pelotard, alias M. Becker); Adolf Engers (Don Esteban Paqueno, Minister of Finance); Ilke Grüning (Augustine the cook); Julius Falkenstein (Ernst Isaacs, banker); Hans Hermann (the hunchbacked conspirator); Georg August Koch (the dangerous conspirator); Max Schreck (the sinister conspirator); and Robert Scholz, von Camphausen, Walter Rilla.

1924   *Der Letzte Mann* [The Last Man]
Eng./U.S. title: *The Last Laugh.*
6 acts – 2,036 metres.
First shown 23 December 1924 at the Ufa Palast am Zoo.
Production: Universum Films A.G. (Decla Film der Ufa).
Script: Original film script by Carl Mayer.
Sets: Robert Herlth and Walter Röhrig.

Camera: Karl Freund.
Music: Guiseppe Becce.
Cast: Emil Jannings (the hotel porter); Maly Delschaft (his daughter); Max Hiller (her fiancé); Emilie Kurtz (his aunt); Hans Unterkircher (the manager); Olaf Storm (a young resident); Hermann Valentin (a resident); Emmy Wyda (a thin neighbour); Georg John (the night watchman).

1925   *Tartüff* [Tartuffe]
First shown 25 January 1926 at the opening of the Gloria Palast.
Production: Ufa.
Script: Carl Mayer, after Molière.
Sets: Robert Herlth and Walter Röhrig.
Camera: Karl Freund.
Characters in the prologue and epilogue: Hermann Picha (the old man); Rosa Valetti (the housekeeper); André Mattoni (the grandson).

Characters in the play: Emil Jannings (Tartuffe); Werner Krauss (Orgon); Lil Dagover (Elmire); Lucie Höflich (Dorine).

1926   *Faust*
First shown 14 October 1926.
Production: Ufa.
Script: Hans Kyser, after Goethe.
Sets and costumes: Robert Herlth and Walter Röhrig.
Camera: Carl Hoffmann.
Cast: Gösta Ekman (Faust); Emil Jannings (Mephisto); Camilla Horn (Marguerite, a part first intended for Lillian Gish); Frieda Richard (her mother); Wilhelm Dieterle (Valentin); Yvette Guilbert (Marthe); Eric Barclay (the Duke of Parma); Hanna Ralph (the Duchess); Werner Fütterer (the archangel, a part first intended for Nils Asther).

1927   *Sunrise.* Sub-title: *A Song of Two Humans*
First shown 23 September 1927.
Gala at the Carthay Circle Theatre, 29 November 1927, with music by Carli Elinor.
Production: Fox Film Corporation.
Script: Carl Mayer, based on *The Journey to Tilsit* by Hermann Sudermann.
Sets: Rochus Gliese.
Camera: Charles Rosher and Karl Struss.
Assistants: Edgar Ulmer and Alfred Metscher for the sets and props.
Assistant director: Herman Bing.
Sub-titles: Katherine Hilliker and H. H. Caldwell.
Music: Dr Hugo Riesenfeld.
Cast: George O'Brien (the man – Ansass); Janet Gaynor (the woman – Indre); Bodil Rosing (the maid); Margaret Livingstone (the vamp); J. Farrell Macdonald (the photographer); Ralph Sipperly (the hairdresser); Jane Winton (the manicurist); Arthur Houseman (the rude gentleman); Eddie Boland (the kind gentleman); and Gina Corrado, Barry Norton, Sally Eilers.

1928   *The Four Devils*
First shown, according to Huff, 3 October 1928; according to *Kinematograph Weekly*, in August 1929.
8 acts – 2,547 metres; 9,450 feet.
Production: Fox Film Corporation.
Script: Carl Mayer, Berthold Viertel and Marion Orth, based on a novel of the same name by Hermann Bang.
Sets: William Darling, from designs by Robert Herlth and Walter Röhrig.
Camera: Ernest Palmer and L. W. O'Connell.
Dialogue added by George Middleton.
Cast of the prologue: Jack Parker (Charles as a child; in the script, Fritz); Anne Shirley (then still Dawn O'Day – Marion as a child; in the script, Aimée); Philippe de Lacy (Adolphe as a child); Anita Louise (then still Anita Fremault – Louise as a child); Anders Randolph (the manager of the circus); J. Farrell Macdonald (the clown).
The Four Devils: Charles Morton (Charles); Janet Gaynor (Marion); Barry Norton (Adolf); Nancy Drexel (Louise); and Mary Duncan (the lady); J. Farrell Macdonald (the clown).

1929   *Our Daily Bread* [*City Girl*]
9 acts – 2,580 metres; 6,171 feet.
First shown 19 May 1930.
Postsynchronized by Western Electric.
Production: Fox Film Corporation.
Script: Berthold Viertel and Marion Orth, based on *The Mud Turtle*, by Elliot Lester. Dialogue: Lester.
Sets: William Darling.
Camera: Ernest Palmer.
Cast: David Torrence (Tristine, Tustine, an old peasant); Charles Farrell (Lem, his son); Mary Duncan (Kate); and Ivan Linow, Guinn Williams, Edith York, Dawn O'Day, Dick Alexander, Tom Maguire, Edward Brady, David Rollins.

Tabu
8 acts – 2,311 metres.
First shown 18 March 1931, a few days after Murnau's death.
Production: Murnau, Robert Flaherty.
Distribution: Paramount.
Script: Flaherty and Murnau.
Camera: Floyd Crosby and Flaherty.
Music: Dr Hugo Riesenfeld.
Cast: Reri (Anne Chevalier, the girl); Matahi (the boy); Hitu (the old chief); Jean (the policeman); Jules (the captain); Kong Ah (the Chinese).

Bibliography

Agel, Henri: 'Un Cinéaste Moderne – Frédéric Murnau', in *Radio, Cinéma, Télévision*, 499. Paris, 9 August 1959.

Alvaroell, Amo: 'Homenaje a Murnau', in *Nuestro Cine*, 52. Madrid, 1956.

Anger, Kenneth: 'Hollywood ou le comportement des mortels (II)', in *Cahiers du Cinéma*, 77. Paris, December 1957.

Anger, Kenneth: *Hollywood Babylon*. J. J. Pauvert, Paris, 1959.

Astruc, Alexandre: 'Le Feu et la glace', in *Cahiers du Cinéma*, 18. Paris, December 1952.

Blin, Roger: 'Murnau – Ses Films', in *La Revue du Cinéma*, 25. Paris, July 1931.

Borde, Raymond; Buache, Freddy; Courtade, François; Tariol, Marcel: '*Le Cinéma réaliste allemand*'. La Cinémathèque Suisse, Lausanne, 1959.

Calder-Marshall, Arthur: *The Innocent Eye. The Life of Robert J. Flaherty*. W. H. Allen, London, 1963. Harcourt, New York, 1966.

Carné, Marcel: 'La Caméra, personnage du drame', in *Anthologie du Cinéma. Textes réunis et présentés par Marcel Lapierre*. La Nouvelle Edition, Paris, 1946.

Carr, Harry: 'When the best guessers in Hollywood guess all wrong', in *Motion Picture Magazine*. New York, August 1926.

Dittmar, Peter: *F. W. Murnau: Inaugural Dissertation zur Erlangung des Grades eines Doktor der Philosophie*. (Doctorate thesis.) Freie Universitat Berlin. Berlin (?1965).

280

Domarchi, Jean: 'Murnau', in *Anthologie du Cinéma*. Paris, July 1965.

Domarchi, Jean: 'Présence de F. W. Murnau', in *Cahiers du Cinéma*, 21. Paris, 1953.

Eisner, Lotte H.: *L'Ecran Démoniaque*. André Bonne. Paris, 1952, 1965.

Eisner, Lotte H.: 'L'énigme des deux Nosferatu', in *Cahiers du Cinéma*, 79. Paris, 1957.

Eisner, Lotte H.: *F. W. Murnau*. Le Terrain Vague, Paris, 1964. (Original French edition of the present book.) German edition; Friedrich Verlag, Berlin, 1957.

Eisner, Lotte H.: *The Haunted Screen* (English version of *L'Ecran Démoniaque*). Thames and Hudson, London, 1969; University of California Press, Berkeley, 1969.

Eisner, Lotte H.: 'Tabu' (review), in *Film-Kurier*. Berlin, 28 August 1931.

Flaherty, David. 'A Few Reminiscences', in *Film Culture*, 20. New York (1959).

Flaherty, Robert J. and Murnau, F. W.: 'Turia, an Original Story', in *Film Culture*, 20. New York, 1959.

Flaherty, Robert J. and Murnau, F. W.: 'Tabu (Tabou), a Story of the South Seas' in *Film Culture*, 20. New York (1959).

Freund, Karl: 'A Film Artist', in *A Tribute to Carl Mayer, 1894–1944. Memorial Programme, Scala Theatre, 13 April 1947*. London, 1947.

Gide, André: *Journal, 1889–1938*. Bibliothèque de la Pléiade. Paris (1940).

Gilson, René: 'Murnau et les courants d'air glacés. Études sur six chefs-d'œuvres', in *Cinéma 63*, 76. Paris, May 1963.

Granach, Alexander: *Da geht ein Mensch*. Frankfurter Verlagsanstat. Frankfurt, n.d.

Grau, Albin: 'Vampire', in *Buhne und Film*, Jahrgang 3, 21. Berlin, 1921.

Griffith, Richard: *The World of Robert Flaherty*. Victor Gollancz, London; Duell, Sloan and Pearce, New York; Little, Brown and Co., Boston, 1953.

Griffith, Richard: 'Flaherty and *Tabu*', in *Film Culture*, 20. New York (1959).

Haas, Willy: 'Ein neuer Regisseur der "Decla-Bioskop"' in *Film-Kurier*, 12. Berlin, 14 January 1921.

Haas, Willy: 'Schloss Vogelöd' (review), in *Film-Kurier*, Berlin, 8 April 1921.

Höllriegel, Arnold: *Hollywood Bilderbuch*. Verlag E.P. Tal, Vienna and Leipzig, 1927.

Huff, Theodore: *An Index to the Films of F. W. Murnau* (*Sight and Sound* Index Series, 15). British Film Institute. London, 1948.

Hauptmann, Gerhart: *Phantom, Aufzeichnungen eines ehemaligen Sträflings*. Fischer verlag, Berlin, 1923.

Jaeger, Ernst: 'Nicht fur Veröffentlichung. Vergessenes, Bekanntnes und Indiskretes aus deutscher Filmgeschichte', erzählt von E.J., in *Der Neue Film*, Wiesbaden, 1954.

Jameux, Charles: *Murnau*. Editions Universitaires, Paris, 1965.

Jannings, Emil: *Das Leben Und Ich*. Deutsche Buchgemeinschaft, Berlin and Darmstadt, 1951.

Jones, Dorothy B.: 'Sunrise – A Murnau Masterpiece', in *The Quarterly of Film, Radio, Television*, Vol. IX, No. 3. University of California Press, Spring 1955.

Josephson, Matthew: 'F. W. Murnau – The German Genius of the Films', in *Motion Picture Classic*. New York, October 1926.

Kracauer, Siegfried: *From Caligari to Hitler, A Psychological History of the German Film*. Princeton University Press, New York, 1947, 1966; Dennis Dobson, London, 1947.

Lane, Tamar: 'The Last Laugh is on Hollywood' in *Motion Picture Magazine*. New York, November 1926.

(Mayer, Carl) *A Tribute to Carl Mayer*. Memorial Programme, Scala Theatre, *13 April 1947*. London, 1947.

Mori, Phil: 'Il Testamento di Murnau', in *Bianco e Nero*, 4. 1951. Rome, 1951.

Murnau, F. W.: 'Étoile du Sud', in *La Revue du Cinéma*, 5. Paris, May 1931.

Murnau, F. W.: Interview in *Cinéa-Ciné*, 22. Paris, 1 April 1927.

Murnau, F. W.: 'The Ideal Picture Needs No Titles', in *Theatre Magazine*, Vol. XLVII, No. 322. New York, January 1928.

Murnau, F. W. and Flaherty, Robert J.: 'Turia, an Original Story', in *Film Culture*, 20. New York (? 1959).

Murnau, F. W. and Flaherty, Robert J.: 'Tabu (Tabou), a Story of the South Seas' in *Film Culture*, 20. New York (1959).

Olimsky, Fritz: 'Deutsche Regisseure – F. W. Murnau', in *Film-Kurier*. Berlin, 11 September 1922.

Scherer, Maurice (pseud. of Eric Rohmer): 'La Revanche de l'Occident (*Tabou*)' in *Cahiers du Cinéma*, 21. Paris, 21 March 1955.

Scherer, Maurice (pseud. of Eric Rohmer): 'Vanité que la peinture', in *Cahiers du Cinéma*, 3. Paris, 1951.

Scognamillo, Giovanni: 'F. W. Murnau', in *Bianco e Nero*, 6. Rome 1953.

Sunrise (Sonnenaufgang), Ein Drehbuch von Carl Mayer mit handschriftlichen Bemerkungen von Friedrich Wilhelm Murnau, Deutsches Institut für Filmkunde, Wiesbaden, 1971.

Treuner, Hermann (ed.): *Filmkünstler: Wir über uns selbst*. Sibylla Verlag, Berlin, 1928.

Ulmer, Edgar G. Interview with Louis Moullet and Bertrand Tavernier, in *Cahiers du Cinéma*, 122. Paris, August 1961.

Wesse, Kurt: *Grossmacht Film*. Deutsche Buchgemeinschaft, Berlin, 1928.

White, Kenneth: 'F. W. Murnau', in *Hound and Horn*, 4. New York, July/September 1931.

Wollenberg, H. H. (under signature Wbg.): 'Satanas' (review) in *Licht-Bild-Bühne* 1920, 5. Berlin, 31 January 1920.

Anonymous articles in the following periodicals:

Ami du Peuple (Paris) (article, 'Murnau – Le Cinéma de dessin', 21 March 1930).

Courier Cinematographique (Vienna) (article, 'Murnau', 16 April 1927).

Film-Kurier (Berlin).

Film und Presse (Berlin).

Licht-Bild-Bühne (Berlin).

Motion Picture Classic (New York).

Neue Freie Presse (Vienna).

Theatre Magazine (New York).

Index

Index

LADIES AND GENTLEMEN:

WILLIAM FOX TAKES PLEASURE IN PRESENT-
ING TONIGHT FOR THE FIRST TIME ON ANY
SCREEN

4 DEVILS

BASED ON A STORY BY HERMAN BANG
SCENARIO BY BERTHOLD VIERTEL
CARL MAYER AND MARION ORTH

DIRECTED BY F. W. MURNAU

AFTER YOU HAVE REVIEWED 4 DEVILS
WE WOULD APPRECIATE YOUR FRANK COM-
MENT:

(1) WHAT IS YOUR GENERAL IMPRESSION
AND OPINION OF 4 DEVILS

(2) WHAT CHARACTERS, WHAT PARTS
OF THE STORY AND WHICH PAR-
TICULAR SCENES ENTERTAINED
YOU MOST?

(3) WHAT PARTS, IF ANY, PROVED UN-
INTERESTING?

(4) IN WHAT RANK OF MOTION PIC-
TURE ENTERTAINMENT WOULD
YOU CLASSIFY 4 DEVILS

(5) WAS EVERY PART OF THE PICTURE
CLEAR AND UNDERSTOOD BY YOU?
IF NOT, PLEASE SPECIFY WHAT
SCENES WERE NOT FULLY UNDER-
STOOD.

YOUR SUGGESTIONS, COMMENTS AND CRITI-
CISMS WILL BE APPRECIATED AND YOU MAY
WRITE A LETTER IN WHATEVER LENGTH YOU
DESIRE. PLEASE MAIL YOUR LETTER OF RE-
VIEW WITHIN 24 HOURS AFTER YOU HAVE
SEEN THE PICTURE.

PLEASE ACCEPT MY THANKS IN ADVANCE
FOR YOUR LETTER.

The Four Devils: the première questionnaire (see page 195)